TOWARD A GENERAL THEORY OF ACTING

Cognitive Studies in Literature and Performance

Literature, Science, and a New Humanities
  Jonathan Gottschall

Engaging Audiences
  Bruce McConachie

The Public Intellectualism of Ralph Waldo Emerson and W.E.B. Du Bois
  Ryan Schneider

Performance, Cognitive Theory, and Devotional Culture
  Jill Stevenson

Shakespearean Neuroplay
  Amy Cook

Evolving Hamlet
  Angus Fletcher

Cognition in the Globe
  Evelyn B. Tribble

Toward a General Theory of Acting
  John Lutterbie

Toward a General Theory of Acting

Cognitive Science and Performance

John Lutterbie

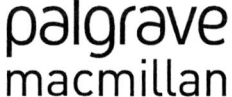

TOWARD A GENERAL THEORY OF ACTING
Copyright © John Lutterbie, 2011.

All rights reserved.

First published in 2011 by
PALGRAVE MACMILLAN®
in the United States—a division of St. Martin's Press LLC,
175 Fifth Avenue, New York, NY 10010.

Where this book is distributed in the UK, Europe and the rest of the world, this is by Palgrave Macmillan, a division of Macmillan Publishers Limited, registered in England, company number 785998, of Houndmills, Basingstoke, Hampshire RG21 6XS.

Palgrave Macmillan is the global academic imprint of the above companies and has companies and representatives throughout the world.

Palgrave® and Macmillan® are registered trademarks in the United States, the United Kingdom, Europe and other countries.

ISBN: 978–0–230–11335–0

Library of Congress Cataloging-in-Publication Data

Lutterbie, John Harry, 1948–
    Toward a general theory of acting : cognitive science and performance / John Lutterbie.
       p. cm.—(Cognitive Studies in Literature and Performance)
      ISBN 978–0–230–11335–0 (hardback)
      1. Acting—Philosophy. I. Title. II. Series.
PN2061.L84 2011
792.02′801—dc22
                                                                          2010048474

A catalogue record of the book is available from the British Library.

Design by Newgen Imaging Systems (P) Ltd., Chennai, India.

First edition: June 2011

10 9 8 7 6 5 4 3 2 1

Printed in the United States of America.

To Simon and Julia who make every day worth living

Previous Publications

Hearing Voices: Modern Drama and the Problem of Subjectivity (1997)

Contents

Editors' Preface	ix
Introduction	1

Part I

Chapter 1 The Language of Acting	21
Chapter 2 Theatre and Dynamic Systems Theory	77
Chapter 3 The Actor's Tools	103

Part II

Chapter 4 Technique	131
Chapter 5 Improvisation	161
Chapter 6 The Actor's Score	181
Chapter 7 In Performance	211
Notes	233
Bibliography	249
Index	255

Editors' Preface

Noam Chomsky started a revolution in human self-understanding and reshaped the intellectual landscape to this day by showing how all languages have deep features in common. Gone—or least retreating—is the idea that the mind is a blank slate. In its wake, fierce debates have broken out about what the mind is and how it works. At stake are some of the most urgent questions facing researchers today: questions about the relationship between brain, mind, and culture; about how human universals express themselves in individual minds and lives; about reason, consciousness, and the emotions; about where cultures get their values and how those values fit our underlying predispositions.

It is no secret that most humanists have held fast to the idea that the mind is a blank slate. Not only has this metaphor been an article of intellectual faith, it has also underwritten a passionate moral agenda. If human beings have no inherent qualities, our political and social systems are contingent rather than fixed. Intellectuals might be able to play an important role in exposing the byways of power and bringing about a fairer world. But, evidence is rapidly piling up that humans are born with an elaborate cognitive architecture. The number of our innate qualities is staggering; human cognition is heavily constrained by genes and by our evolutionary past. It is now known that we are born with several core concepts and a capacity for developing a much larger number of cognitive capabilities under ecological pressure.

Beyond that bold headline, however, the story gets murkier. Each of the mind sciences is filled with dissonant debates of their own. In her magisterial investigation into the origin of concepts, Susan Carey writes that her goal "is to demonstrate that the disciplines of cognitive science now have the empirical and theoretical tools to turn age-old philosophical dilemmas into relatively straightforward problems."[1] Notice her sense of being on the verge rather than on some well-marked path. The terrain ahead is still unmapped. But notice, too, her sense that scientific methods will eventually transform fuzzy questions into testable ones.

How brave, then, are language and performance scholars who, driven by their passion to understand how the mind works, seek to explore this new terrain? Brave, but increasingly in good company. The Modern Language Association discussion group on cognitive approaches to literature has grown exponentially in the last decade.[2] And the working group in cognition and performance at the American Society for Theatre Research is flourishing. Many scholars are fascinated by what cognitive approaches might have to say about the arts. They recognize that this orientation to literature and performance promises more than just another "ism." Unlike the theories of the last century, the mind sciences offer no central authority, no revered group of texts that disclose a pathway to the authorized truth. Indeed, cognitive approaches to the arts barely fit under one broad tent. Language-processing, reader and spectator-response, pragmatics, embodiment, conceptual blending, discourse analysis, empathy, performativity, and narrative theory, not to mention the energetic field of literary Darwinism, are all fields with lively cognitive debates.

Cognitive approaches are unified by two ideas. The first is that to understand the arts, we need to understand psychology. Humanists have uncontroversially embraced this idea for decades, as their ongoing fascination with the now largely discredited theory of psychoanalysis suggests. Now that psychology has undergone its empiricist revolution, literary and performance scholars should rejoice in the fact that our psychological claims are on firmer footing. Second, is the idea that scholarship in this field should be generally empirical, falsifiable, and open to correction by new evidence and better theories—as are the sciences themselves. Of course, this epistemological admission means that many of the truth claims of the books in our series will eventually be destabilized and perhaps proven false. But this is as it should be. As we broaden our understanding of cognition and the arts, better science should produce more rigorous ideas and insights about literature and performance. In this spirit, we celebrate the earlier books in our series that have cut a path for our emerging field and look forward to new explorations in the future.

BLAKEY VERMEULE AND BRUCE MCCONACHIE

Introduction

The two actors, both women, come from very different backgrounds and have two distinct approaches to the art of acting, yet the metaphors they use to describe their rehearsal process are strikingly similar. Deborah Mayo grew up in a theatre family that moved from the United States to England when she was a child. By the age of nine or ten she was playing lead roles, mostly britches parts because of her height; she eventually grew to almost six feet tall. In high school after playing one of the fathers in John Gay's *A Beggar's Opera*, she was asked to play the part of Richard II in the next year's production, but her family moved. Despite her disappointment, Mayo said it gave her confidence to know that an English director considered her ready to play the role. While attending school, she was exposed to a steady diet of English acting. "So it was pretty clear that was what I loved doing pretty early on, I guess. During the time I was living in London, all those years I saw Laurence Olivier and Maggie Smith, and Robert Stephens and Peggy Ashcroft, and Ralph Richardson. So I was hooked."[1] After returning to America and attending Wheelock College, she went to graduate school in acting at Yale. She describes her training at the School of Drama as

> Hodge-podge. [Laughter] We weren't taught *a* technique, we were exposed to different teachers, different ideas. So I would characterize my training as three years of being in the trenches, acting all the time in different venues. That was the value of it for me. That we...Not that we were self-taught...We learned by doing, because twenty-four hours a day, we were in plays. That may be unkind to say to my teachers—we had good teachers for sure—but the focus was on the doing.[2]

She is not comfortable describing her approach to acting, saying that actors tend to latch on to techniques that work, regardless of the source. However, Mayo recognizes that her training can be characterized as "traditional," in the sense that there was little emphasis on improvisation and that she was not exposed to alternative training methods, such as those of Joe Chaikin and the Open Theatre. Mayo has worked primarily in text-based theatre in regional theatres and has done some work on Broadway.

Margarita Espada was born and raised in Puerto Rico where her initial training in performance came from work in the martial arts, specifically karate. Less interested in the fighting aspects of the form, she fell in love with the *kata*, set sequences of moves that emphasize the specificity of each gesture and the fluidity of the sequence. "I was very curious about how you manipulate energy, how you can really play with timing, and play with the audience."[3] Her introduction to theatre came when she saw *La vida es sueño* (*Life Is a Dream*) by Calderón de la Barca, in sixth grade. Until that time she was unaware of theatre, coming from a working-class background in a poor country. "And when I saw it I knew, 'I want to be there.'"[4]

Her first formal training in theatre came in 1984 when she entered Puerto Rico University. The training was traditional conservatory and based on the precise execution of exercises. Her work on the *kata* prepared her well for this approach to training in courses such as mime. However, she found the strictures of repetition-based techniques frustrating—"This structure bothers me. Like, 'Stay here on the line.' I need to jump."[5]—and joined an alternative theatre company founded on the popular theatre principles of Augusto Boal's *Teatro del Oprimido*. The improvisatory nature of this work created a tension with the precision demanded by her formal university training; that tension began to be reconciled when she attended an international theatre festival in Cuba. There, for the first time, she encountered Eugenio Barba. It was a turning point for her because she began to see the possibilities of combining specific, physical work with a more improvisational approach to the making of theatre. She now runs her own company, *Teatro yerbabruja* on Long Island.

Espada's process begins with the generation of images, which are then structured into a performance and rehearsed until ready for an audience. In the early stages she prefers to go into the rehearsal space alone to center, focus, and quiet the voices of the day. Once she has achieved the right degree of silence Espada begins to move, seeking a deep relationship between herself and the images that are generated. She attends to the feelings and images that arise from the physical experience of moving, letting each movement suggest the next, and acknowledging the sensory effects that arise. At this point she is less interested in what the experiences mean than the unanticipated associations that arise, seemingly unbidden from her subconscious. As she moves and recognizes images without judging or evaluating them, she is also aware of the emotions that are evoked, allowing them to spur the next emotion, to underscore the next association. This feedback loop—from movement to image to emotion to movement—carries forward particularly strong images, while allowing others to dissipate or recede into the background. "I don't want to think, just to see what comes. Suddenly I have an image of someone walking. Then other images open up. Suddenly there is a flood of different images and I have to work with them to get a clean image."[6] In this way material accrues; each image carries its own potential. The concepts, as they arise, do not maintain a neat sequence; as their contents become clearer, they fold back on each other or suggest alternative directions to explore. As she works with the material, certain images gain intensity and become more insistent, defining a basic structure that may or may not find a place in the final performance, that may or may not appear in the particular form that arises during the exploratory process.

The two qualities that are central to the generation of material are the suspension of judgment and responsiveness to the changing dynamics of the body. The moving body goes through a series of movements that reflect past experiences and certain pleasures, pains and anxieties. But while moving and focusing on the initial image, impulses or other images arise that suggest different kinds of engagement. As the work proceeds, the dynamic proliferation of subsidiary images intensifies and transforms the original concept, enriching its potential or giving rise to unexpected and divergent possibilities or, failing to find the impetus to continue, the process stops. The exercise may also come to an end because of a surfeit of material, when judgment can no longer be suspended, when concentration is broken either by the singularity of an image or the overload of the senses—when it is not possible to clarify a "clean image." Most difficult to describe is the suspension of judgment. It is not conceptually difficult but is far from easy to achieve in the process and to define:

> Where everything is blank. I try to get to this point where I am just pure energy. No past, no present, just here, now. Not necessarily Zen...The neutral mask of Lecoq, what it means to carry a neutral mask. Almost impossible.[7]

The distinction between Lecoq's concept of neutrality and a Zen state is one of movement. Zen is associated, rightly or wrongly, with a passive, meditative state, while creativity in the theatre is active. In drawing the parallel between Lecoq and Zen, she is creating an interesting binary between passive and active states, suggesting that the two qualities can exist simultaneously.

Mayo works primarily with texts and the development of character. She goes to rehearsal with a certain amount of homework done—a relatively clear idea of her character's objectives, a breakdown of the actions, and as many of the words learned as possible. When entering the rehearsal space she has a set of structures that guide her explorations, but equally important is what she does *not* bring to the rehearsal. She refers to these negative aspects as clutter, which she defines as "judging, self-judging, any mental activity, i.e. focused on anything other than the given circumstances, any ego concerns, ideas of right and wrong choices."[8] The value of this avoidance of the cognitive is what it allows to happen: "loose enough to let [the character] in, it is so gratifying. There is an awareness that it happens, but that is what the 'uncluttering' is: standing back and letting that happen."[9] Mayo knows that the idea of the character taking over sounds like "hocus-pocus"; nevertheless, "It feels like you empty yourself.... It's not that you are making but responding. There is a moment when [the character] seems to take over and does what she wants to do."[10] However, it is not work done in isolation. Much of the discovery process comes from the presence of the other actors:

> It is almost always the other actors that are the stimuli, the way they listened or the way their characters were reacting to me that somehow bolstered or affirmed my going out on the limb I was going out on. So much is response and attentiveness.[11]

The rehearsal process requires being open to the moment, investing the given circumstances without concern for what might happen or has happened. What am I being given now? What is the response I make? After the response has happened it is possible to reflect on what this tells her about the character or the action of the play and whether or not the response was appropriate. But at the time there needs to be openness to what is happening, an attentiveness that is not interrupted by cognitive oversight. In common acting parlance, you have to be in the moment.

The idea of "being in the moment" is important to both actors, and I suspect it is one of the more universal concepts in acting. It is constituted, at least for these two actors, by avoiding the intrusion of discursive thought, which is seen as a negative influence, as interfering with the actor's availability to unexpected images, as clutter that disrupts the reciprocal exchange between actors. For Mayo and Espada, it involves a suspension of the intellect in favor of attending to the physical and emotional impulses that arise from the flow of images in one case and from the exchange of responsive behavior defined by the structure of the script in the other. Reflection and decision making is something that happens later, after the exercise is completed, whether in an improvisation or scene work.

It is interesting that two artists from such different backgrounds and with such dissimilar approaches to training describe their work using the same primary metaphors—metaphors that are central to understanding the creative process. First is the binary of intellect and emotion. Rational thought needs to be put on hold so that the experience of images and emotional responses can play freely across and through the body. It is only *after* the improvisational experience that a process of reflection allows for a rational evaluation of the images and emotions evoked in the rehearsal. A second binary perceives the self as a container that can be emptied and filled with fresh contents. The self is perceived to be a force of containment that impedes the creative process and that requires a relaxing of the boundaries, a move into a neutral state to be productive in rehearsal. Linking these binaries is the need to be in the moment. The assumption is that subjectivity and rational thought take one out of the moment (if such a thing is possible) and that when concerns about the past and the future are bracketed, artistry becomes most compelling and vibrant. Two very different actors rely on the same metaphors—negation/affirmation, emptying/filling and being in the moment—to describe the states necessary for making theatre. Yet, to see them on stage is to see very different styles of acting. Is there a way of talking about acting that can account for these similarities and differences? There is a fairly new discourse in theories of theatre and performance that holds that the study of the cognitive sciences has the potential to improve our understanding of such questions, if not to provide answers to them. This book takes up the challenge by arguing that integrating Dynamic Systems Theory (DST) with findings in a number of disciplines, including linguistics, movement studies, gesture studies, and the neuroscience and psychology of memory, provides a better understanding of acting at no cost to our respect for the complexity and wonder of the art form.

The Author's Sad Confession

I am not an actor. I am a theorist, trained as a director who sometimes acts. Most of the years when I was acting more or less regularly, I did not have a clue about the art or craft, other than the most rudimentary basics. Told I am blessed with a natural sense of comic timing, I suspect it has carried me through a number of performances without which I would have been rather hopeless on stage. Most of what I knew about acting came from being a director. When dealing with texts, I tried to help actors make connections and develop scores that would result in performances that transcend an audience's expectations; or, on occasions when the work was devised, I tried to create a performance based in the performers' experiences and that allowed their work to guide the structuring of the final piece. So, why a book about acting?

Early in my academic career, when my research was lacking a focus, I had the good fortune to participate in a National Endowment for Humanities (NEH) summer seminar with Herbert Blau. He said, "Write a book about directing." Instead, I wrote a book about the ethics of intersubjective relations. The comment stayed with me, however. Thinking about a book on the director, I realized that I first needed to understand acting. For the past eight years I have been trying to satisfy that need by reading and teaching theories of acting—even those with which I have little sympathy—talking with actors, seeing theatre of all kinds, (brilliant and mediocre—a benefit of living near New York City), and finally taking the opportunity to act again. The part was Granpa Joad in *The Grapes of Wrath*, a Stony Brook University production directed by Nick Mangano. The part was ideal mainly because it had a limited number of lines and because the character dies on page 26 (a good thing for an aging memory) and because for the most part, it fed into my comic abilities. Though brief, it gave me an opportunity to experiment with what I had been learning and to learn what I either thought I knew or had not yet encountered. It was a very rewarding experience.

The more I thought about the actor, the more I felt the need to understand what it is that makes acting possible. The early stages of research revealed that there is nothing in the actor but flesh and bone, blood, and organs. There is nothing there I could identify as imagination, memories, emotions, intellect—and no "little room" from which a homunculus directs traffic. I needed to read science. This recognition occurred by pure coincidence. As I was struggling with this problem, Antonio Damasio's *The Feeling of What Happens:*

Body and Emotion in the Making of Consciousness was published. The rest, as they say, is history. Words like amygdala, hippocampus, sensory-motor cortex, synapse, and ion gates started creeping into my vocabulary as my reading led to exploring the different parts of the brain, how neurons work, how memories are created and retrieved, and what makes improvisation possible.

What was lonely work ceased to be when F. Elizabeth Hart put together a conference where my first paper on cognitive science and Samuel Beckett was presented. Shortly thereafter came the publication of an essay on improvisation in *Performance and Cognition: Theatre Studies and the Cognitive Turn*, edited by Hart and Bruce McConachie. Research groups were formed at the American Society for Theatre Research, and the Humanities Institute at Stony Brook reinvigorated a faculty seminar in science and art. Conversations I was having with myself started happening with people in the arts, humanities, sciences, and social sciences, leading to a grant (a study of actors, emotion, and memory with colleagues in Psychology) and much of what is in this book. A pivotal moment came when McConachie said I might want to read Evan Thompson's *Mind in Life: Biology, Phenomenology, and the Sciences of Mind*, wherein I encountered DST for the first time. Pieces began to fit together in new and exciting ways. Ideas that were being forced into place suddenly worked together cooperatively; and a book that was to be about the "embodied actor" became "a general theory of [Western] acting." The most exciting aspect of this research has been that the further I examined and dissected the art of acting, the more respect I gained for the creativity of actors and the wonders of acting. The more I understand—or think I understand—about how acting happens, the more I marvel at the work of good actors and those who strive to understand the art.

A Word on Science

A second admission: I am not a scientist and spent most of my life with a resistance to science bordering on antipathy. This is, perhaps, typical of people who do not understand the thing they dislike: if you can't do it, hate it. Needless to say, my attitude has changed drastically. I have a growing respect for the work scientists do, but at the same time I see its limitations. Paul Adams, a neuroscientist at Stony Brook, at the opening of a Science and Art seminar rethinking C. P. Snow's seminal lecture, "The Two Cultures," suggested that the question was not whether the arts and sciences should talk to each other, but whether such a conversation was even possible. After many readings and healthy debates the jury is still out. For instance, in the arts and humanities to be reductive is unthinkable because it removes from consideration the richness and complexity of the arts. Pollock's paintings become nothing more than spattered paint; and *Hamlet* is the story of an unhappy son. In the sciences, being reductive is an absolute necessity if the experiments are to be meaningful and anything proven. All variables need to be accounted for or there can be no surety about what is discovered in the laboratory. As a second example, theory in the arts is deduced from the examination of existing texts; in the sciences it serves an inductive function, allowing the scientist to predict what will happen in an experiment.

Despite these differences, interdisciplinary work across the divide can lead to interesting projects. Suparna Rajaram, a behavioral psychologist, is energized in thinking about implicit memory and improvisation after listening to jazz trombonist Ray Anderson discuss entering "a state of grace" when playing with his ensemble. Rajaram and neuropsychologist Hoi-Chung Leung, regretting that the costs of longitudinal experiments make long-term investigations into collaborative learning difficult, begin to consider the possibilities and problems of studying the ensemble interactions of actors who rehearse together intensively for a relatively short period of time. The growth of cognitive studies in literature, music, political science, linguistics and, of course, theatre indicates that the interaction of the arts and sciences can be an exciting and productive conversation.

However, the scientific need to be reductive creates problems for the theatre theorist. The removal of variables inevitably means that experiments look at extremely specific, one might say microscopic, objects. The neurobiology of memory seeks to understand the chemical bonds that allow specific neurotransmitters to generate an electric charge in a single type of neuron in a specific part of the brain. When it comes to discussions about acting, such information while interesting is not very useful. It is only when the results of numerous experiments from a variety of labs are brought together that the bigger picture becomes comprehensible. The paradox is that as the discussion becomes more general, the number of variables increases, making the conclusions more speculative. In other words, the more scientists try to communicate to a wider audience, the farther they get away from science and into conjecture. One needs to be suspicious of what is published for public consumption.

INTRODUCTION

The relatively recent desire to communicate the complex workings of the brain by scientists to a wider audience as a means of countering certain misconceptions began with Joseph LeDoux, Antonio Damasio, V. S. Ramachandran, Sandra Blakeslee, and Steven Pinker. The excitement that their work elicited was palpable until contradictions between the different theories began to appear, for instance between connectionist and computational theories of the mind, requiring a reassessment. Looking into these discrepancies revealed the depth of the speculation and the vast areas of research still to be undertaken. The scope of a project can be a warning sign. The closer an author comes to providing a "theory of everything," the more skeptical the reader needs to be. As questions arise, the greater is the need to go back to primary and secondary research. The virtue of reading the results of experiments is that they tend to be short; the difficulty is they can be virtually incomprehensible to the nonscientist without a clear understanding of the context. I remember enthusiastically reading an article on some aspect of memory only to realize I did not have a clue what they were talking about. Summary articles in recognized scientific journals written for readers across a number of scientific disciplines proved to be a great asset because they provide background, summarize competing theories, and digest experimental findings in relatively comprehensible language. In such circumstances, decisions about what constitutes the best evidence to support a theoretical model ceases to be about finding the truth and revolves around finding a point of view that is supported by the preponderance of evidence from a wide range of reliable sources across a number of disciplines. For instance, the decision to use DST to develop a theory of acting was determined in part by the number of sources using this model productively in neuroscience, neuropsychology, linguistics, gesture and movement studies, computer science, phenomenology, and poststructuralist theory. It proved to have an explanatory power commensurate with the complexity and creativity of the acting process.

Finally, one of the most valuable concepts to be taken from the sciences is the Principle of Falsifiability. What is believed to be true can always be disproved by an experiment whose findings undermine the foundations of an accepted theory. Even ideas as seemingly incontrovertible as gravity are eminently falsifiable. As experiments are repeated with the same results and challenges to the hypothesis are unsuccessful, the weight of evidence makes it increasingly unlikely that the rule will be overturned. Nevertheless, it remains potentially falsifiable. This is certainly true of this work.

Acting and Actors

A general theory of acting needs to take into account a vast array of training methods and types of theatre. Over the past half-century approaches to and theories about the training of actors have multiplied even though the rise of the cinema intensified the belief that psychological realism was the sine qua non of good acting. Prior to the 1950s, at least in English-speaking countries, there were two dominant approaches: extensions of the work of Stanislavski and apprenticeship. In the second half of the twentieth century conceptions of theatre changed as practitioners became aware of the work and writings of Bertolt Brecht, Antonin Artaud, and Michael Chekhov, leading to experimentation in theatre with the work of the Living Theatre, the Open Theatre, and new forms of playwriting by writers such as Samuel Beckett, Eugene Ionesco, Sam Shepard, Adrienne Kennedy, Marie Irene Fornes, Luigi Pirandello, Dario Fo, and Franca Rame, and so on. Fresh approaches to thinking about theatre encouraged new ways of talking about the actor. In particular the work of Jacques Lecoq, Jerzy Grotowski, Kristen Linklater, and Cecily Berry, to name but a few, caught the attention of a new generation of actors who found the Method espoused by Lee Strasberg and the emphasis on technique of the Royal Academy of Dramatic Arts in London limiting. While versions of Stanislavski remain dominant, when seeing an actor perform it can no longer be assumed that her work is based in emotional identification. For instance, Geoffrey Rush, whose work on screen and stage is perceived as psychological realism, studied with Lecoq, whose mime-based approach to acting is counter to traditional methods that work from the "inside out." As styles of acting increase, the search for new methods of teaching the art intensifies. For some, the encounter with Asian traditions of performing resulted in hybrid forms of acting by such directors as Peter Brook, Eugenio Barba, and Ariane Mnouchkine, whose companies have looked to the East for inspiration and acting techniques (however politically problematic some may find their appropriation of the forms[12]). Other actors, such as Deborah Mayo, seldom claim allegiance to only one approach, but combine a number of different training methods to craft an approach to acting that works for them in a variety of contexts.

Seemingly every day new books appear that claim to provide a uniquely different way of showing young actors how to achieve success. Most can, for purposes of discussion, be traced to the work of either Constantin Stanislavski or Vsevelod Meyerhold. The realist vision of Stanislavski (rightly or wrongly associated with working "inside out") and the biomechanics of Meyerhold ("outside in") coexist in an uneasy tension that mirrors the complex relationship between the two men. Both went through profound changes in thinking about theatre as they responded to unexpected experiences and changing times. These two currents split into new streams of thought as their theories were challenged by the likes of Bertolt Brecht and Antonin Artaud, or embraced by acting teachers such as Lee Strasburg and Stella Adler. These in turn have engendered new tributaries in the work of Sanford Meisner, Uta Hagen, Jerzy Grotowski, Michael Chekhov, Jacques Lecoq, and Eugenio Barba. This is far from a comprehensive list; and all flow into the sea of actor training methodologies.

Even more complex is trying to encompass in a satisfactory way all the forms of performance that can legitimately (or not) be called theatre. For purposes of clarity and following the lead of Hans-Thies Lehmann, I identify three dominant forms: realism, non-realism, and the postdramatic. Realism is identified as character-driven narratives, which include not only traditional realism but also classics such as the work of Shakespeare, Moliere, Wilde, and so on. Non-realism includes text-based theatres that challenge traditional linear structures, including works by Georg Büchner, Alfred Jarry, Samuel Beckett, Eugene Ionesco, Luigi Pirandello, Gertrude Stein, Heiner Müller, Adrienne Kennedy, Sarah Kane, and again the list goes on. The postdramatic is the most unwieldy, encompassing a range of styles including Eugenio Barba and Augusto Boal, Ariane Mnouchkine and Ann Bogart, Reza Abdoh and John Jesurun, Bill Irwin and Rinde Ekert, Ping Chong and Richard Foreman, the Wooster Group and the Builders Association. It also includes a myriad of artists who do "devised" work such as KRAKEN, Forced Entertainment, Rachel Rosenthal, Katie Mitchell, Tadeuz Kantor, Complicite, Crossroads, Swamp Gravy, Gruppe 38, and Societas Sanzio Raffaello. Also under its umbrella are the many community-based theatres, political actions such as Act Up and the protests of the WTO, and street mimes and companies such as Blue Man Group and the Cirque du Soleil.

It is assumed that you as a reader have a preconception of what constitutes good acting, and preferences for particular kinds of theatre. Some of you have tastes that are quite specific, while others are more eclectic. To be comprehensive, my approach in writing has been to be as inclusive as possible, so there may be times when you identify a bias for a particular type of acting or are dismayed by the generality of the discussion. These are unavoidable pitfalls of writing a general theory for a field as vast as acting.

Some may also question a theory that argues for universals. My response is as follows. Everyone—actors or not, and recognizing differences in ability—engages the environment using more or less the same cognitive processes that work according to the same biological rules: the body has a structure that determines how—but not what—we think, feel, and act. At the same time, everyone has different experiences in different contexts that lead to the formation of different patterns of behavior, memories, and identity formations. The diversity of experience creates different frames of reference and preference for certain types of behavior, which some may argue reflect genetic patterns while others hold that it demonstrates the power of culture. Regardless, these distinguishing characteristics determine—always acknowledging the potential for change—a predisposition for a particular approach to the world. In other words, although the machinery works the same, what comes out can be vastly different depending on the biological make up and personal history. When it comes to acting, this means that there is no right or wrong way of approaching the art, and that artists commit to specific techniques of acting because they work for them. At the same time, the strong claim of this theory is that regardless of the method or system our cognitive processes (conscious and unconscious) utilize the same mechanisms, and regardless of outcome the basic operations are the same. These processes define flexible forms of interaction that determine our relationship with the environment.

An underlying assertion is that experienced actors are experts, regardless of how they approach their art and craft. Hubert and Stuart Dreyfus, using a study by Patricia Brenner, define five stages people go through in the acquisition of expertise. The five steps begin with novice and proceed to advanced beginner, competence, and proficiency before achieving the stage of expert.[13] The defining quality that the last stage possesses that the earlier phases do not is the ability to respond "intuitively," that is, without the need to go through an analytical process. "An expert's skill has become so much a part of him [sic] that he need be no more aware of it than he is of his own body."[14] A standard example of an expert is a professional athlete. A beginning tennis player analyzes where an opponent is, how fast the ball is coming and where best to place his/her shot. Professional players do not need to think, but respond "intuitively." "*When things are proceeding normally, experts don't solve problems and don't make decisions; they do what normally works*" (italics in original).[15] A professional actor in performance does not need to think about projecting his/her voice or holding for a laugh; professional actors do it as a matter of course because that is "what normally works." An expert performer still needs to concentrate because, whether playing tennis or acting, focus and attention are necessary if she is to adjust to changing circumstances. These abilities are not "natural" but are learned techniques that have become "second nature" through repetition.

This book is not only for experts. Many of the examples and the discussion are relevant to all stages in gaining expertise as an actor. Indeed, the explicit hope is that everyone will go away with a better understanding of what acting is and how it happens.

The Lie of the Land

Toward a General Theory of Acting is divided into two parts. The first part, which looks at different approaches to training and the actor's tools, sets the stage for the second, which divides the work of the actor into three areas of expertise, all of which are integrated in performance.

Chapter 1 looks at dominant approaches to the training of actors. The examples presented are by and large teachers of acting in the West who have established careers and have written or spoken about the approach to training that they advocate. The focus is on the language and metaphors used to discuss a particular system. Surprisingly, despite the array of very different and contradictory systems, the terminology is consistent across methods, although used for different ends. This foundational discussion establishes the terms of engagement for the rest of the book.

A model for understanding human cognition based in DST is the subject of chapter 2. Originating in mathematics, DST has become widely recognized as a powerful explanatory tool in numerous areas of study. Most relevant to a discussion of acting are philosophy, neural linguistics, gesture and movement studies, and cognitive studies more generally. The basic premise is that a dynamic system is always in a state of relative instability and subject to perturbations or disruptions that give rise to patterns that are responsive to the disturbance. Basic elements of a dynamic system are the attractor states and boundary conditions. Attractors are memories that promote patterns that have worked in the past, while boundary conditions are limits on behavior. A batter awaiting a pitch in baseball has less than a second to decide whether or not to swing. If she does swing (the decision indicates a specific attractor), certain techniques are put into play—focusing on the ball, shifting the center of gravity, bat speed, and follow through—all of which are boundary conditions that increase the likelihood the ball will be hit. Making the right choice of attractor and the appropriate boundary conditions does not guarantee success—hitters are doing very well if they get a hit once every three at bats. These elements are part of a model for understanding how an action happens, whether in baseball or on stage.

Chapter 3 explores the six tools that most actors have at their disposal. They are movement, gesture, language, memory, intention, and executive control. The first three can be grouped as physical manifestations of behavior, while the last three are associated with cognitive functions. Although gesture is usually associated with movement, it is in fact more intricately connected to speech, at least in everyday life. Gesture helps us to think and organize thoughts into words. In traditional forms of acting, a spontaneous gesture is transformed into a sign because of its usefulness in communicating the role. The second triad reflects common concepts (remembering, desiring, controlling) that have rather precise analogs in cognition. They determine how an actor improvises, presents a speech, and understands a role.

The second part of the book is divided into chapters on technique, improvisation, creating a score, and performing on stage. Technique defines a set of skills the actor learns and in which she becomes an expert. It is seldom pure but rather a hybrid that integrates other skills into a productive approach to acting. Improvisation uses techniques to explore different associations between thoughts and patterns of behavior. It is liberating because it increases the range of possible responses to a situation; and can give rise to novel solutions to challenges. The actor's score is a step-by-step template that gives shape to the performance. Most frequently associated with text-based productions, it is just as necessary in the postdramatic works of Robert Wilson or the mime of Marcel Marceau. Creating a score in terms of dynamic systems is the identification of attractors and the definition of boundary conditions that allow for performances that are repeatable night after night.

The final chapter, chapter 7, examines the actor on stage by breaking the performance into three parts. The first looks at the performer's relationship to space, the second at work with other actors, and the third at interactions with the audience. The common denominators of all three are that they involve technique, improvisation, and a set score. Foundational to understanding the art of performing is the fact that the actor is a dynamic system, capable of responding to internal and external cues, aware of changes in the performance (self-generated or an effect of the work of others), and in tune with the ebb and flow of audience involvement. The same holds for the audience, who are continually responding to what is happening on stage. If theatre has a purpose, it is to create a reciprocal relationship with the spectator that engages her thoughts, feelings, and imagination.

The purpose of the book is not to solve the mystery of acting. In fact, this study raises many new questions as it attempts to answer a few. The implicit dedication of this book is to all those who engage—successfully or not—in the art of acting. The more I think I know the more marvelous seems their work.

Acknowledgments

This is perhaps the most painful part of the writing process because it seems inevitable that someone deserving of recognition is going to be forgotten. It is also difficult because so many people have influenced my life in ways that led to this book that it is impossible to name them all. If your name does not appear and it should, please know that you are remembered and that your thoughtful contribution to this work is deeply appreciated. However, if your name does appear and you grimace—thinking "I told him..."—please accept my apologies; and dear reader, realize the flaws are of my own devising and not those who have taken the time to work with me on this book.

There are four people who have had a profound effect on my work in the theatre. Francis Hodge, from whom I learned to direct, Mavourneen Dwyer, who had faith in my acting when I had none, Herbert Blau, who has given unflagging support and direction to my work, and E. Ann Kaplan, whose faith in me as associate director of the Humanities Institute and as a scholar has been of immeasurable value. I should also add to this list Bill Burford, perhaps my oldest friend, with whom I have enjoyed innumerable discussions about theatre and life, recognizing that the two are inseparable.

Theatre and Cognitive Studies form a new paradigm for unpeeling another layer of the onion known as performance. What seemed at first like a lonely road to travel turned out to be populated by some wonderful scholars and friends. F. Elizabeth Hart and Bruce McConachie published my first work in this area in their profoundly important book of edited essays, *Performance and Cognition: Theatre Studies and the Cognitive Turn.* Particular thanks to Amy Cook, whose unwavering curiosity and sense of humor have pushed my thinking and lifted my spirits. Equally important to this work are Rhonda Blair, whose close reading of this manuscript has been invaluable, Pil Hanson, and Bruce Barton. I have also been enriched by the interviews conducted with Deborah Mayo, Margarita Espada, Alison Armbruster Russell, Colin McPhillamy, and Marie Danvers.

My work has also been deeply affected by my colleagues at Stony Brook University. Most notable is Robert Crease with whom I shared many breakfasts at Strawberry Fields where we discussed phenomenology and performance, the understated foundations of this book. The Arts and Science seminar sponsored by the Humanities Institute gave me the opportunity to present and discuss my work, especially with Ira Livingston, Judy Lochhead, Paul Adams, John Bailyn, Mary Kritzer, Elza Mylona and, of course, the Institute's director E. Ann Kaplan. I would also like to acknowledge the support of faculty in the Psychology Department, Nancy Squires, Richard Gerrig, and Nancy Franklin; with special gratitude to Suparna Rajaram and Hoi-Chung Leung, with whom I share a grant, for their unending patience as I climb the steep learning curve of experimentation. Thanks is also owed to Christa Erickson, Margaret Schedel, and Jonathan Levy; and Nick Mangano, who agreed to give me time to complete this manuscript at a time when the need for teachers was the greatest.

I would be remiss if I did not recognize the students with whom I've worked and who put up with my initial stumbling as the research moved from the study to the classroom. In particular, I want to thank Amy Jensen, Matt McMahan, Adrienne Sowers, Lorien Reese Mahay, Anneka Esch-van Kan, James Cockroft, and Cordelia Chenault. There are many others, in the past and in the present, who are deserving of recognition.

This book would not be possible without the diligent and expert work of the publishers. Thanks, again, go to Bruce McConachie, who has supported this work from its inception and has provided excellent editorial advice and encouragement. Thanks also go to Blakey Vermeule, who along with Bruce edits the Cognitive Studies in Literature and Performance series for Palgrave Macmillan. Brigitte Shull, Samantha (Sam) Hasey, Joel Breuklander, Rohini Krishnan, and the rest of the staff at Palgrave Macmillan and Newgen Imaging Systems are owed a deep debt of gratitude for the time and effort they have taken in the publication of this book.

Finally, I need to thank Lauren Neefe and Rachel Walsh for their careful and patient editing and indexing of the manuscript; and the Faculty of Arts, Humanities and Social Sciences at Stony Brook University for a subvention that allowed me to secure their assistance.

One Christmas Sara, recognizing that my interest in acting was leading toward neuroscience, gave me Antonio Damasio's *The Feeling of What Happens.* It was a turning point in my life, but one not nearly as important as when we met. Her support has been unfailing, both encouraging me to pursue the work and editing each draft of each chapter as it came off the printer. For this and so many, many other things, thank you, "because I'm still in love with you / On this harvest moon."[16]

Part I

Chapter 1

The Language of Acting

Every night thousands of actors step on stage before an audience. Every year an even greater number sign up for acting classes at private studios, art schools, universities, and colleges. All hope to thrill an audience and, not insignificantly, put food on the table. From each teacher or colleague they seek techniques that will make their work more powerful and striking to spectators, directors, and casting agents. Wherever theatre books are sold, the shelves are chockablock full of texts touting the latest fashion in acting, promising readers that the secrets to a successful career can be found in their pages. In the United States, most strive to make it on Broadway or in regional theatres, some are happy to work Off-Broadway or Off-Off-Broadway, and then there are those who eschew the traditional and dedicate their talents to avant-garde or community-based performances. There are two things they all have in common, regardless of origin, talent, drive, and personal contacts: they are alive and have bodies.

This may seem an anticlimactic conclusion, but in reading texts about acting it is astounding how many of them take the body for granted; although, the body is discussed more frequently than the mind. Most are "how to" books that focus on techniques for generating emotions or discovering powerful images and, when they do address the physical apparatus, it is subdivided into resonators, articulators, and so on. For most the body is seen as a tool to be used to achieve desired ends, especially by those who take a more theoretical or intellectual approach to acting. Despite protests to the contrary, an underlying assumption of most acting systems is that the mind and the body are separate entities, and that both are subservient to emotion. The body is seen as a vessel that contains the mind and the centers of emotion, or as in the excesses of Antonin Artaud a material to be rendered abject because it impedes the communication of the creative impulse. The mind is perceived as useful when analysis is needed to enhance understanding, but an obstacle when it comes to creating a strong performance. The primary tenet of this book is that ignoring the body is not only wrongheadedness, it is simply wrong.

Some may ask: "What difference does it make, if it works?" Perhaps it doesn't matter *if* it works; or if you believe that every time an audience jumps to its feet, it is a sign of a great performance rather than a means of convincing itself that it has gotten its money's worth.[1] It is my contention that the body does matter, *if* you think the theatre should aspire to a level of excellence that does not depend on technique to get the actor through the performance, or is not simply a means of keeping a roof over her head. It is also my belief that the vast majority of actors strive to create performances that *transcend the everyday expectations of the audience.* So why does that happen so infrequently? One among the myriad reasons that theatre fails is that we do not have an adequate understanding of how acting works, a misunderstanding that arises from an inaccurate understanding of the actor's instrument and what it means to be embodied. This fault, perhaps as dangerous to theatre as the San Andreas fault is to California, arises because we have come to believe that there are three categories—mind, body, and emotion—and that these are somehow as separable in fact as they are in discourse. At least since 1994, the date of the publication of Antonio Damasio's seminal speculation on developments in neuroscience, *Descartes' Error,* it has become increasingly clear that these three are integral parts of a single system; that you cannot have one without the other and still be an animate, living being. Actors are, for all their failings, animate, living beings.

It may be only now that we can speculate about what is happening as a performer works. Funded research in Behavioral and Neural Psychology is beginning to look at actors not only for insights into the art but also to identify techniques that may be useful in treating people with autism and addiction disorders. Helga and Tom Noice are investigating the strategies actors use to memorize[2]; Fiona Shaw performs while undergoing a functional Magnetic Resonance Imaging (fMRI)[3]; and with two colleagues in psychology, I am exploring how emotion affects the actor's ability to learn lines. More importantly, as pieces of the puzzle are found that provide clues to how the mind works, scientists are becoming bolder in speculating about cognitive processes. Drawing on physics and mathematics as well as neuroscience, genetics, and psychology, scientists create models that have yet to be proven but take into account major developments in a range of empirical and theoretical fields. The question I am asking is: Can we create a model of acting that is supported by findings in the sciences, resonates with working actors, and has the potential for improving our understanding of the creative process?

I begin to answer this question by asking another: What does it mean to be embodied? If you believe some of the Artificial Intelligence (AI) people including the performance artist Stelarc, or are enamored of William Gibson's view that in cyberspace subjectivity can be downloaded onto a computer and exist without this "too, too, solid flesh" (at least until the server crashes), the body can be transcended. If you are skeptical of this vision of the future, and believe the living and breathing body is necessary for life, a concept of the body as more than a lump of clay or a conduit for words and emotions is needed. This is where the concept of embodiment becomes central.

This chapter lays the foundations for the trajectory of this book, which is coming to grips with what it means to be an embodied performer in the theatre. It begins with a brief discussion of the relationship between the body and the mind, followed by a section that recognizes the complexities of developing a general theory of acting in a field as diverse as the theatre. The preeminent theories of acting in the West are examined in some depth to understand how the art is approached in the training and practice of the actor, with particular emphasis on the language used to talk about it. Certain of these fundamental concepts are then identified because they appear in most if not all of the systems discussed. This common terminology forms the basis for the development of a theory of acting using evidence from the cognitive sciences. The chapter concludes by looking briefly at the limitations of science in thinking about the arts, and the claim that despite the shortcomings of using the empirical disciplines, they provide a framework that can significantly improve our understanding of the art of acting.

The Yin Yang of the Body Mind

The body continues to be defined according to binaries: mind/body, emotion/reason, creativity/technique, transcendence/materiality, inside/outside, and physical/spiritual. Depending on such dualisms makes it difficult if not impossible to conceive of the human organism holistically, that is, as an integrated, interdependent system. The binary problem does not belong to theatre alone, but permeates thinking in the arts, academia, and virtually every area of everyday life. It is the major contention of this book that such thinking is limiting, even crippling when engaged in the art and craft of acting, or any other creative enterprise. There is, of course, value in creating categories that provide focus when working on specific problems, articulating theories, writing books about acting, and for communicating in general. The problem arises when these divisions lead to privileging one category over all others, as Stanislavski realized when he reached the limits of emotional recall and moved toward the more inclusive theory of physical actions. We need taxonomies, but we also need a theory of acting that sees the actor as thinking, feeling, moving, speaking, perceiving, and continuously engaged in the rehearsal hall, on stage, and in everyday life. It is only when we understand that these different qualities are intertwined in the creation of a performance that we can begin to grasp what it means to act. It is by seeing the actor as embodied that we can begin to rethink how we talk to and train actors, ultimately improving the quality of the theatrical performance.

The term "embodied" is not ideal. Philosopher Maxine Sheets-Johnstone argues that it once again diminishes the importance of the body by seeing it as a container for the brain.[4] Her preferred term is the "mind-full body," believing that it recognizes that the mind is integrated into physical being, not a separate entity. While I continue to use embodied because it is less awkward and is the term currently in use, it is meant in the sense expressed by Sheets-Johnstone: the mind is of the body, the body of the mind, and their integration is central to all of the processes that we associate with being alive.

But what is meant by embodied? Artaud argued for a "body without organs." He developed the image of the flesh as a unified organism to fight the tyranny of language, believing words constrain life by dissecting the world into discrete parts, denying the artist the opportunity to communicate the full range of intensities that seek expression through the body. Without going to the extremes that Artaud sought with such great passion, there is some value in moving away from the categories of mind, body, and emotion, and embracing a conception of the actor as a unified being. She is not, however, an autonomous being. To be embodied is to engage the world utilizing all our abilities. Differentiating between the self and the environment diminishes self-understanding. There is a reciprocal relationship between thought and experience that marks the inextricable intertwining of the environment and the actor. Those interactions are the source of behaviors and attitudes; of values and desires. A person cannot retreat from the world; it is inherent in every aspect of experience. Remembering an emotion involves a physical reinvestment in a past event; thoughts are grounded in metaphors based on bodily experience; communicating with others integrates language, gesture, and thought. All we do, we do in the flesh. Maurice Merleau-Ponty addresses the question of the flesh, defining its phenomenological limit as the farthest reaches of the senses: the flesh extends as far as it can see, hear, touch, or smell; and what it perceives exists in relationship to the body.[5] Sentient beings are continually and inextricably immersed in the world, capable through thought, feeling, and experience of differentiating themselves as individuals, but not as autonomous beings.

In thinking about the actor, it is useful to draw on a mathematical concept that has found purchase in a number of different disciplines, including physics and neuroscience. Dynamic Systems Theory (DST), a topic discussed in greater detail in chapter 2, states that a "system" is generally defined as elements that function together to create a complex whole; and a "dynamic system" is one that exists in a constant state of disequilibrium, responding to perturbations (disturbances) that further destabilize the whole. The forces that upset the near stable state can come from proprioceptive or internal sources ("I don't feel well") and perceptual or external ("It is cold outside"). This agitation of the system gives rise to patterns that usually take the form of behavior (she takes medicine; or puts on a coat). Sometimes an adequate resolution does not appear and we experience states of confusion or inaction, such as writer's block. The stimuli that perturb can originate in passive or active engagements with the world, but the response to a perturbation is never singular but a complex form that involves thoughts, emotions, and physical sensations. The director tells an actor, well into rehearsals, that a certain choice is not working. This perturbation, whether it comes as a surprise or a relief, unsettles the actor, requiring the identification of a different form of behavior or activity that will solve the problem. Drawing on all her available resources, she searches for a pattern of thought, feeling, movement, and intonation that can be integrated into the world of the production and work with others, returning her to a state of relative stability and an improved performance. Acting is the activity of an embodied, dynamic system.

The Complexities Involved in Proposing a Theory of Acting

If the actor is a dynamic system, equally so is the theatre. Anyone who has been involved in theatre knows that it is not a stable system; and the closer it comes to being one, the more boring it is likely to be. The actor needs to expect the unexpected and know that it is likely to influence the performance. Even when everything is running smoothly, the performer must be attentive to differences in the flow of performance, and respond to nuances in the intensity and rhythms of what is happening on stage and in the house. The audience brings a different energy to each performance, and the actor has to adapt to unexpected laughs, or to spectators who are not particularly responsive. Happenings on stage also require attention, in obvious situations such as when one actor goes up on a line and in the more subtle differences in playing out of the action. Engaged acting requires sensitivity to the shifting dynamics of the production.

In addition to the vagaries of each performance, there is a bewildering array of types and styles of theatre and locales in which they take place. In the West theatre can be thought of as a wheel. The hub represents what most people think of when they think of theatre: major cultural centers, such as New York, London, Paris, and Berlin, each providing a wide range of traditional forms. The spokes house the regional theatres, civic centers where road companies perform, colleges and universities, amateur community theatres, and theatre for young audiences; while at the very rim are nontraditional companies of restless practitioners who play havoc with conventional norms. The latter include theatres that work with communities to create performances addressing local issues; companies whose work is based on a special technique; experimental groups who combine media in the search for new forms; and political theatres that seek to foment change. Avant-garde performances can take place in traditional theatres, art galleries, dance spaces, churches, lofts, warehouses, streets or, as with Boal's Invisible Theatre, in restaurants. The performers can have traditional theatre training in acting, dancing, and singing; focus on specialized techniques such as the mask work of Lecoq or circus techniques like juggling and gymnastics; or be enthusiastic amateurs. Others who decided not to focus on performance can be involved in research such as Grotowski's work with Theatre of Sources in Pontedera, Italy, or Barba's work at the Odin Theatre in Denmark. All of these approaches to theatre and the many others not mentioned are engaged in a reciprocal relationship, influencing each other through variations in form and by offering models that are embraced, or resisted in favor of a more appealing methodology.

For purposes of argument, I divide the variety of theatrical forms into three categories based on the relationship to a written play: realism, non-realism, and postdramatic. Each is defined in greater depth in chapter 6 as a prelude to discussing the actor's score; but it might be useful to outline them briefly. The predominant form of realism is expanded beyond its accepted definition to include all plays that present a narrative driven by characters motivated to perform acts within the boundaries of personal objectives and the given circumstances. Therefore, Shakespeare, Molière, Schiller, Calderón de la Barca, Aphra Behn, and many others are lumped together with Ibsen, Strindberg, Chekhov, Shaw, Miller, Williams, Albee, Wesker, Wasserstein, and so on. Non-realism consists of written works that openly violate the tenets of the more traditional form and range from the "absurdist" plays of Genet, and Beckett to the introverted works of Büchner, Maeterlinck, and Pirandello to the political forms of Brecht, Müller, Bond, Churchill, Bensussa, and formalist explorations such as the early works of Sam Shepard and plays by Mac Wellman.[6] The postdramatic, as defined by Hans-Thies Lehmann, refers to the range of theatrical events that are not based primarily on the presentation of a play, although the work may involve written texts as a starting point or incorporate them during the creative process.

> The adjective "postdramatic" denotes a theatre that feels bound to operate beyond drama, at a time "after" the authority of the dramatic paradigm in theatre. What it does not mean is an abstract negation and mere looking away from the tradition of drama.[7]

The search for new paradigms includes the work of Robert Wilson, Ariane Mnouchkine, William Forsythe, the Wooster Group, Blue Man Group, Cirque du Soleil, Socìetas Raffaello Sanzio, Forced Entertainment, Split Britches, Richard Foreman, and the list goes on.

The primary argument of this book is that when speaking of the cognitive processes involved in acting, the type of theatre does not matter. To talk about acting, then, is to talk across all three categories of theatre. The brain is structured more or less the same for everyone; and operates the same, although in disabled performers it can reorganize itself to compensate for differences.[8] This does not mean that acting in a realist production is the same as postdramatic, or that one method can serve all kinds of theatre. Every production in any of the categories privileges those skills that make a performance unique; and in so doing may place emphasis on one set of cognitive functions. For instance, in a traditional production of William's *Streetcar Named Desire*, an actor may consciously assess the patterns of emotion that are evoked during rehearsals, while a performer in Robert Wilson's *Einstein on the Beach* or *Quartett,* may be concerned less with the affective, focusing instead on the precise mechanics of the movements. This does not mean that the actor in *Streetcar* will ignore the technical requirements of the character or that there is no emotional content in *Quartett*. Acting does not work that way; no one works that way, unless there is a severe loss of cognitive ability. Everything is integrated: thought, emotion, motor skills, and imagination. They are all part of a dynamic system that quite miraculously interleaves these different aspects into a performance. So it is, in principle, possible for any actor to perform in any type of production. The limitations that make realizing this potential rare are imposed by habitual patterns that are learned through years of training and by that ineffable quality, talent.

Approaching Acting

Every program in acting, whether professional or academic, founds its approach on a set of assumptions about the actor and the techniques that she needs to develop if she is to succeed in the profession. To understand acting it is useful to identify the theoretical foundations and metaphors on which a method is based.[9] Interestingly, when such an investigation is undertaken it becomes clear that rather than a wide range there is a relatively small number of basic principles. What vary are the aspects a particular teacher privileges in structuring the training. For instance, virtually every methodology takes a position on whether it is better to approach developing a performance from the "outside in" or the "inside out." While the distinction does not matter if it works for the student, it does reveal a bias. By understanding these prejudices, we gain insight into how theatre practitioners view the art, and by defining the similarities and differences come to a better understanding of the issues that must be addressed by a cognitive theory of acting. To that end, I examine texts that promote a particular point of view about acting in the realist, non-realist and postdramatic traditions of theatre as practiced in the West. Because of the scope of such a project, I focus on those teachers of indisputable reputation who have written about their methodologies.[10]

Stanislavski

Constantin Stanislavski is the obvious choice to begin a discussion of Western approaches to acting. There is no question that he had an immeasurable influence on how we think about acting. It is now generally recognized that Stanislavski's thinking changed from a theory of emotional recall to an interest in physical actions. Despite this shift in focus, however, he remained committed to core principles, which run throughout his writings. I will focus on two readings. The first, "*On Various Trends in Theatrical Art*," written and revised between 1909 and 1922, is an extended critique of the acting conventions of his day and a manifesto articulating his vision of theatre. The second is the chapter on *The Government Inspector* in *An Actor's Work on a Role*, the last of the three volumes in which he set out the principles of his system for actor training. After discussing these writings in some detail, his work will be contextualized in comparison with the theories of his life long friend and nemesis, Vsevolod Meyerhold.

Stanislavski identifies three types of acting in his early writing: craft, presenting a role, and emotional identification:

> Whereas the art of emotional identification implies getting the feel of the role every time, at every performance, and the art of presenting a role means living through it just once at home in order to comprehend it and make up a form for it, expressive of its essence, craft forgets about "living the part" and strives to work out, once and for all, ready forms to express the emotions and scenic interpretation for all the roles and trends there are.[11]

The relation between the three types is hierarchical, craft being the lowest and emotional identification the most elevated. This triad is perceived as a continuum encompassing the binary of craft and art. The two poles of the craft/art binary are not equal in Stanislavski's eyes; rather, they too form a hierarchy in which art is seen as the equivalent of emotional identification. Actors capable of achieving the heights of acting are, therefore, the artists, while those who, for whatever reasons are not able to attain this goal are seen as craftsmen. The verticality of these relationships is important not only because it validates Stanislavski's own striving, which was to develop a system for helping actors become artists, but also because being an artist holds special status.

The metaphorical associations with being on top are numerous. The person who occupies the position on the uppermost rung of a ladder is understood to have the greatest authority and the most power; in this case that position is occupied by the artist who achieves emotional identification. However, there is another meaning attributed to hierarchies that is more resonant with Stanislavski's point of view. Up is connected with heaven, the realm of spiritual purity, while down is linked to earth and the mundane. The mundane in

Stanislavski's universe is associated with technique in its most negative sense: "ready-made clichés for illustrating all human emotions, and established patterns for aping all human characters. Techniques, clichés, and patterns greatly simplify the work of the actor-craftsman." His vision of the artist is one who aspires *"to create on the stage a live life of the human spirit."* The end of art is a spiritual accomplishment: the creation of a human spirit that is shown *"in artistic scenic form."*[12] While we need to address the concept of "creating a live life of the human spirit," it is important to note that he here introduces yet another hierarchical structure. Creativity is associated with emotional identification and art, while technique (at least in the negative sense) is linked to craft. To strive to be an artist is a spiritual quest that seeks to transcend dependence on clichés and patterns and seeks creativity in the realm of the human spirit.

The process of creating the "live life of the human spirit" by those who have the ability and the commitment is a journey that has three possible end points: craft, presenting the role, or emotional identification. This structure parallels Plato's allegory of the cave in *The Republic*. For Plato the promise of philosophy is the ability to break the bonds of illusion that keep us in the darkness of the cave and to climb out into the sunlight of truth. For Stanislavski, the light of truth is emotional identification. As in Plato's allegory there are three stages to Stanislavski's theory. To be chained in place so that one sees only the light reflected on the walls of the cave is the equivalent of craft. The actor creates an image but there is no greater value outside the performance. Once free from the bonds of illusion—seeing the flickering images on the wall for what they are—Plato's would-be philosopher recognizes that there is a reality that gives rise to false representations. In the world of Stanislavski this stage is "presenting the role." The actor who can present a role creates the emotional life of the character and then solidifies it into a repeatable performance. What is missing is the creation of a "living" character in front of an audience. There is an element of creativity, but it is formalized and stripped of its live spiritual content before the performance begins. To climb fully out of the darkness—into Plato's realm of truth and philosophy—is to leave the mundane theatre and step into the light of living art and the knowledge of how to *live* the emotions in performance.

For this to happen, an actor needs to develop and have access to creativity, "that spiritual and bodily state which best stimulates his inspiration." The creative state is not a static concept but a dynamic process for Stanislavski. "Art is not a *game,* not *artificiality,* and not *technical virtuosity,* but a *conscious process of spiritual and physical nature.*" The actor needs to define a process that will allow her to achieve emotional identification:

> The actor has to prepare his emotional and physical apparatus for coping with all the creative stages and processes necessitated by his work on a role, starting with his first acquaintance with it, then analyzing it, creating inner and outward circumstances, bringing them to life, conceiving a verity of passions, and finally embodying the lived-through inner image in an outward image and its actions.[13]

Creating a role is a journey that begins with developing a relationship to the character by engaging the circumstances of the text. If done correctly, this relationship elicits the necessary emotions in the actor who gives them form, and concludes with the communication of the role to the audience. The actor uses three elements in developing a role: "emotions, will, intellect." Note that these functions are conventionally considered to be internal to the actor, not visible to others, and that the body is excluded. Stanislavski may have assumed the body, for he typically talks about the emotional and physical components of performance; nevertheless it is significant that he does not specifically include it. In this text at least, he does not address the physical, other than to acknowledge that the work of the actor must be given a form in order to be communicated to the spectator, which work requires bodily techniques. Beyond this acknowledgment, Stanislavski understands the body to contain the work done by the actor, without playing a role in accessing emotions. The physical must instead be "slavishly obedient to the bidding of [the actor's] inner feeling"; while emotional identification, therefore, utilizes the *actor's creative state.*

The value of the creative state is the access it provides to the emotional history of the actor. For theatre to have power, the emotion needs to be intense, what Stanislavski calls a "primary feeling." In everyday life, we seldom experience such emotions; rather they are "cluttered with incidental extraneous details, often unrelated to the substance of the matter." When the actor achieves an "inner creative state," the actor experiences "repeated feelings he has known earlier in life and revived from memory," which then need to be "cleansed of everything superfluous."[14] By purifying the recalled emotions, getting rid of the clutter of ambiguity, the actor can portray the character with the emotional intensity necessary for theatre that is truly artistic—provided she can find the form suited to the character.

Of the three components involved in developing a role, the intellect is the least valued. The importance of the emotions and the relevance of the will to accessing the affective are evident. Intelligence is negligible and plays a role only in analyzing the circumstances of the play, supplying the information necessary for the process of emotional identification. In comparing hierarchies in this writing, the intellect parallels craft: a necessary technique but not a crucial player in creating the living human spirit on the stage. Similarly, the body is at this point a simple container, a crucible if you will, in which the living spirit is created, nurtured, and in which the spirit matures. The body's other function is to provide a conduit for expressing the spirit that has come into being through the process of emotional identification.

Later in his life, when he wrote *The Actor's Work on a Role,* Stanislavski rethought the role of the body. Instead of seeing it as simply a vehicle for expression, physical action became a means to arouse emotions. The significance of the shift in approach is not lost on the students of Tortsov (Stanislavski's alter ego for the purposes of his trilogy) who are at a loss for how to proceed when it is suggested they approach a role without first reading the play. Instead of analyzing the action, they are supplied with the given circumstances and asked to improvise within those limits. As the improvisation proceeds they discover that their emotions are being activated and an understanding of the character in a particular situation starts to form. The journey of the actor in creating a role has undergone a significant alteration or perhaps it is more accurate to say it has a new beginning point. What caused Stanislavski's change in direction is not clear. His continued association with Meyerhold may have contributed or, as is sometimes suggested, his work on Maeterlinck's symbolist play *Blue Bird* made him aware of the limitations of emotional recall. Whatever the reason, Stanislavski came to understand or at least appreciate the role of physical action in producing emotion.

The core of his theory did not change, however. He maintains the central metaphor of his work, with a slight but important shift. The "actor's creative state" becomes the "inner creative state."[15] When the body is not significant, Stanislavski may feel compelled to locate the creative process, but once the physical becomes a player in the acting process, it assumes a spatial relationship to the other aspects of creativity (emotion, will, and intelligence): they take place inside the body. Despite the newfound relevance of the body it remains for Stanislavski an adjunct to the creative process, continuing to be a container for the crucial work of the actor.

However, the metaphor is more complex than that of a simple container. In the earlier articulation the body is a vehicle of expression, a conduit that communicates a "spiritual" energy to the audience. It is a bridge across which what is internal becomes external. With the change in function, the body engages in a dynamic relationship with the creative state. Instead of being merely expressive, it is generative as well. Intentional movements based on given circumstances stir up feelings, which in turn give rise to new motivated activities, which in turn lead to longer sequences that are validated by the intensity of the emotions:

> [Long] periods have been created out of individually different actions, and an unbroken line of logical and sequential actions out of those periods. They are pushing forward and that produces movement, and movement, a genuine inner life. The more I repeat this scene, the stronger the line becomes, the greater its momentum, life, truth and belief.[16]

The relationship between the body and emotions is reciprocal. Physical actions generate an inner life, and the emotions validate the truthfulness of the sequence and offer direction to defining the next stages in the action. "Belief" in the appropriateness of the actor's work supports pursuit of a given direction, which in turn intensifies the emotional trajectory. At the same time that the body is engaged in this process, it continues to have the function of expressing the "truth" of the inner life to the other actors and/or the audience. By pursuing this truth through a succession of cycles the character emerges and gains fullness in the interaction of physical behavior and the emotions. The body negotiates between the internal and external worlds, between creativity and expression. In both theories it generates structures that define the performance, yet it also remains subservient to the "genuine inner life."

The script may define it, but the actor creates the character—with the caveat that the role must come to life within the given circumstances of the play. It is a cause-and-effect relationship. Identifying the circumstances and improvising with different physical actions initiate emotional responses that combine with the inner creative state. The conjunction of the emotions aroused through the improvisations and the actor's creative state gives rise to a "creative working state." "I taught you how to create a real sense of the life of the role not only mentally but physically.... This awareness arises of its own accord in the inner creative state previously established, combining with it to form the so-called *small creative working state*."[17] The work on a role engages the actor's creativity, giving rise to the definition of a specific character that draws on the material available through the more profound creative state shaped by the actor's training. In this lesser state, the appropriateness of the actions is determined by the identification between action and feeling, which gives rise to faith in the truthfulness of the character. The benchmark for this truth is the performer's judgment—through feeling rather than analysis—that her creativity is being fully engaged to produce a synthesis of the performer and the character: "[Whatever] role the actor is playing, he must always do what he does as himself, at his own risk. If he doesn't or if he loses himself in his role, he kills the character, because he has deprived it of living feeling."[18] If she does find herself *in* the part, the character will come to life, and the actor will create on the stage a *"living human spirit."*

There are two other structures present in both the articles. One is the absence of the intellect in Stanislavski's discussion of creating a role, and the other, not yet mentioned, is the need to free the self from constraints. There is no sustained critique of the intellect; rather it is a case of benign neglect. When it is referred to directly, it is always in combination with other, warmer elements: "I analysed my physical actions in the given circumstances but not just coldly, intellectually. All the elements helped me. I analysed my mind and body." Instead of valuing the conventional cool collectedness of reason, Stanislavski here embraces the functions usually associated with the passions. While intelligence is included, it is not regarded as the most important function. Indeed, analysis occurs only after the investigation has given rise to the character and even then it is not primarily an intellectual exercise: "It is only then that we can proceed to analyzing and studying a role, not with a cold heart, with our heads, but with the participation of the elements of the inner creative state and the active help of all the creative forces, mental and physical of our creative apparatus."[19] There is a clear effort to minimize the intrusions of reason (i.e., "a cold heart"). Analysis that occurs too early in the process, when one is trying to find the life of the character, is an obstacle that dampens the emotions that are key to creating a role.

The inner creative state is not a given, except in the few exceptional actors who are gifted with ready access to the emotional centers. Most aspiring actors need to develop the ability to access creativity. Like the slaves to images in Plato's cave, actors need to free themselves from the mundane aspects of life and develop sensitivity to the generative activities of the inner creative state. That is the purpose of training:

to learn that by freeing the spirit one becomes an artist. The liberating process in Stanislavski's system is designed to provide easy access to the emotions, whether through emotional recall, as he argues in his early writing, or through physical actions, the emphasis in his later writing. The assumption is that the emotions are deadened or repressed in everyday life and need to be enlivened or released so that they can be experienced and used in the art of acting.

Despite the inseparable connection between physical actions and emotion, the inner creative state is understood to be separate. In a striking image, Stanislavski figures the relationship between action and the creative state as an additive process:

> But, as I have already said, that is not sufficient to bring all the "elements" alive, to lead to the study and analysis of the play and the role with your whole self, not just with your head. That state needs to be informed by *a real sense of the life of the role and given circumstances.* That produces a wonderful transformation, a metamorphosis in the creative actor.[20]

The inner creative state of emotion, will, and intellect exists prior to the work on the text. The work in rehearsals is "informed by" the actor's sensitivity to "the life of the role" and gives rise to affective states. If the actor uses the given circumstances to improvise correctly, past emotional experiences will be retrieved as vital energies that fuel the acting process. The result can be figured as a chemical, if not alchemical, reaction that gives rise to the metamorphosis out of which the character emerges. But it is not a one-way street. The circumstances defined by the play create limits and boundaries, and the actor must find herself in the role. She must identify the emotional intensities and physical sequences that bring about the appropriate patterns for making the embodiment of the text seem alive and natural to an audience. What results from this work, when expressed in performance, is nothing less than the creation of a "living human spirit."

Stanislavski's concept of the actor is based on a hierarchical construct that privileges the artist as someone who can rise above the everyday and access the realm of art through an inner creative state. Attaining this state requires a process of sensitization to the internal workings of the soul, defined as the conjunction of emotion, will, and intellect. Physical actions determined by the circumstances given in a particular play engage the actor's creativity, activating emotional contents that define the "life" of the character. By infusing sequences of actions with these energies the character comes to live "naturally" and appropriately in the given circumstances, which include the actions of other character/actors in the play. When done with commitment and honesty, acting succeeds in using the actor's life to "breathe" life into the text, vibrantly creating the role.

The prevalence of the Stanislavski system in the West—particularly in the United States—makes his approach to training seem the *right* and *natural* way to think about acting. Therefore, it is useful at this time to examine an alternative to his system as a means of foregrounding the core assumptions of his approach to acting. The purpose is not to refute, but rather to underscore the fact that any theory of acting is a construct that seeks to explain and validate a particular way of working. The goal is also to make clear that there are other ways of thinking about what constitutes good acting, that there is not one truth. Vsevolod Meyerhold, who worked alongside Stanislavski, developed a very different approach to the actor's work.

Meyerhold

Meyerhold, like Stanislavski, changed his thinking about acting over the course of his career. While the reasons for Stanislavski's shift in thought are not completely clear, Meyerhold's transformation seems to be linked to the Russian Revolution. His early work in the symbolist theatre of Maurice Maeterlinck, or what Meyerhold calls "stylized theatre," reflects the supremacist movement in Russian art, with its emphasis on form rather than content. This focus is replaced later in his life by theories associated with Russian constructivism, a movement that recognized the role art could play in building a postrevolutionary society that rejected outmoded forms of social thought and sought to revitalize the country's industrial economy after years of political unrest. Meyerhold's decision to call his new approach to the training of actors biomechanics, underscores his support of the new aesthetic regime and its objectives. During this transition the language he uses to talk about the actor changes from one who "*freely* reveals his soul."[21] to that of "economical" expression that ensures "precision of movement."[22] Yet despite this radical rethinking, the tropes he employs remain consistent. His approach is in clear opposition to the theatre of Stanislavski, but both practitioners use the same metaphors for similar purposes.

Throughout his career, Meyerhold held fast to the belief that the actor-spectator relationship should be the focus of the theatre. Like Stanislavski, he believed the director and playwright should guide and support the creativity of the actor. Unlike his colleague, however, he believed more fully in the creative function of the audience: "the spectator is compelled to employ his imagination *creatively* in order to *fill in* those details *suggested* by the stage action." He rejected naturalism (his term for the work of the Moscow Art Theatre) because fleshing out the character's "living human spirit," left no room for the play of the spectator's imagination. It provided everything for them. By focusing on form, the actor could "transform the spectator into a vigilant observer."[23] The audience as active participant continued to be a central tenet of Meyerhold's theory.

Being interested in the experience of the audience does not mean that Meyerhold was only interested in presenting an external form. In his early work, he believes, like the Supremacists, that through form the actor reveals his soul. Meyerhold rejects the "histrionics of the old theatre,"[24] in favor of plasticity. "I employ *plastic movement*.... Plasticity itself is not new, but the form which I have in mind is new. Before, it corresponded closely to the spoken dialogue, but I am speaking of a *plasticity which does not correspond to the words*."[25] The movements and compositions created by the actors are not designed to support the meanings of the words, but to create a tension between the visual and aural. This is the gap that the audience fills through its own creativity. This process releases the performer from depending on the "exaggerated tremolo"[26] of the spoken word, allowing her to act "with everything light and unforced."[27] The actor's self-presentation within the parameters of this acting style involves an "exterior calm which covers volcanic emotions."[28] Like Stanislavski, Meyerhold was interested in the internal emotional state; but rather than making it the primary function of the actor, he sought to make its communication a by-product of acting. Naturalism, in reference to the Moscow Art Theatre, creates the illusion of everyday life by asking actors to present emotionally driven characters. Meyerhold insisted that the presentation is stronger if the actor detaches the emotions from the physicalization of the character; and allows the role to be communicated through the intensity of feeling. A volcano, before it erupts, creates tremors in the earth and belches smoke and stones. Without a direct demonstration of its force, the destructive potential is well understood. Meyerhold was interested in the actor conveying this intensity without having it take center stage as in expressionist acting. By presenting a calm surface that *contains* the feelings that are generated in the actor through the action and circumstances of the play, a stronger and more powerful theatre could be created.

The body *is* used to convey the emotional content, not as a vehicle for it, rather as a form—"the eyes, the lips, the sound, and manner of delivery"—that can communicate the "internal mystic vibration,"[29] which Meyerhold believed to be the source of dramatic power in the plays of Maeterlinck and other Symbolist playwrights. Rather than setting the tone of the presentation, the emotional content becomes an overtone, something that emanates from the actor without obvious effort. The actor still needs to generate the emotional content but needs to keep it below the surface and allow its intensity to be conveyed through what Roland Barthes calls "the grain of the voice,"[30] the qualities of expression that allow us to know the passion someone is feeling despite a seemingly calm exterior. The dichotomy between the volcanic emotions and the surface of the performance asks the audience to resolve the disjunction between what the actor is feeling and the formal plastic movement of the production. This engagement creates "an unbroken circulation of creative energy"[31] between what is experienced by the spectator and the work of the actor.

At this early stage, Meyerhold is less explicit about how the actor is to achieve the emotional intensity that lies below the surface of the performance. From the images that he uses, there are indications that the source of the material lies, as it does for Stanislavski, in the actor's subconscious. The gap the actor needs to create in order for the spectator to be engaged requires the performer to "penetrate *behind* the mask, *beyond* the action into the character as perceived by the mind; we want to penetrate to the *inner mask*."[32] Two metaphors are worth noting. One is that of the mask; the other is the interiority that lies within the surface of the body.

The mask is a façade that conceals the face beneath it. The purpose of penetrating the mask is to find what is being hidden from view. In Meyerhold's theatre, it is not the hidden face, but the emotional foundations of the character that are being sought. He does not expect the revelation of an essential emotion, however, he expects another mask, the "inner mask." The interior is multilayered and peeling away one layer does not give access to an essential truth, but to another boundary that conceals another interior. The image is one of containers within containers, similar to a nesting doll, except the removal of each layer does not reveal another face; it reveals an emotional intensity. Once revealed the force of the feelings can be used to drive the character. The body is not a vehicle here, but a membrane that allows the intensities of the unconscious to be expressed indirectly, not as the mask but through the mask, "the eyes, the lips, the sound, and manner of delivery." The unraveling of the character in the course of the action frees these emotional contents, making them available to the spectator. To use a different metaphor, one not used by Meyerhold, the evocation of emotion is like the bouquet of a wine. As air mixes with the body of the wine, pheromones are released. The olfactory experience of the aroma reveals the wine before it is tasted. The emotions are freed by the interaction of the actor with the context of the play. There is no need to perform them. If they have reached the intensity of a volcano, they will manifest themselves without explicit effort.

The keys to finding the emotions appropriate to the character are found in "the rhythm of the language and the movement."[33] As in the later Stanislavski, physical actions (speech and movement) evoke within the actor the feelings necessary to create the intensity and therefore the gap between a calm exterior and a volcanic interior. While Meyerhold loses interest in the "mystical vibrations," his fascination with the body continues in the development of his biomechanics.

In his early career Meyerhold devised a simple diagram of relationships in production. Unlike a model in which the actor is at the beck and call of the playwright and director, the performer is the creative force. Guided and supported by the other artists, she uses the circumstances provided by them to assume responsibility for creating the interaction between herself and the audience. In biomechanics the actor remains at the core of the theatre experience, but the focus shifts to the different stages she needs to go through in developing a performance. In a now famous formula, Meyerhold defines the two primary functions of the performer.

$N - A_1 + A_2$
(where N = the actor; A_1 = the artist who conceives the idea and issues the instructions necessary for its execution; A_2 = the executant who executes the conception of A_1).[34]

The actor has become responsible for devising as well as executing the concept. Meyerhold further subdivides acting into two parallel phases: pre-acting and acting. Pre-acting "prepares the spectator's perception in such a way that he comprehends the scenic situation fully resolved in advance and so has no need to make any effort to grasp the underlying message of the scene."[35] The actor is no longer expected to create a gap between the text and the physical action, but now to prepare the audience for what is to come: the communication of the text. This binary is further divided into the three parts that form the acting cycle. They are intention, realization, and reaction. In preparing the audience, the actor needs to define an intention, which is then realized through the performance of the text. The enactment concludes with a reaction, or an assessment of what occurs, which in turn provides an impetus for the next intention. The intention, like the conceptualization of the part (A_1) is an "intellectual assimilation of a task"[36] and is followed by the performance of the task (A_2), which is "volitional, mimetic and vocal."[37] The dissection of the actor's work into discrete parts rejects the idea of "mystic vibrations" without becoming a purely intellectual exercise. Rational analysis has a role to play in the rehearsal process, but the work of the actor has more to do with the body and emotions than the intellect. Biomechanics defines a journey that prepares the performer's instrument.

Meyerhold's formula reflects the time-action studies of Frederick Taylor, who at the beginning of the twentieth century observed workers in factories and proposed removing extraneous effort in order to make the process more efficient.[38] Similarly, the actor is expected to hone her performance to the essentials: "In so far as the task of the actor is the realization of a specific objective, his means of expression must be economical in order to ensure that *precision* of movement which will facilitate *the quickest possible realization of the objective.*"[39] To this end, biomechanics consists of a series of exercises, designed to prepare the body for performance.[40] Each step of the sequence involves a precise movement to improve the flexibility of the actor and to eliminate extraneous activity. Less evident is that each gesture in the sequence is also designed to stimulate the affective centers of the actor.

> All psychological states are determined by specific physiological processes. By correctly resolving the nature of his state physically, the actor reaches the point where he experiences the *excitation* which communicates itself to the spectator and induces him to share in the actor's performance.[41]

The performer has greater access to her emotions because biomechanics helps to identify "points of excitation."[42] Continuous training with biomechanics provides the actor with the keys to creating a role: "(1) *the innate capacity for reflex excitability*...(2) 'physical competence', consisting of a true eye, sense of balance, and the ability to sense at any given moment the location of his centre of gravity."[43] The emotional response is connected to the movement, which when properly facilitated causes the initiation of the emotion through the physical action. The training also has the effect of replacing the techniques of everyday life with a body that is attuned to the necessities of the stage. The connection between physical actions and emotional intensity is strengthened. Meyerhold never loses sight of the fact that the theatre is not an intellectual exercise, but that the core of the theatre is the emotional connection between the actor and the spectator.

The purpose of the relationship between the performer and the audience changes with the shift to biomechanics. In the stylistic theatre the meaning of the performance arises from the distance between the plastic movement of the actor and the emotional intensity that supports the calm surface. The goal is to "penetrate the mask." Biomechanics maintains the image of the mask, but it foregoes the purpose of revealing the inner mask; rather, the actor "lifts the mask of the character to reveal his true nature to the spectator; he does not merely speak the lines furnished by the dramatist, he uncovers the roots from which the lines have sprung."[44] The objective of this unveiling is not the revelation of a "living human spirit," but service to the state as an actor-tribune.

> The actor-tribune sets himself the task of developing scenic situations not in order to impress the spectator with the beauty of their theatricality, but like a surgeon whose task it is to uncover what lies within. The actor-tribune acts not the situation itself, but what is concealed behind it and what it has to reveal for a specifically propagandist purpose.[45]

The theatre serves a political function: showing the reality behind reactionary behavior and revealing the virtuous behavior of the representatives of the state.

Nothing could be further from Stanislavski's vision of the theatre. The evocation of a "living human spirit" has nothing to do with the espoused propagandist intentions that Meyerhold sets for the actor. However, despite their vast differences, they share a common metaphorical language. The body is a vehicle for the communication of a text, which is defined less by the written word than by the role the actor develops within specific circumstances. Physical actions are useful in stirring the emotions and creating a body that is useful for communicating them. Both theorists argue that everyday life needs to be transcended if the world of the play is going to be communicated and that creating the world of the play requires a revelation of what is inside the performer—something that needs to be discovered and intensified so that it can be shared with the audience. Despite the emphasis on the actor's intellectual engagement, emotional communication is the most significant aspect of the performance.

Bertolt Brecht and Antonin Artaud

Bertolt Brecht and Antonin Artaud did not train actors. In that sense, their inclusion in this chapter may seem curious. However, both continue to have an immense impact on acting, not only in the postdramatic theatre but in non-realism as well. Their extreme positions are particularly valuable in putting the ideas of Stanislavski in perspective and for understanding the impetus behind the work of those who choose realism as their preferred acting style. Equally if not more important, Brecht and Artaud use many of the same concepts as Stanislavski uses, if for very different ends.

When Brecht began writing, his plays were heavily influenced by expressionism, the non-realist form of his day. Expressionist playwrights used theatre to critique the alienating forces of contemporary life. As an acting style it was an inversion of Stanislavski's realist theatre. Instead of focusing on the surface of everyday life and using emotional intensities to reveal the inner workings of the characters, expressionists attempted to use the text as a vehicle for expressing the power of the unconscious. Brecht's involvement in World War I and his exposure to the writings of Karl Marx led him away from expressionism and to search for new overtly political forms . He came to see the theatre as a pedagogical device for awakening his audiences to the oppressive truth of Capitalism. Instead of bewailing his state of alienation, he turned expressionism on its head and used alienation as a tool for teaching.

Brecht rejected Stanislavski's concern with the "living human spirit" just as he moved away from the overt emotionalism of the expressionists. He believed empathy was a trap that made society appear unchangeable. If theatre were to play a role in improving life, it needed to increase awareness of the repressive forces of society by making its audience adopt a critical attitude and actively critique the status quo as represented on stage. The alternative was, as he understood realism, to provide an emotional experience that distracted the spectator from facing the inequities and hypocrisy of the world. To this end Brecht transformed *alienation* from a word that describes a state of being, to a word that evokes an active force for awakening a sleepy population; and in so doing he developed a new way of thinking about acting and its relationship to emotion.

Like Meyerhold, Brecht focuses on the spectator. Unlike his Russian counterpart, however, he wants a particular kind of audience: the spectator of a sporting event. Like today's "armchair quarterback" who critiques the play calling and the performance of the team from a distance, the Brechtian audience should adopt an active attitude when seeing a play. During a football game, the sports enthusiast becomes involved in the play; but, when the play is over, sits back and evaluates it, only to be brought back into the game when the action resumes. The actor's responsibility is, according to Brecht, to encourage this kind of behavior, and he called the actor's means of doing so the *Verfremdungseffekt*, a word that can be translated as "alienating," "distancing," "estranging," "or making the familiar unfamiliar." By distancing the audience from the particular acts of the characters, the spectator enters into a concentrated, active critique of the play.

Brecht, in his thinking about the *Verfremdungseffekt*, employs one of the major metaphors of Western thought: the Cartesian distinction between mind and body. The mind, associated with cool rationality, is clearly distinguishable from the body, associated with heated emotions. In becoming distanced from the action, the audience could bracket its emotional response and use it as a springboard to critical reflection. The question of emotion, therefore, becomes pivotal in his thinking about theatre and, as we shall see, an issue that plagued him throughout his career.

Brecht identifies two types of acting. One he labels "imitation," linking it to Stanislavski's use of empathy or the ability to reproduce what another is feeling in oneself; he labels the other, "demonstration," which makes use of the feelings one has when relating a story about an emotional event:

> Empathy alone may stimulate a wish to imitate the hero, but it can hardly create the capacity. If a feeling is to be an effective one, it must be acquired not merely impulsively but through the understanding. Before a correct attitude can be imitated it must first have been understood that the principle is applicable to situations that are not exactly like those portrayed. It is the theatre's job to present the hero in such a way that he stimulates conscious rather than blind imitation.[46]

The mixed metaphor Brecht uses is telling. Empathy is blind, while "alienated" emotions are subject to understanding. Blindness means sightlessness—dwelling in darkness—or that vision is at best clouded. Understanding, on the other hand, signifies vision, enlightenment, and clarity. The conundrum Brecht faced was how to bring about the latter while limiting the force of the former. He found his answer in Hegel's dialectic.

The dialectical structure of thesis-antithesis-synthesis requires the juxtaposition of two contrasting points of view that allow for a new understanding to be synthesized from the complementary antagonisms. Brecht's name for this process is "an exercise in *complex seeing*."[47] The complexity arises from a disjunction between what the audience is led to expect and the reality of what is presented. Without a system of expectations there is no distancing effect. One needs to be alienated *from* something; it is a spatial metaphor that implies a dislocation. The audience needs to move from a state of clouded vision to the clarity of understanding. The actor, therefore, pulls the spectators *in* before taking them *out* of the action. "In" implies intimacy, while "out" implies perspective. "Intimacy" implies an emotional connection, while "perspective" implies detachment. The difficulty lies in creating an effective connection that can then be broken without appearing schizophrenic. The problem with translating *Verfremdungseffekt* as "alienation" is the danger of turning the audience "off" the production, so the spectator ceases to be engaged. Without the engagement, there is no dialectic. The emotion portrayed by the actor needs to keep the audience present in the performance while at the same time making it critical of what is happening and what it is feeling. That is why Brecht prefers demonstration to empathy. Demonstration allows the viewer to recognize the emotion as it relates to the action without identifying with or "feeling" it. This connection between effect and critical thinking clarifies what Brecht means when he says, "It is perhaps more important to be able to think above the stream than to think in the stream."[48] (Brecht, 44). To know that one is "above the stream" is to know what it is to be in it. The actor must demonstrate the emotion to let the spectator know what is being felt but she must do so without encouraging identification. The audience must never be allowed forget that the actor portrays a character; in other words, the performer can never appear to "become" the role she is playing.

In his famous essay "The Street Scene," Brecht argues that witnesses to an accident do not attempt to live the emotions felt in the moment either by themselves or by those involved, but use emotion to tell the story from a particular point of view. Instead of living the truth of what a character might be feeling, as Stanislavski advocates, Brecht insists the actor focus on the surface of the events, depicting the character's role in what happens rather than losing the self in the retelling of it:

> It is most important that one of the main features of the ordinary theatre should be excluded from our street scene: the engendering of illusion. The street demonstrator's performance is essentially repetitive.

The event has taken place; what you are seeing now is a repeat. If the scene in the theatre follows the street scene in this respect, then the theatre will stop pretending not to be theatre.[49]

The goal is not to create the illusion of the first time, but to retell an event that can then be evaluated. To this end, Brecht adopts two terms to convey what he wants: *quotation* and the *gestus*.

Quotation is to use someone else's words for a particular effect. The speaker acknowledges that the words are not hers and, therefore, not original or spontaneous, but memorized. For an actor to present a role as a quotation is to refuse "becoming" the role in the sense that Stanislavski conceives of becoming. There is no illusion of an inner spirit; rather the focus is on presenting the form:

> Once the idea of total transformation is abandoned the actor speaks his part not as if he were improvising himself but like a quotation. At the same time he obviously has to render all the quotation's overtones, the remark's full human and concrete shape; similarly the gesture he makes must have the full substance of a human gesture even though it now represents a copy.[50]

The actor is not transformed into the character and therefore makes no attempt to create the illusion that she *is* the character. Instead the performer presents the shape but not the psychological energy that Stanislavski demands of creating a role. The presentation of the part exhibits the fully developed surface of the character without the inner heat. Quoting someone is done with conviction and force, but it does not create the illusion that the actor is the person who wrote the words. The emotion that fuels the performance belongs to the actor and what she wants to communicate about the role and the action of the play. Brecht's acting is not cold and intellectual; it is driven by the actor's passions and not the character's.

The *gestus*, a means of maintaining the qualities of a quotation, is a complicated notion because Brecht uses it to signify a number of theatrical functions that are subject to the *Verfremdungseffekt* (e.g., making lighting fixtures visible, using titles for scenes, the interjection of songs and poetry), as well, as to signify acting.[51] The purpose of the gestus is to provide a distilled gesture stripped of any superfluous movement and carefully crafted to draw attention to it. In this regard it is akin to Meyerhold's biomechanics. The actor shapes the action to make the spectator aware that the character's everyday actions define a relationship to the world, that gestures are socially constructed. In rehearsal, improvisations are subject to scrutiny; choices are examined for content and their relationship to the structure of the play in question. Specific elements of the improvisatory work are selected and refined to make them specific and resonant with the play's political discourse. The gestures are simplified and clarified:

> Here it is essential that the actual playing should be infused with the gest of handing over a finished article. What now comes before the spectator is the most frequently repeated of what has not been rejected, and so the finished representations have to be delivered with the eyes fully open, so that they may be received with the eyes fully open too.[52]

The purpose of the gestus is not to make the acting simple—a move that shows contempt for the intelligence of the audience—but to make the spectator aware of the conflict between the values the characters espouse and their actions: "The coherence of the character is in fact shown by the way in which its individual qualities contradict one another."[53] Rather than showing a character as a unified subject in a state of emotional distress, Brecht's theatre portrays people who are alienated from themselves—a state made apparent through the sequence of actions that open for examination the characters' internal contradictions. For example, Mother Courage worries about the safety of her children but in the next scene haggles over the price of saving their lives. The specificity of the *gestus* will signify the internal dilemma of the characters in external form; at the same time, it will communicate their political position in the social matrix of the play.

The actor uses quotation and the gestus to allow the dialectic to take place through the alienation (in the sense of "making strange") of the character's actions.

> The contradiction between acting (demonstration) and experience (empathy) often leads the uninstructed to suppose that only one or the other can be manifest in the work of the actor.... In reality it is a matter of two mutually hostile processes which fuse in the actor's work; his performance is not just composed of a bit of the one and a bit of the other. His particular effectiveness comes from the tussle and tension of the two opposites, and also from their depth.[54]

The synthesis of the demonstration and the experience of emotion is a fusion of the public and the personal, of the visible and the invisible. In the fusion there is no room for the private feeling of emotion; rather what is presented is what of the emotion can be made visible:

the effects on the body and in the voice. It is not the pulses that define the depth of emotion, but what can be made visible of the affective state.

Whereas Brecht sought to eliminate any reference to metaphysics, Antonin Artaud attempted the precise opposite: to bring to the stage the metaphysical intensities that underlie the emotions. Artaud was a member of the surrealist movement until he had a falling out with André Breton over the future direction of the movement. Breton favored joining forces with the nascent French Communist Party, while Artaud wanted to follow his own passionate research. Heavily influenced by Freud's work on the unconscious, surrealism sought to overcome the repressive and alienating effects of society by searching for a way to unite the unconscious with conscious life. This endeavor took two forms: One married dream images with everyday life, as in Luis Buñuel's film *Un chien andalou* (*An Andalusian Dog*) or the paintings of René Magritte, Salvador Dali, and Georgio de Chirico. The other sought evidence of the unconscious as manifest in everyday life, such as Breton's novel *Nadja*, which combined an imaginary love story with photographs of hauntingly empty locales in Paris, or Eli Lotar's photograph of an abattoir, or slaughterhouse.[55] Artaud adopted neither approach and forged his own path, using the "theatre of cruelty" as a crucible for releasing the pure intensities of desire.

Artaud agreed in principle with Stanislavski's concept of bringing the "living human spirit to the stage." He believed, however, that rather than illusion, it was the actor's living spirit that should be brought to the stage. He likened the process to alchemy where dross is transformed into gold. His base materials were the body of the actor or, more specifically, his own body. Extant recordings of Artaud's performance are painful to hear for the excruciating sound of his screams as he attempts to release the spirit from his flesh through self-laceration.[56] Beneath the excesses of what is clearly a tormented mind, there is a vision of acting that has inspired such diverse theatre practitioners as The Living Theatre and Jerzy Grotowski. Developing a clear image of Artaud's theory of acting requires an understanding of his deepest principles because they form the foundation for the structures that some actors emulate in performance.

One of the founding metaphors in Artaud's writings on the theatre is the concept of the "double." In the terms of surrealism, the double manifests the alienating split between the conscious and unconscious. The visible is associated with everyday life; while its double dwells in the realm of the repressed. Artaud sought a means of releasing this other energy in its pure form, unadulterated by the flesh or society.

He believed the theatre had the potential to be such a means, but what he found in his attempts to bring the double to light was an unrelenting resistance.

Throughout his life Artaud struggled with forms of expression. Even the most flexible modes of communication lacked the suppleness and spontaneity he needed to convey the intensities of his ideas. Neither the languages of the stage nor that of poetry could contain or transport the content he felt compelled to release. They debased what he wanted to say because these forms of signification were incommensurate with the images that roiled inside him. In their failure, he felt they "stole his breath away."[57] Artaud associates the respiratory movement of air in the body with the life of the spirit. The release of the breath has the potential to release the spirit but it requires a reorganization of the actor's body, which needs to be transformed from a repository of the habits of everyday life into a conduit for transmitting the pure energy of the double.

Artaud locates this spiritual force in the unconscious and links it to Freud's concept of the repressed. Society produces forms such as language and the conventions of bodily behavior that impede our ability to express ourselves directly, and it is only by overcoming these obstacles that the soul is set free. The soul is not contained in any one location but infuses every molecule of the body. To release its energy, Artaud claims, the actor needs to become a "body without organs." The body, whole at birth, becomes fragmented into discrete structures through the analytic processes of a scientific society that develops taxonomies in order to come to an understanding of how the body functions. This process distorts our thinking about the physical self and represses our power and creativity. Only by "a meticulous and unremitting pulverization" of all social and cultural forms can the energies of the "body without organs" be released.[58] Underlying this system of metaphors is the belief that there is a natural body that is capable of releasing pure forms of energy without the intervention of the organizing principles of society. Artaud's quest is an ontological search for origins: the desire to recover an essential state that has been contaminated by culture.

This appears to be an inversion of the Cartesian mind-body split. Instead of privileging the mind, Artaud glorifies the body, or at least the energy of the unconscious; and there is little room for reason in the equation. Artaud does not dismiss the intellect, however, insisting that there is a bodily intelligence that is sublimated by an alienating society. In his attempts to define this alternative intellectuality, Artaud reconceptualizes semiotics. The sign in the work of Ferdinand de Saussure and Charles Sanders Peirce assumes that for every signifier there is a signified and that it is this relationship that makes communication possible. Artaud posits a sign for which there is no denotative signifier: "These spiritual signs have a precise meaning which strikes us only intuitively but with enough violence to make useless any translation into logical discursive language."[59] Indeed translation is *impossible*. As Artaud argues in his correspondence with Jacques Rivère, language is not sufficiently supple to contain the meaning of the double, which can only be glimpsed obliquely in the interstices of the juxtaposition of words.[60] Its force is not rational, and its meaning lies in its *felt* intensity. Nor is the double simply irrational: "Everything that might correspond to immediate psychological necessities, corresponds as well to a sort of spiritual architecture, created out of gesture and mime but also out of the evocative power of a system."[61] It is a system that does not participate in the discourse of reason, but is understood through physical gesture in performance.

Seeing a performance by Balinese dancers was a turning point for Artaud, because in their performance he found a meaning that was more than a simple emotional response.[62] The gestures of the dance were moving, three-dimensional hieroglyphs: "mysterious signs which correspond to some unknown, fabulous, and obscure reality which we here in the Occident have completely repressed"[63] The theatre from Bali communicated through the language of temporal images (visual and aural) that rendered conscious thought irrelevant. What *was* significant in the dance was the visceral communication between the bodies of the performer and the spectator:

> this physics of absolute gesture which is the idea itself and which transforms the mind's conceptions into events perceptible through the labyrinths and fibrous interlacings of matter, gives us a new idea of what belongs by nature to the domain of forms and manifested matter.[64]

The content lies neither in the surface narrative nor, *pace* Stanislavski, as subtext—although it bears a resemblance to both—but in a reality that appears in the interstices of text: "that intellectual space, psychic interplay, and silence solidified by thought which exist between the members of a written phrase is here, in the scenic space, traced between the members, the air, and the perspectives of a certain number of shouts, colors and movements." The intellect that interests Artaud is one that responds to a "primitive" unity, that elicits content without reason or language, before a distinction is created between mind, body, and world, before the body *with* organs—. The function of the actor—and this is why it is a "cruel" theatre—is to provoke this nonrational intellectuality through performance, to create through the body the visceral hieroglyphs. It requires an unremitting process of self-negation, or the elimination of the effects of culture from the body.[65]

Should one succeed in freeing the body from habitual modes of behavior, the breath is the vehicle that will release the spirit from its material bonds. Artaud differentiates between two types of breathing: that which supports the physical activity of the athlete; and that which is supported by the body of the actor in the theatre.[66] The ability to sustain the exertion of sport necessitates constant and deep breathing. The actor does not depend on the quantity of air but on finding the correct breath for every gesture (in the broadest sense of the term): "For every feeling, every mental action, every leap of human emotion there is a corresponding breath which is appropriate to it."[67] Artaud's critique of the acting of his day is the lack of respect given to the body and breathing. "Since they do nothing but talk and have forgotten they ever had a body in the theater, they have naturally also forgotten the use of their windpipes."[68] The ability of the actor to perform is limited by such neglect of the physical. Without the body supporting the breath and supple "windpipes," actors lack the emotional force necessary to communicate: "The same points which support physical effort are those which also support the emanation of emotive thought."[69] Breath has the potential to express the spirit, if the deforming forces of language and behavior can be kept from stealing it away and returning performance to mundane illusion.

Artaud's theory of the double continues to be a powerful force in thinking about acting, perhaps because of its relationship to Stanislavski's subtext, which is the motivating energy in the character's pursuit of objectives and defines the character's responses to the action of others. Yet Stanislavski's is a lineage that Artaud would have denied as vehemently, I suspect, as Stanislavski would have rejected the excesses of the theatre of cruelty. The idea of an essential energy that is tapped for the actor's performance continues, however differently inflected, in the next generation of European acting theorists and teachers: Jerzy Grotowski, Jacques Lecoq, and Michael Chekhov.

European Theories of Actor Training

These three theorist-practitioners seem to have little in common. Grotowski, who saw himself as continuing the work of Stanislavski, pursued a transcendental approach to acting through a process he called *via negativa*. Lecoq used masks to find a neutral creative state in his mime work; and Michael Chekhov, nephew of the playwright, employed the psychological gesture (PG). The differences between them are profound, yet there are significant similarities in their thinking about the work of the actor.

Over his lifetime of research into acting Grotowski defined four stages: theatre of presentation, paratheatre, theatre of sources, and art as vehicle. Bordering on the theological, he believed firmly in the importance of self-discipline and commitment as a means of transcending conventional theatre in pursuit of "carnal prayer."[70] There are two important concepts here: (1) a journey and (2) the link he identifies between the carnality of the body and a higher, spiritual presence. The religious overtones are not coincidental or merely rhetorical. Grotowski expects his actors to dedicate their lives to training with an almost monklike determination: "The work takes at least eight hours a day (often much more), six days a week, and lasts for years in a systematic way."[71] To appreciate the necessity of this intense commitment, the *via negativa* needs to be defined.

While his research is based on the systematic pragmatism of Stanislavski's pursuit of the "living human spirit," Grotowski's work is strongly influenced by Artaud's vision of the theatre of cruelty: "We propose to the actor that he should transform himself before the spectator's eyes using only his inner impulses, his body, when we state that the magic of the theatre consists in this transformation **as it comes to birth** we once more raise the question: did Artaud ever suggest any other kind of magic?"[72] To help an actor achieve a performance "using only his inner impulses" Grotowski echoes Artaud's "meticulous and unremitting pulverization" by demanding a scientific rigor in his laboratory. He understands that the actor is structured by physical and mental habits that are ingrained in the body and mind. These behaviors, arising from repetitions in everyday life, function to express unconscious impulses in socially acceptable ways. To restore the intensity of the impulse the actor must rid the body of cultural inscriptions, making it a conduit for the release of pure intensity:

> We attempt to eliminate his organism's resistance to this psychic process. The result is freedom from the time-lapse between inner impulse and outer reaction in such a way that the impulse is already an outer reaction. Impulse and action are concurrent: the body vanishes, burns, and the spectator sees only a series of visible impulses.[73]

Whereas Artaud never developed a technique for achieving this ideal state, Grotowski used his Wroclaw facility to find the means to this end.

The actor's "organism" keeps in the energies of the unconscious, preventing them from direct expression. These obstructive behaviors need to be eliminated; and this is the work of training. True to *via negativa*, the performer does not seek an end through the exercises; she seeks rather to "eradicate blocks" by working through the resistance: "One does not '**want to do that**' but rather '**resigns from not doing it**'"[74] Seeking a particular goal requires concentration on a specific objective, which in turn limits the actor's openness to impulses. By "resigning," the tensions of goal-oriented work are released and the performer becomes open to an alternative energy. In principle, once the resistances to impulses are released, the body ceases to contain the forces of the unconscious, becoming the means of expressing them in performance: "the body vanishes, burns, and the spectator sees only a series of visible impulses." Like Artaud's desire to "let the spirit take its leap" at the "incandescent edges of the future,"[75] Grotowski envisions "all the actor's psychic and bodily powers which emerge from the most intimate layers of his being and his instinct, springing forth in a sort of 'translumination.'"[76] He is not interested in alchemy, but in preparing the body for the release of creativity. And, unlike Artaud, his vision of theatre is not a form of psychic anarchy, but of a disciplined revelation of what is most intimate through a carefully crafted performance.

In Grotowski's theatre of presentation, the actor is not asked to create a character as defined by a play. The script and the performance are rather shaped by a parallel relationship between the text and the actor's work. Determining the structure that the audience sees is the function of the director, who molds the production so that the revelations of the performer are synchronized with the narrative of the text. There is, therefore, no necessary correlation between character and actor, between the action of the play and the performer's score. For the parallel between performer and role, performance and story to be effective, the score must be detailed with precision: "We believe that a personal process which is not supported and expressed by a formal articulation and disciplined structuring of the role is not a release and will collapse in shapelessness."[77] The articulation of the score requires precise choices and a weeding out of anything that is not necessary. For the communication with the audience to be effective, the performer must "subtract, seeking **distillation** of signs by eliminating those elements of 'natural' behavior which obscure pure impulse."[78] The actor must be prepared to "resign" herself to the specific actions that most concretely and specifically allow for the release of the impulse.

Grotowski cites as an example Ryszard Cieslak's performance of Julius Slowacki's adaptation of Calderón de la Barca's *The Constant Prince*. The play, according to Grotowski, concerns a martyr whose ability to endure extreme suffering gains the respect of his torturers as they kill him. This is the story presented to the audience, but it is not the story on which Cieslak based his performance:

> All the river of life in the actor was linked to a certain memory, which was very far from any darkness, any suffering. His long monologues were linked to the actions which belonged to that concrete memory from his life, to the most minute actions and physical and vocal impulses of that remembered moment. It was a relatively short moment from his life—we can say some tens of minutes, a time of love from his early youth.[79]

This is not the emotional recall of Stanislavski, which is based on the character's actions and the given circumstances of the play, Ciezlak's performance was an expression of the emotions associated with the event through physical actions. The actor began working alone with Grotowski "months and months" before rehearsals for the production began.[80] The score developed during this time focused on the memory of adolescent love. The joys and pains of that transitory experience were distilled, structured, and amplified into a performance that paralleled and fueled the speeches of the play. This work was never intended to turn the actor into the character. The distance between the source materials and the role is important in understanding Grotowski's approach to the theatre. The material that fueled Ciezlak was not derived from the text and the associations that created the emotional through-line of his performance were highly personal and never explicitly communicated to the audience. He did not create the illusion that his performance was based in the Slowaki/Calderón play.

Grotowski was at the end of his career when he related this story from the first stage of his journey in the theatre. He undoubtedly told it because of what it says about his early period, but he must also have told it because of its relevance to his later work. "Art as vehicle" can be characterized as adding a spatial dimension to the primarily temporal focus of "theatre as presentation." In the latter, the score of the actor and the text run on parallel tracks, each complementing and supporting the other as they unfold for the audience. The work Grotowski did in the later stage of his career was not intended for public presentation; he saw it as research into the art of acting. The score had by then become subordinate to the verticality of the carnal prayer.

Combining the carnal with the act of praying is a complex metaphor. Carnality is associated with the sensual, earthy body, with materiality and appetites. Prayer, meanwhile, is a transcendent and spiritual form of communication with God. This theological interpretation is supported by the numerous biblical allusions in Grotowski's writing, for example his reference to the story of Jacob and the ladder to heaven: "The Bible speaks of the story of Jacob who fell asleep with his head on a stone and had a vision; he saw, upright upon the earth, a great ladder, and perceived the forces or—if you prefer—the angels, who ascended and descended,"[81] The aesthetic experience is one that raises the artist above the mundane to the ethereal realms of the spiritual. It is not simply a prayer, however, because the actor is not asleep with her head on a stone. She remains in her body—the vehicle—and is, if we push the metaphor, dreaming of angels while very much awake. Grotowski insists on the actor's alertness when he develops the image.

> For this ladder to function, every rung must be well made. Otherwise the ladder will break; all depends on the artisanal competence with which one works, on the quality of the details, on the quality of the actions and the rhythm, on the order of the elements; all should be impeccable from the point of view of craft. Instead, usually if someone looks in art for his Jacob's ladder, he imagines that it depends simply on good will; so he looks for something amorphous, a kind of soup, and he dissolves himself in his own illusions.[82]

The carnal is not simply lust for the spiritual; it is subject to the same rigorous discipline and specificity of the theatre of presentation. The ability to rise to the heights of creativity requires detail in the physical actions, immersion in the internal rhythms of the text, (or, in art as vehicle, a song) and an ordering of parts that lets the angels rise up and come down the ladder, creating a spiritual circulation that uses the performer's carnality to express the intensity of the impulses.

Dreams and rituals take advantage of liminal spaces, defined as the thresholds between the worlds the performer occupies as someone betwixt and between, in neither the one nor the other, or in both simultaneously. The carnal keeps the actor grounded in the material world through specific and detailed actions, while the prayer releases the spiritual to emanate through the body. The carnal prayer is not a form of schizophrenia—two states existing "independently" in the body—but a fusion of the effable and the ineffable, the physical and metaphysical. Without Jacob's head firmly at rest on the stone, there is no dream of a ladder reaching to heaven on which angels ascend and descend.

There is continuity between Grotowski's early and his late thinking about acting. They both depend on a parallel structure. In the early stage the parallel exists between the actor's score and the text; in the later stage, it exists between the carnal and the spiritual. In both instances Grotowski defines the binaries as discrete realms that are linked by a rigorous discipline, which allows for a liberation of the performer's creative energy. Whereas Artaud believes the spirit can only be freed through the demolition of all forms, Grotowski understands the freeing of impulses to depend on a form defined by specific physical actions. *Via negativa* is not simply the negation of culturally formed tensions in the body. When the performer "resigns from not doing it," she develops a technique, a structuring of the organism that allows the "living human spirit" to express itself in performance.

Jacques Lecoq also sought to "rewrite" the habits of the body in order to release the actor's creativity, but he subscribes to the metaphysics of neither Artaud nor Grotowski. His interest in removing everyday habits was to help the actor access the "universal poetic sense."[83] This "sense," a metaphysics of a different kind, is the "*essence* of life"[84] It is "draw[n] from the material of real life" which he identifies as being "composed of time, space, tension, thrust, colour, light, and matter"[85] While Grotowski seeks to free the internal impulse through memory, Lecoq looks to the external world for inspiration. Grotowski and Lecoq do agree, however, on the importance of memory and the body's suppleness and openness to the creative act.

The first stage in Lecoq's path to the "universal poetic sense" is gaining an understanding of the body freed from everyday tensions, which is accomplished through the "neutral mask." Neutrality to Lecoq is not a passive state but one of potential energy: "the *state of neutrality* prior to action, a state of receptiveness to everything around us, with no inner conflict."[86] The neutral mask is, therefore, one that has been stripped of individual characteristics and has no signs of emotion. In using the neutral mask the actor releases the tensions that resist simple, direct movement—which are the effect of "inner" conflicts, the by-products of everyday life. The objective of the mask is to achieve "a state of discovery, of openness, of freedom to receive...a state of perfect balance and economy of movement...a stable position."[87] It also consists of identifying fulcrum points, centers that signal an equal distribution of weight and the ability to move efficiently, effortlessly, and simply. By developing a neutral body, the actor frees herself of idiosyncratic movement, of the little tics and habitual gestures that make her recognizable as her individual self.

The openness for which Lecoq strives requires what can be called a soft focus. A hard focus looks at the detailed outline of a single object, while the soft attempts to take in as much of the field of vision as possible without singling out a specific set of perceptions. In soft focus the mind does not attend to anything in particular and is calm—freed of the competing demands of everyday life. In order to achieve this state, the performer needs to be relaxed but ready; her breath will be regular and slower than usual; the skeletal frame will be centered and aligned. This configuring of the performer takes place in the context of a task: *"In a state of repose, relaxed, lying on the ground, I ask the students to 'wake up for the first time'. Once the mask is awake, what can it do? How can it move?"*[88] The actor's attention to the command cannot disrupt the neutral state; it must rather be attentive to the interaction between the implications of the task and the performer's responses as the task is carried out. There is no correct way to do the exercise but there is an awareness of those moments when the balance between attention and action falter and the continuity of the performance is disturbed by an "inner conflict." I focus on this because it is an aspect of acting that is addressed later in the book and is generally called "split attention," that is the ability to perform an action while monitoring it at the same time. This metaphor of divided attention is virtually a universal in the discourses on acting and a challenge to a cognitive understanding of the mind-full body.

Work with the neutral mask has at least two objectives. The first is to introduce the actor to working with images, as in the abovementioned exercise of "waking up for the first time." Other work may deal with more abstract assignments such as embodying fire from its first flames to its dying embers. The goal of this exercise is not to represent or become flame but to investigate how the performer embodies the image of fire through the imagination. The second objective of the neutral mask is to help the actor understand herself. "The neutral mask, in the end, unmasks!"[89] The performer is liberated: "The mask will have drawn something from him, divesting him of artifice. His face will be beautiful and free."[90] Lecoq's principle is that we are constrained by the roles we play in everyday life and we carry tensions associated with those roles into the studio. By releasing the tension, the performer becomes aware of a different physical, mental, and emotional state—all three interconnected and inextricable—that is neutral, akin to if not identical with her "natural" asocial state of being.

The second stage in Lecoq's work is "down into the depths: "It brings us into contact with the *essence* of life, which I call the *universal poetic sense*. Here we are dealing with an abstract dimension, made up of spaces. Lights, colours, materials, sounds which can be found in all of us."[91] Unlike Grotowski who views such explorations as a vertical move to the higher realms of the spiritual, Lecoq figures the work as a downward exploration (using the physical metaphors of uncovering and revealing) consisting of analyzable qualities related to a perceptual experience of the material world. This phase of the actor's work is designed to strengthen creativity through the *"mimodynamic* process."[92] It involves the development of *mimages* (a conflation of mime and images), which reveal "hidden gestures, emotions, underlying states of a character...which express, through a different logic, the character's state at a given moment."[93] The mimage finds expression and therefore its dynamics in performance. Lecoq defines the qualities of the movement that embody the image through a system of binaries.

For Lecoq, movement is analogous to sound: the one is defined in relation to stillness, the other in relation to silence.[94] Movement is also seen in opposition to a still point that allows us to recognize motion, underlining the importance of contrast in his theory of acting. Furthermore, every gesture consists of both a movement and a countermovement, the latter defined as anticipation or preparation. The mime must move in the opposite direction before going in the intended one. He uses the French clown Monsieur Hulot as an example: "In order to start walking, [he] makes a little jump backward. One could say he steps back to take a step forward."[95] While in everyday life the countermovement is not evident, it is nonetheless present. There is a further complexity in his understanding of movement that explores the oscillation between equilibrium and disequilibrium.— Walking, for instance, is in this sense a process of losing and regaining one's balance.[96] It is by taking command of these binaries that the rhythm of performance and a dynamic use of space are generated. While this oscillation takes place in everyday life—Lecoq encourages his students to study people on the street. The mime must learn to incorporate these binaries into her technique.

Masks are used in this process to focus on the expression of the body rather than the plasticity of the face. In addition to the neutral mask, larval, character, and utilitarian masks are used. Each one poses a different set of problems for the performer. An additional binary is then added to the advanced work in order to give fullness to the character: the mask and counter-mask. The character suggested to the actor by the mask—a process of using the mask and allowing it to determine movement makes close study of the mask or working before mirrors unnecessary. It is the task of the director (or teacher) and collaborators to comment on the appropriateness of the gestures. The counter-mask provides the performer with a second approach to the role:

> [T]he *counter-mask,* revealing a second character behind the same mask, lending it a depth which is much more interesting. In this way we discover that people's faces do not necessarily fit what they are and that for each character there is a depth of field. A third stage can be reached with certain masks: to perform, in the same character, both mask and counter-mask.[97]

Some may argue that this strategy fails to give a role the psychological depth that many look for in acting. Lecoq's purpose is not, however, to create realistic characters but to help the actor achieve and communicate a "universal poetic sense," not to be confused with the "living human spirit." Indeed the difference between Lecoq's vision of acting and Stanislavski is echoed in their approach to memory.

Lecoq's exploration down in the depths is not an immersion in personal memory or in the psyche of the actor. The memories that are important to Lecoq are those that are retrieved through attention to the "external" world: "I never ask students to search within themselves for the true memory. I have no wish to enter into their intimate secrets."[98] Instead he is interested in the "dynamics of memory" because "they are more important than the memory itself."[99] The contents of a memory are secondary in his view of the creative impulse. What is more important is how the energies implicit in the memory are manifest in the body. The implication is that memory is not merely thought and emotion but that it also stimulates sensorimotor responses that emerge in the performance.

Memory is aroused through the physical action of exploring the mask and is of value only if it provides an impulse appropriate to the character. The emphasis on working from the "outside in" places him closer on the theoretical continuum to Meyerhold and Brecht, than to Stanislavski, Artaud, and Grotowski. Michael Chekhov also emphasizes the external but the acting style he valued is closer to that of Stanislavski.

Chekhov, a nephew of the playwright Anton, believed that the "creative individuality of the artist"[100] derives from the exercise of willpower and the responsibility of the actor is to tap that source and release it in a form suitable to the production. The willpower is defined as "our wants, wishes, desires, longings, lusts, yearnings...always mixed with feelings."[101] The "key" to unlocking this energy is found in "movement (action, gesture)."[102] Rather than seeking subjective memories that ignite and direct the well-tuned body, shaping the body through movement frees the creative impulse of the actor. "So we may say that the *strength* of the movement stirs our will power in general; the *kind* of movement awakens in us a definite corresponding *desire*, and the *quality* of the same movement conjures up our *feelings*."[103]

The three aspects of movement—quality, kind, and strength—parallel a triad that defines what Chekhov calls the "individual psychological state" through a combination of "Images...Feelings and Will-impulses."[104] The actor identifies the movements that provide access to the creative state, or, to use Chekhov's term for the key to unlocking the emotions, to the *psychological gesture*. The purpose of the PG is "to influence, stir, mold, and attune your whole inner life to its artistic aims and purposes."[105] The concept, as befits his outside to inside orientation, is both physical and imaginary.

The PG bears a clear resemblance to the Jungian archetype. Carl Jung, a contemporary of Freud with whom Jung disagreed on many points, believed that there are universal qualities that define personality, such as the anima and animus (male and female principles) and the shadow (a secret and potentially sinister side of the self). Chekhov defines seven characteristic gestures, which reflect emotional states and are linked to character qualities. Each gesture involves putting the body into dynamic tension with itself and is described according to its effect on the will of the character or on a linked-character type. One such position has the actor standing, weight on the left leg, right leg extended, right arm pointing to the ground at a spot on which the eyes are focused, and it is identified with a strong-willed personality with "a *definite desire* for *dominating* and *despotic* conduct,"[106] Another position shows a crouching man embracing one knee, his head touching the knee; it is "entirely introspective.... A strong brooding quality permeates its whole being. It might enjoy its loneliness."[107] The training of the actor involves adopting the physical position and exploring the emotional and bodily responses that arise as a result of putting the body in the necessary shape. To understand the effect, the performer needs to focus on the energy required to fulfill the gesture, to commit to it completely. The tensions in the body give rise to a limited range of emotional responses (it is difficult, if not impossible, to feel despotic when assuming the introverted gesture), which in turn provide insight into the character being portrayed.

Once the gestures are explored and their effects "memorized," the actor no longer needs to take the position to gain the benefit of the psychological gesture. By simply imagining the shape the actor can feel the emotional impact in her body and provide the affective content needed to perform the action. No single gesture is sufficient to portray a complex personality. Rather, as the character passes through the series of actions in the play, different gestures key the performer to the shifts in emotional intensity, shape, and quality required by the part. By carefully modifying the sequence of gestures and identifying valences in feeling, the actor devises the foundation of a score that is nuanced and repeatable. While every psychological gesture has universal qualities, each performer will have individual responses to its shape according to autobiographical experience and the circumstances of the play. There is a parallel between Chekhov's acting score and Grotowski's. The major difference between them is that Grotowski's actor derives the emotional foundations of the role's physical actions from personal memories, whereas Chekhov uses universal gestures to elicit the affective reality of the role. For the latter, "body memories," or physical feelings are the link to emotional intensity.

Chekhov believed that defining psychological gestures is the first step in defining the score of actions for a character; analyzing the role and play is a secondary task, if it is necessary at all. Like many of his predecessors and contemporaries, he had little use for intellectual analysis:

> You can do this either by using your analytical mind or by applying the PG. In the former case you choose a long and laborious way because the reasoning mind, generally speaking, is not imaginative enough, is too cold, and abstract to be able to fulfill an artistic work. It might easily weaken and for a long time retard your ability to *act*. You may have noticed that the more your mind "knows" about the character, the less you are able to perform it. This is a psychological law.[108]

The reasoning mind can be circumvented by using the physicality of the body to evoke the feelings necessary to realize the emotional through-line of the character. Chekhov's approach may involve moving from the outside to the inside, but it nevertheless depends on that binary as a measure of good acting. The key, as in Stanislavski's approach and that of many others, is where the emotions and the spirit of a character are to be located, how the reasoning mind may interfere with the process of the actor, and how penetrating the psyche of the performer is necessary to developing a psychologically believable character. Brecht, the only practitioner to reject the psychological, believed that reason and intellect were the primary tools for avoiding the emotional intensity of a part and the assertion of its "spiritual" existence (however illusory).

The debate over the psychology of the character or the place of the intellect in creating a role is not at issue in twentieth-century–American approaches to actor training. What varies from one approach to the next is the means by which the actor gains access to the emotional truth of her character.

The Method and Its Alternatives

If Stanislavski's system is the polar star that Western practitioners use to orient their approaches to acting, Lee Strasberg's Method serves the same purpose in the United States. It is not coincidental that he claims to bear the mantle of Stanislavski. For better or worse, the mystique of The Actors Studio parallels that of the Moscow Art Theatre as the birthplace of a new style of acting. The critique frequently leveled at Strasberg is that he embraces the emotional recall of Stanislavski's early work, represented in *The Actor Prepares*, but never engages the later work on physical actions with equal vigor. And there is no doubt that Strasberg's focus is on "inner technique."[109]

Inner technique is a concept that participates in the inside-outside binary. Strasberg rejects the outside-in strategy because he believes it leads to "mere" imitation: "Even in an external technique there can be this search for reality, but then the actor simply settles for details of reality, how to behave or how to drink or how to burst out. It is an imitative kind of reality."[110] Imitation is a problem for Strasberg for a couple of reasons. Foremost it does not engage the emotions; and because repetition of external reality leads to cliché, neglecting the emotions limits the actor's creative potential: "That's what we mean by clichés. That's what we mean by the conventional way of doing it, the thing you think should be done because you have seen people...do it that way."[111] Theatrical conventions arise from the reproduction of people's behavior on and off the stage, but the imitation of other actors is the least acceptable. The actor should depend instead on her creativity, which is evoked through the inner technique.

At the heart of Strasberg's approach lies the unconscious, the source of impulses that, when expressed freely, give a performance the emotional truth necessary to elevate acting from a craft (imitation) to an art (creativity). The release of impulses cannot be random but needs to be controlled by the will, which is in turn directed by the actions of the character and expressed through the actor's instrument, the body. The impulses that lie at the heart of the Method are not real emotions—Strasberg perceives real emotions as being too unruly and unreliable. The appropriate emotions are those that can be generated through memories to create the effect needed for the performance in relation to the action and to the other characters. An additional value of produced rather than spontaneous emotion is that it allows the actor to have a "divided consciousness," or the ability to express the impulse while being aware of what is happening onstage. The elements of this schematic need some elaboration for a fuller understanding of the Method's complexity.

Strasberg divides the actor's instrument into the mind, the emotions, and the body, although his conception is not consistent. Sometimes he includes all three; at other times he seems to speak only of the body. He generally views the body as a vehicle for the expression of inner feelings. As long as the body is relaxed it can manifest the thoughts and emotions that are released from the unconscious: "Without relaxation a lot of things an actor may rightly want to do will be deformed as they enter his instrument, because the instrument itself sets up resistance through tension"[112] The key to relaxation is "inner concentration"[113] on the work done for the role. As long as the focus is on the evocation of the impulses and the step-by-step sequence of actions, the instrument will be relaxed and relay the emotional intensities. The body, then, is a container that depending on its permeability (i.e., freedom from tension) has the potential for restraining or releasing its contents.

The power that can be released by the body is grounded in the actor's capacity—"the habits, the thought processes, the emotional patterns that are already in him" which can be accessed and improved through technical training: the more sophisticated the technique, the greater the capacity.[114] Therefore, training is not designed to develop new skills per se, but to make it easier for the performer to utilize her cognitive and personal experiences. It is difficult to measure an actor's capacity, however, because it is largely unconscious and unquantifiable. It can only be evaluated by the intensity of the thoughts and emotions and their appropriateness to the circumstances in performance. Issuing from the depths of the performer the emotions will be truthful if a technique is well used. If the work on the text has been done properly and concentration is on the task at hand, the emotions will satisfy the demands of the role.

Technique is a means but not the driving force in the theatre. The actor releases the intensities of the unconscious through the exercise of the will, a force that mediates the internal affect and external expression: "Will is seldom the engine. Much more often it functions as the master control station that starts the engine and directs its power in the proper channels." The engine, to continue the metaphor, is the unconscious, which needs to be engaged by the will so that it can release its energy:

> "Will" may properly be described as that which first leads the actor to the use of his unconscious resources and finally allows him to permit these resources to flow through his instrument. Much training of the will is actually training in self-awareness. It involves expanding the actor's consciousness of how his organism functions unconsciously, what impulses rise under what conditions, what happens when he tries to feed these impulses into expression.[115]

Through Strasberg's technique the performer learns to control the will so that it can use the unconscious in the service of the character. This does not mean that the same emotions are elicited every time, because the actor's circumstances change from day to day. While the thoughts determined during rehearsal remain constant, the feelings that arise from the same preparation vary.

The mere exercise of the will is not sufficient to bring the specific emotion needed for the execution of the character. The text as rehearsed provides images that elicit the appropriate memory: "You need a mental picture that unconsciously incites more than a mere memory of the picture, a picture not chosen accidentally, but somehow related to yourself so that your subconscious can thereby be started to work"[116] The image is only useful if it connects to the performer directly and personally, allowing for an identification to be made between the actor and the part. This intimate connection bridges the distance between the person and the role, allowing the character to be depicted believably and truthfully, giving the illusion of the "life of the human spirit." The image discovered through rehearsal is found "back of the words" and gives them "life, so they stem logically from the character on the stage."[117] Like the thoughts and emotions that fuel the performer, the structures that make action believable are found in the subtext, the "unconscious" of the play, so to speak. Strasberg equates his approach with Chekhov's vision of the theatre: "He liked the kind of painting which is simple and easy and yet has a texture through which something less obvious shows. That was what he was trying to get at in his plays."[118] The text and the performer need to be translucent, if not transparent, if the truth of the play as conceived in the production is to shine through.

It is the ability of the audience to experience this alternative reality that gives the theatre its power and underscores the importance of having good technique. Positive technical ability allows for the play to come to life, but not all such skill works toward this end. The actor's "intentions are deflected by habits of which he is unaware most of the time. Instead, he often does things of which he is equally unaware because they are mannerisms—automatic and unconscious behavior." The purpose of training is to rid the actor of these habitual practices, to make her aware of the choices that will achieve an emotional verisimilitude. The difference between the intensity of the emotions that arise from memory through the use of images and the knowledge that the feelings aroused are not real but illusory gives the actor her purchase on the "divided consciousness." This split awareness is an "essential part of the actor's training...[making] him aware of what he is doing at the time a thing is happening."[119] This is the key to the actor's art because she needs to find a balance between the feelings and an awareness of the score as it unfolds during the course of the performance.

Uta Hagen, whose approach to training actors is in many ways similar to Strasberg's, identifies good acting by means of two binaries. Realism as a constant, which she differentiates from formalism and naturalism. Formalism, which she identifies with "international" acting styles, focuses on "outer techniques." The formalist approach, identified by such terms as *indicate* and *illustrate*, is defined as a technique **"in which the artist objectively *predetermines* the character's actions, deliberately watching the form as he executes it."** Realism is based, as it is for Stanislavski, on inner technique whereby,

> the actor puts his own psyche to use to find identification with the role, allowing the behavior to develop out of the playwright's given circum-

stances, trusting that a form will result, knowing that the executions of his actions will involve a moment-to-moment *subjective* experience.[120]

The form will evolve through the use of inner technique, rather than being the focus of the process. Nonetheless, inner technique poses a greater risk in "trusting that a form will result," than the formalist approach does, wherein the danger is mitigated by the emphasis on external presentation. The trade-off for Hagen is the depth of characterization. One depends on "charisma and panache...effective theatricality...the bravado of their startling choices, the grandeur of their gestures, and their ability to *illustrate*"[121]; while the other offers "recognizable human behavior...[shaking] off all theatrical conventions."[122] Formalism is fixed and predictable, while realism is spontaneous and fresh.

Hagen's second binary opposes realism and naturalism. The latter "implies a desire to be ordinary and leads to a search for the habitual, for the trivial details of daily life, to an irrelevant imitation of nature." Hagen insists on the relevance of the theatre as a cultural form, rejecting an approach to acting that "water[s] down the truth [to] make it palatable in the mistaken notion that *that* will be an answer to false histrionics."[123] Her preferred approach uses the actor's experiences in everyday life as a starting point for creating a character, rather than as an end in itself. "**Realism** entails a search for *selected* behavior pertinent to the characters needs within the prescribed circumstances of the dramatist. We must take *from* life in order to create the reality of our *new* life on stage."[124] The actor draws on personal experience as a foundation for creating a character, as a source of psychological energy that can spark an imaginative and original portrayal of the role as written by the playwright. Realism is therefore poised between these two extremes: on the one hand external histrionics and on the other a pedestrian imitation of life.

Central to her approach to acting is the maxim "I must find myself in the role."[125] Hagen calls the method she uses to accomplish this goal "transference," citing the dictionary: "to convey from one person, place, or situation to another."[126] These spatial metaphors are instructive, but they are not precise. The character is conceived of as outside the self (i.e., something that can be entered into) and yet it is animated through the body of the actor. Both the character and the animation of it, however, carry the sense of a journey—one a trip of discovery, the other a conveyance from one place to another. The challenge that Hagen sets for herself is to help the actor gain an understanding of and the techniques necessary for the journey, however conceived.

She begins with a discussion of the body, the vessel of transference through which the discoveries about the "self in the role" are expressed:

> THE BODY is the outer manifestation of the actor, the most visible of his tools, capable of communicating the slightest nuance of thought and feeling, of regal bearing and Olympian carriage as well as the physical frailties and distortions that may be demanded by a given role.[127]

The range and scale of information to be communicated—from the godly to the most human of weaknesses—requires a reflexive instrument that is able to respond to the strongest and weakest creative impulse. Yet the greatest and most supple tool possessed by the actor is the voice. Hagen has little tolerance for regionalisms, insisting on the virtues of knowing and speaking "Standard American Speech." The well-trained vocal mechanism allows "language [to] take shape on your tongue until it begins to spring from your soul."[128] The bodily voice is what allows the result of internal technique to be communicated to the audience and fellow performers. However, an instrument that is limited by cultural habits, such as regional dialects, is ill-suited to the task of realistic acting.

Emotional recall, as in Strasberg and the early Stanislavski, is central to the inner technique, but Hagen recognizes that it is not necessarily the first stage in the process:

> You will need to supply personal psychological realities *only* when direct contact with the events, the objects, and your partners fails to stimulate you, when the imagination alone fails to support your specific actions during the moment-to-moment give and take which will prove that you are alive on stage.[129]

Emotional recall is necessary when the rehearsal process fails to supply the motivations and inspiration necessary to fully develop the role. When this happens the actor asks, "If I were..."—which is the key to finding past experiences that can provide the emotional impulse to drive the action. Answering this question is not a matter of simply finding an adequate substitution, but rather involves reciprocal connections between the physical and psychological senses and the use of associative reflection. The five senses are not only imperative for our interaction with the world but are, moreover, linked to memories that can be triggered by the imagination: "**The *realistic* actor learns that, at will, he can induce specific, imagined stimuli to produce an organically correct behavioral response in order to arrive at the essence of the experience.**"[130] Using the imagination, the actor can develop an image that evokes a physical state that brings with it, through association, a psychological response: "*Physical* responses evoked by these stimuli are, of course, accompanied by *psychological* ones."[131] The correct physical stimulus is found through a process of "particularization," or the specific detailing of a memory until the trigger is found that will initiate the impulse and its attendant feelings. Finding the right image releases the material hidden in memory and, along with it, the emotional force necessary "to discover and execute the consequent *actions* (what we *do* about what we feel) and to give substance to the *actions* which are the true communicators of our character."[132] The technique of emotional recall uses sensory images to recover the psychological states associated with the memories triggered.

The journey to locate the impulses leads the actor into the depths of self-awareness. The psychological states, such as anger, depression, and joy, are to be found in the self, or what Hagen refers to as the soul: "The soul, the psyche (the Greek word for soul), and the self are one and the same, with different semantic connotations."[133] Only retrieving the appropriate memories and their emotional content can give the character the depth and realism demanded by Hagen. This technique is not only to be used during rehearsals but also should be part of the actor's everyday discipline. The work of the actor throughout life is to develop a store of triggers that she can access when needed to give depth to the character: "Sensory stimuli can be stored in a treasure chest to be recalled and transferred selectively to a particular character's stage life."[134] Once discovered, they can be employed to animate the role, bringing it to life in a way that satisfies the demands of the text and of substantive, emotionally driven, realistic acting.

There are also striking similarities between Strasberg's Method and that espoused by Sanford Meisner, which may explain in part the intensity of their rivalry.[135] Both claim to be followers of Stanislavski, both place a premium on emotional truthfulness and both recognize the significance of the "as if." The primary difference lies in their determination of the best practice for developing the connection between emotion and character. Meisner, somewhat surprisingly, cites George Bernard Shaw as a source for his definition of the actor's work: "Self-betrayal, magnified to suit the optics of the theatre, is the whole art of acting."[136] What is less surprising is the definition that Meisner gives for the idea of "self-betrayal": "By 'self-betrayal,' Shaw meant the pure, unselfconscious revelation of the gifted actor's most inner and most private being to the people in his audience."[137] The accuracy of this reading of Shaw is less important than the insight it gives into Meisner's approach to acting. His theory of acting is based on the actor's emotional truthfulness and her ability to communicate it to the audience.

The metaphor that Meisner uses to communicate his theory is that of a canoe on a river. The canoe is the text that is propelled by the currents of a stream of emotions: "The text floats on the river. If the water of the river is turbulent, the words will come out like a canoe on a rough river. It all depends on the flow of the river which is your emotion."[138] The objective of his method is to create in the actor an emotional flow of sufficient strength and intensity to keep the text afloat. Implicit in the image is that the river needs to be moving before the canoe is put in the water. Indeed, the largest part of *Sanford Meisner on Acting* is given over to the preparation: "Preparation is what you *start* with. Preparation is to acting what warming up the motor is to driving a car on a cold day."[139] If the actor does not know how to get ready to go onstage for a rehearsal or performance, the results will lack the emotional depth Meisner deems the most important aspect of acting. Without emotional depth the actor's performance is just a combination of words and clichés.

The text is not merely a vessel that rides on the currents of emotion, however. There is a reciprocal relation between text and emotion. The given circumstances of the play provide parameters that define the direction of the emotional flows, while the intensity and continuity of the emotions shape the interpretation of the production. What makes a performance unique is the emotional truth the actor brings to the portrayal of the character: "The foundation of acting is the reality of doing."[140] But it is not just any reality "*Real* pianists who play it will play it differently, but they will all play the same notes./Are you saying...that if they play the same notes, the color or emotional tone will be the same?/More or less."[141]

What makes the theatre interesting for Meisner is the "more or less." This equivocation is based on what the actor brings to the play each time she goes onstage. The structure of the performance remains the same but the nuances of the emotional foundation vary with the preparation: "By that time you may have had fifty different preparations, but the particularizations—the *as ifs* which have been worked out in rehearsal and are now those elements that give form to your role—remain constant."[142] It is not only the text and the preparation of the performer that determine the "reality of doing."

The other key ingredient is the work of the other actors. They bring their own preparations, their own emotional rivers. There are a number of streams and it is their confluence that keeps the canoe moving in the "right" direction. This is a second and, for Meisner, the more important reciprocal process. The given circumstances are not defined by the world of the play alone but also by the interaction among the actors. It is important to note that the interaction is among the performers and not among the characters. The communication between the actors is carried out not only through the text, but also through what Meisner calls the "emotional dialogue."[143] The preparation readies the actors for going on stage, providing them with a starting point. Once they have entered the scene, the direction, taken by the emotions activated by the preparation will vary depending on what the actors provide one another. The importance of being open to the emotional currents of the other actors is underscored by the two principles basic to Meisner's approach to acting: (1) *"Don't do anything unless something happens to make you do it"* and (2) *"What you do doesn't depend on you; it depends on the other fellow."*[144] The actor's task is to be open to the performance of the other actors.

Being receptive to what the other performers offer requires openness and sensitivity. The work of the actor is to overcome the obstacles that keep her from responding truthfully to what is offered. Using a formulation that resonates with Lecoq's neutral mask, Meisner requires the actor to begin in a neutral state.

> Neutral—what's that mean? Open to any influence, right? If you are neutral, you will achieve a kind of emotional flexibility, won't you? If you're tense, if you're unrelaxed, like John was at the beginning, you're not responsive to the influence.[145]

Tension makes the body unresponsive and therefore unreceptive to the emotional currents of the other—a problem that actors face because society does not encourage emotional availability:

> It's difficult to do because we've been trained since we were children to be restrained emotionally—at least some of us have—and every day we're constantly aware of what our proper limitations are. We always know what our boundaries are and it's difficult to break them, even in

an acting class. But emotional freedom gets easier when you try to go along the path your inner life is sending you.[146]

The potential for being receptive is always present in the form of an "inner life." The difficulty is to clear the path for its expression. The other major resistance to the emotional dialogue is being overly intellectual: "The more brainless it is the chances are the better off you'll be."[147] Reason gets in the way of emotional honesty: "I wanted to eliminate all that 'head' work, to take away all the mental manipulation and get to where the impulses come from....I'm listening and there is an absolute elimination of the brain."[148] Eliminating the noise—whether physical tension or mental manipulation—allows the actor to engage in the emotional dialogue of the production, both as listener and speaker.

The preparation, the warming up of the engine, needs to put the actor in contact with the emotions appropriate to the beginning of the scene. Once the initial intensity is reached and the action begun, the performer follows the path of the emotion until circumstances change and she is forced into a new emotional state. The actor knows the correct emotional path to follow not by analysis but by following her impulses, by responding truthfully to what is given by the other actor. "Acting is all a give-and-take of those impulses affecting each person."[149] The difficulty arises when the actor is unable to respond to the given circumstances of the play because she lacks the experience that would provide an appropriate response. Meisner calls the process of resolving this problem "particularization":

> When you come up against a text that's cold to you, which doesn't mean anything because the circumstances are alien to you, you use a particularization—another way to say that is *'as if'*—to describe for yourself a situation that would bring you *personally* to the emotional place you need to be in for the sake of the scene.[150]

The imagination is brought into play as a bridge between the actor's experience and the demands of the play: "It's your personal example chosen from your experience or your imagination which emotionally clarifies the cold material of the text."[151] Once the appropriate particularization is determined—through the interactions between the actors and the director—it becomes a fixed part of the performance. What may change is the preparation that accesses the necessary emotions for the scene:—"By that time you may have had fifty different preparations...the particularizations...remain constant."[152] Similar to Grotowski's concept of the actor's score, Meisner's "stream" denotes the performer's personal response to the situation in the text, which she need not share with anyone: "He's not going to reveal his preparation, but he's going to have it! If anybody says to him, 'Where did you get that feeling of being a conqueror when you knocked at the door?' his only answer is, 'None of your business.' That's how private the personal preparation is."[153] He does not go as far as Grotowski in distancing the score from the text, however, because the preparation is always constrained by the given circumstances of the play. The emotions, whatever their source, are what brings the "heat" to the "cold" text.

The creation of the character seems to take place in three stages. The first is the identification of the actor with the currents of emotion as defined by the given circumstances of the play. At this point the performer attends to the emotional impulses that derive from the instincts: "Now, that happens in an exercise, which changes the dialogue. The instinct changes the dialogue. Then it continues until the instinct changes it again."[154] The actor's score or stream forms the foundation for the development of the character and prepares the way for the second stage: "Now we're beginning to edge up on the problem of playing the part. The emphasis has been primarily on 'This is what I'm doing and I'm doing it truthfully.' Now the question coming up is '*How* do I do it?'"[155] The preparation has defined the inner character through the identification of the emotional through-line with the particularizations needed to connect the actor with the role. Once this process is complete—or at least sufficiently finished—the second stage can begin, which is to create the "outer component, the external portrait."[156] This can be accomplished with makeup and costume, or techniques for creating the character's physicality. The work will succeed provided the emotional score is defined and the actor is open to the impulses of the other actors onstage. The final stage is to make the performance big enough: "You have to raise it to a level above real life. Otherwise it doesn't communicate."[157] The emotional stream needs to be sufficiently vibrant to allow the audience to experience the actor's work.

Common Ground

When all is said and done there remains a question about what is meant by the "emotional stream." Emotion is certainly a key component of acting and, from a cognitive perspective, impossible to escape, despite Brecht's best efforts to advocate otherwise. Yet there remains considerable debate about what an emotion is. Neuroscientist Antonio Damasio provides a succinct definition:

> In short, emotional states are defined by myriad changes in the body's chemical profile; by changes in the state of viscera; and by changes in the degree of contraction of varied striated muscles of the face, throat, trunk, and limbs. But they are also defined by changes in the collection of neural structures which cause those changes to occur in the first place and which also cause other significant changes in the state of several neural circuits within the brain itself.[158]

I suspect this is not, at first glance, very useful to actors who are in the process of constructing an emotional through-line for a character or trying to resist observable effects of emotion in creating the *Verfremdungseffekt*. Its value may become clearer when *emotion* is differentiated from *feeling*.

> I have proposed that the term *feeling* should be reserved for the private, mental experience of an emotion, while the term *emotion* should be used to designate the collection of responses, many of which are publicly observable. In practical terms this means that you cannot observe a feeling in someone else although you can observe a feeling in yourself when, as a conscious being, you perceive your own emotional states...but some aspects of emotions...will be patently observable to others.[159]

A feeling is what an actor experiences when she has an emotion. An emotion, then, is largely an unconscious experience that will manifest itself for the actor as a feeling, or the proprioceptive (internal sensory) experience of a change in a body state. However, an emotion is perceptually visible to an observer, indicating that there may be some scientific foundation for Grotowski's via negativa: reducing tensions in the body allows for the physical manifestations of emotion to be more "publicly observable." It also suggests that to elicit an emotion requires a change in the body's physical state, in its "chemical profile." This may explain why Stanislavski moved away from emotional recall to physical action: focusing on the activities of the body can evoke emotions at the same time that it enhances their communication. These distinctions may also explain why many of Strasberg's greatest successes were film actors. Emotional recall creates changes in the musculature that are sufficiently visible for the camera to pick up but that are not necessarily perceivable in the theatre. Finally, Damasio's distinction suggests that feeling an emotion may not be the same thing as communicating it. Emotions may not be consciously recognized; and what is felt may not find expression if the body is not active and engaged. The relationship between emotion and physical expression raises concerns about the binary that differentiates actors who work from the outside in from those who work from the inside out. The question should not be which approach is better, but how the whole of the actor's instrument can be engaged to create a powerful and meaningful performance.

There are other terms that all or most of the approaches to actor training have in common, which for purposes of clarity will be marked in bold. These terms have been chosen because they are prevalent in discourses on acting, but also because the meaning of each is ambiguous even though it may seem self-evident. **Acting is not the same as everyday life**. It is a form of **communication** through **conscious** and **unconscious** means between a performer and an audience. It is seen as a movement of the **soul** or **spirit** that is expressed through the **body**, which is viewed as either a **container** or a **conduit**, but can also be understood as a permeable membrane, distinguishing the **inside** from the **outside**. The evolution of a **performance** involves developing a **role** that is derived from a **text** (however broadly conceived) and draws on the actor's internal tools of **imagination, technique, impulses, creativity**, and **intellect**. It is a form of **self-expression** that, when well performed, has the potential to transcend the expectations of the audience. The rest of this book interrogates these concepts, directly and indirectly, to tease out their significance to the art of acting and to question the common usage to which they are put. The objective is to clarify their meanings using cognitive sciences, not in order to ground them in empirical studies but in order to provide definitions that are useful to the actor and the teacher of acting. This requires challenging values and beliefs that form the foundations of how we think about acting in the West. Science does not provide us with answers, but with a way of reframing our understanding of acting that offers a more useful and dynamic way of talking about the actor's art.

The Limits of Science

An exceptional performance is seldom simple, although it will seem effortless. It provides an experience that is resonant and causes the spectator to feel and think in complex and unexpected ways. These qualities are anathema to science. While the theatre seeks to expand our understanding of the vicissitudes of human experience, scientists seek to remove all variables that could cast doubt on the conclusions they draw from experiments. For them, being reductive is a virtue. For artists, it is synonymous with being overly simplistic, verging on the boring. The mime on a street corner is not investigating the foundations of a particular movement, but using it to entertain by evoking a visceral and thoughtful response to her expertise from passersby. The arts tend to expand, the sciences to limit the field of investigation. Reading scientific journals can be frustrating and seem meaningless until it is put into a larger framework. As experimental results are generalized, they become more useful to theatre practitioners, but more suspect for those working in the laboratory. The challenge in using the sciences is, in part, to recognize the speculative dimensions of writings that seek to understand how the specific can be used to draw conclusions about the global.

Perhaps *the* fundamental principle of science is that all theories are falsifiable. That is, every theory is provisional because it is possible that at some point an experiment may be done that contests its truth value. Things we take for granted, like gravity, may yet be falsified. This does not mean that all theories are equally viable. The greater the number of experiments that successfully support a truth claim, the more confident scientists are that it can be used as a basis for further explorations. It is humbling to think how much confidence theatre practitioners have in their approaches to creating a performance and how little evidence, other than personal experience, supports that confidence. This does not mean that theories of acting should be based on empirical principles. In fact, I believe quite the opposite is true.

Scientists remove as many variables as possible so that they can conclude the probable. Similarly, artists need to be confident that their work is valid if they are to perform with conviction. Actors draw on whatever sources they can to craft an experience that will be meaningful to an audience. They need to be masters of creating illusions, not as a questionable but as an empowering enterprise. Yet turning to the sciences is not a fool's errand. The project of this book is to look across the divide that separates the disciplines and to identify those theories that are based on the most solid evidence and to evaluate their usefulness to understanding acting. The language of theatre has evolved over time and certain terms and concepts have come to be accepted as self-evident. If we are to improve the way we train actors and approach the creation of a role, these assumptions need to be challenged, not necessarily to invalidate them, but to clarify how they are being used and to rethink the positive or negative impact they have on actors and the way we think about acting. If theatre is the art of the possible, then it is our responsibility to make sure that our visions of what can be are constructed as powerfully as possible, so that it *is* possible to provide those for whom we perform with an experience that transcends expectations.

Chapter 2

Theatre and Dynamic Systems Theory

The claim on the floor is that both overt behavior and brain behavior, properly construed, obey the same principles.[1]
—J. A. Scott Kelso

If actors worry that science is going to take the mystery out of the creative act, they have little to fear. The cognitive and neurosciences are still in their infancy when it comes to understanding how the mind works. When asked to explain the simplest of actions—for instance, how is it possible to pour a glass of water?—science can only answer: *I don't know*. The science can describe certain mechanisms that involve the sensorimotor cortex and areas of the brain associated with hand-eye coordination, but when it comes to the specifics of why a glass of water is wanted or which neural processes allow the body to move to the tap, turn it on, and then off again when the glass is full are too complicated for our current understanding. Experimentation, like rehearsing a play, is a labor-intensive process that works incrementally toward understanding phenomena. The difference is that science tries to eliminate as many variables as possible so that the object of investigation can be understood in isolation, whereas rehearsals explore as many avenues as possible in order to select the one best suited to the production. Neuroscientists are still trying to understand the intricacies of what happens when a synapse fires in the brain, and why and how it does so, not to mention why it happens at a particular time or how it connects with other synapses to create the complex sequence of events that lead to a simple action like pouring a glass of water.

The laboratory paradigm does not stop speculation, however, and in recent years there has been a proliferation of theories to explain the workings of the mind. Like Sherlock Holmes, who is able to deduce complex crimes from the tiniest piece of evidence, scientists, philosophers, psychologists, and many others seek to explain the complexity of the mind from the very few clues available. For example, in 1996 mirror neurons were first discovered in monkeys.[2] Mirror neurons activate parts of the brain associated with carrying out a specific activity even when the action is being watched rather than actually performed. From this discovery whole theories of creativity and empathy have been developed despite the limited evidence that mirror neurons exist in human beings.[3] This does not mean that current theories are pure fiction, nor does it mean that they are wrong. We simply do not know enough to assess the truth-value of the claims. Therefore, in reading theories of how the mind works—including the one presented here—it is best to proceed *caveat emptor*. In most cases the work is done with the greatest integrity and based on hard evidence—when such evidence is available. But the majority of the theories utilize inductive reasoning—generalized claims based on prior experience—and combine similar conclusions from a variety of fields to make claims about questions such as "What is an emotion?" or "What is creativity?"

There are at least two advantages to the proliferation of theories of mind. One is an increased public understanding of how the brain operates. Seminal works such as Antonio Damasio's *Descartes' Error* or Joseph LeDoux's *The Synaptic Self* have made sense of the "dark and mysterious" world of science by pulling together different strands of knowledge in a format that is readable and comprehensible to the general public. The second and more important use of popularized science is the debunking of myths that permeate public discourse, such as the belief that emotion can be eliminated from logical decision-making processes. Positive concepts of how the mind works are most valuable in challenging theories that cannot be reconciled with existing evidence. For example, cognitive studies received a boost with the advent of the computer and the assumption that the binary paradigm of linear computing corresponds to the human brain's operation. Through advances in imaging technologies and increased understanding of neural networks, theories of parallel processing have replaced the earlier model of linear on-off switching. The hope is that by challenging accepted modes of thinking, we are moving closer and closer to a more accurate model of how the creative mind works, if only by negation.

The theory presented here draws on a combination of popular theories and conclusions drawn from laboratory experiments in the neurosciences and neuropsychology. It focuses on those aspects of cognitive theory with strong support in the science community which seem to have the greatest relevance to the work of the actor. Four primary principles underlie this discussion. One is a respect for the complexity and mystery of the creative process, alongside the recognition that theories about the process are rife with cultural biases that distort while they honor the art of acting. The second, taken from the biological sciences, is that efficiency is a prime determinant in the evolution of the brain. When a problem is confronted, new ways of using existing structures will be found before entirely new structures are formed. Third, the brain is intimately intertwined with the body and the environment in which the body lives. Dynamic Systems Theory (DST), one of the most powerful and attractive concepts for understanding the cognitive process, argues convincingly for the integration of thought with the everyday processes of living. In other words, dynamic systems theory effectively refutes Descartes's claim that the mind and the body are distinct, insisting instead on the intricate, inextricable interweaving of mind, body, and world. The fourth principle is that the brains of artists are fundamentally the same as everyone else's but that experience has led to the privileging of different ways of processing information. Computers solve complex mathematical equations with the same hardwiring that others use to play the latest computer game. The results are very different, but the circuitry is the same.

With these caveats and principles, we can begin to articulate a theory of mind. In the next section, a theatrical metaphor for how the mind works will be outlined and contrasted with a brief topography of the various regions of the brain and what is known about the primary function of each. The outline is followed by a description of DST and an examination of various topics relevant to the art of acting, such as memory, emotion, creative association, and the relationship between self and other. Throughout, connections between the abstract and the concrete will be sought and, if successful, will lead to a better understanding of how science can be used to enrich our understanding of the creative process.

The Theatre of the Mind

The theatre is often used as a metaphor for the mind. The brain is viewed as a staging area, where the elements of the cognitive process (the actors), weave together perceptions, memory, emotions, and concepts to form the through-line of our lives. Bernard J. Baars in his book *In the Theater of Consciousness: The Workspace of the Mind*, takes this metaphor a step further by developing a useful if not altogether convincing theory that links cognitive functions to the topography of the brain. He divides the mind into the areas of the theatre: stage, backstage, auditorium. The stage is associated with consciousness; it is the place where the actors—the elements of thought—form coherent and continuous images that define the performance of everyday life. As any theatre person knows, what happens onstage depends on the technical support and preparations that happen off stage. For Baars, off stage is the realm of the unconscious, where the mechanics and decisions of everyday life take place, usually out of our awareness. Actors do not generally need to think about the word or movement that comes next; props are where they need to be, and the lights change, all without apparent effort. Baars locates the director backstage, where the focus of attention and appropriate responses to changing circumstances are determined. The role of the audience, also an unconscious function in this formulation, is not simply to receive.

> In the audience are a vast array of intelligent unconscious mechanisms. Some audience members are automatic routines, such as the brain mechanisms that guide eye movements, speaking, or hand and finger movements. Others involve autobiographical memory, semantic networks representing our knowledge of the world, declarative memory for beliefs and facts and the implicit memories that maintain attitudes, skills, and social interaction.[4]

The spotlight also finds a place in Baar's metaphor, singling out what we are conscious of at any given moment. The score requires the actor to pay attention to the dialogic exchange at one moment, then to shift focus as the audience response is gauged or preparations are made for the next sequence of the performance. The actor's experience is continuous despite the shift in intentional focus. Actors seldom think they are anywhere but on the stage and they experience what happens there as a continuous flow. It is only when the unexpected happens—a prop out of place, a line forgotten—that attention is drawn to a new set of perceptions and the experience of time and space may feel temporarily disjointed.

The metaphor of mind as theatre is useful in identifying different areas of cognition, defining their primary functions, and providing insights into how the areas work in concert. However, mapping each aspect of the trope onto the organization of the brain is difficult, not because there are not areas associated with particular cognitive functions. The problem arises rather because most areas of the brain act in concert with one another and are involved in multiple functions at the same time. These complex interactions make it difficult to speak decisively about how the mind works. Nevertheless, identifying different regions of the brain and their primary functions is of use. The following discussion is not exhaustive because the brain is simply too complex and multifaceted. Instead, it presents a general topography of the principle areas of the brain, highlighting those areas that are most relevant to understanding the art of acting. The subsequent chapters will clarify particular cognitive processes with more specific information about particular parts of the brain.

Two of the standard paradigms for discussing the brain are evolution and lateralization. Evolution defines three stages of development: reptilian brain, limbic system, and neocortex; lateralization differentiates the right from the left hemisphere of the brain. There is value in making these distinctions, but it should be kept in mind that these categories are also limited. The interconnections among the different areas are so pronounced that these divisions are only useful for defining a general topography, seldom for defining the function of a particular region.

The reptilian brain evolved first and, as the name suggests, replicates structures that appear in reptiles, as well as in all vertebrates. Consisting of the brainstem and cerebellum, it controls autonomic functions such as breathing and heart rate, and is associated with sensorimotor activities and the emotional dimension of survival instincts such as "fight or flight." Memories of experiences that require reflexive responses are contained here, allowing an animal to respond to new situations in ways that led to positive outcomes in the past. In humans, this part of the brain can be monitored and, in some cases, inhibited by other, more recently evolved areas of the brain that involve conscious intervention and decision making. Conversely, the reptilian brain can override rational decision-making processes, as in the case of road rage or stage fright. The reptilian brain is intimately linked to the spinal column and is the conduit through which pass perceptual information from the body and impulses for physical action.

The limbic system, the second area of the brain to develop, initially served to integrate sensory perceptions and coordinate motor control of the body. Therefore, it has links to the brain stem and cerebellum. Yet it has also developed a more sophisticated function as a mediator and facilitator between the "primitive" brain structures and the neocortex. The limbic system consists of a number of different parts;

most notable are the hippocampus, amygdala, cingulate gyrus, and thalamus. They are associated with emotional responses, consolidation of long-term memory, social functioning, spatial memory, and attention processing. Initially, serving primarily to provide feedback about body position, the generation of emotions, and the fine tuning of movement, there is increasing speculation about the limbic system's role in the adequate functioning of the organism: its processing of perceptual and proprioceptual experience and its facilitation of cognitive decision-making processes. The limbic system is located in the "heart" of the brain, adjacent to the brain stem within the neocortex.

The newest part of the brain is the neocortex, the locus of most higher-order functions associated with consciousness—imagination, language, and complex decision making. The largest part of the brain, it consists of a number of subsidiary cortices (the motor cortex, auditory cortex, visual cortex, prefrontal cortex, associational cortex, etc.) that differentiate mammals from other fauna. Each cortex is further subdivided into areas of specialization. For instance, the visual cortex is divided into six areas (in some cases further subdivided), each with a particular function such as spatial mapping, color, attention, or eye movement. The neocortex is the area of the brain that Descartes saw as the seat of rationality and as distinct from the body and emotion. I hope to clarify how this differentiation does more to distort than explain our cognitive processes. Nevertheless, the neocortex is the locus of the operations that allow you to read, understand, and remember, plan, and create blends or associations between memories of different kinds of experience. In terms of the theatre, it plays a central role in analyzing the text, making decisions about a character, and creating a performance score. However, it is worth repeating that the functioning of the neocortex depends on the transmission of information and the work of the reptilian and limbic areas of the brain.

The distinction between the right and the left hemispheres of the neocortex is frequently overstated. Imaging studies of the patterns of neural activation indicate that the left side of the brain is responsible for analytical and rational thought processes, while the right is responsible for creativity, synthesizing, and intuition. To derive from these findings that some people are "right-brained" while others are "left" grossly oversimplifies the dynamic. The halves of the brain are interdependent, obscuring the boundaries between subjective and objective processes and crucially linked in the synthesis and coordination of various operations. At the same time, the two hemispheres are not symmetrical and different locations are associated with different functions. As for other parts of the brain, these distinctions are not definitive. For instance, the left side of the brain is associated with language in the vast majority of people, but there are significant instances of speech activity from the right side or even both sides. Therefore, in tandem with the evidence that supports the differentiation of the two hemispheres, a supple appreciation is needed to begin to understand an activity as complex as acting.

Throughout rehearsals and performance an actor continually draws on her analytical abilities and her skill in improvisation, the intensification of emotion, and the retrieval of memory. These complex processes require the coordination of more than one area of the brain, but this basic topography will be of use in identifying the roles the different areas play in acting. Keeping this topography in mind, we will turn our attention to a theory that indicates how interactions among the different parts of the brain allow us to function in the world and onstage. First, however, the elements of the theory will be introduced through an analogy with a theatre performance.

Dynamic Systems Theory and *Waves*

The challenge for any theory of mind is modeling how the neural networks in different areas of the brain work in concert, allowing us to function in the world and to engage in abstract thought. The fact is that no one yet knows how the networks function together, and any attempt to develop a model is based more on speculation than on scientific fact. One promising direction for understanding embodied cognitive interaction is DST, a concept based on the idea of parallel processing and the emergence of sensorimotor activities and mindfull representations through the integration of inputs and outputs from different areas of the brain.

DST is not an outgrowth of the cognitive sciences, but a set of mathematical formulae designed to explain phenomena that occur in the physical world, such as the patterns that form when certain liquids are heated to its boiling point. The formulae also describe how nonlinear systems pose a challenge to linear cause-and-effect paradigms. I draw on the work of three scholars working in very different areas to address this shift in thinking about cognition: Evan Thompson, a professor of philosophy, specializing in phenomenology; Marc Lewis, professor of applied psychology; and J. A. Scott Kelso, professor of complex systems and brain sciences. Working separately but drawing on each other's work, these three scholars provide the tools necessary for understanding how DST is useful in modeling cognitive processes. A definition of nonlinear systems will be followed by an outline of the major concepts of DST and how those concepts inform our understanding of the brain/mind/body/world complex. In the process, I hope to show how DST provides a concrete basis for the philosophical abstractions presented in the preceding chapter.

Actors, particularly in realistic approaches to acting, focus on developing an acting score based on cause and effect: A does to B; B does to A. While actors are aware of other circumstances that impinge on this narrative structure, they accept that this equation is an adequate model for understanding behavior. Similarly, in everyday life we create linear narratives for events, although we are frequently confronted with complex motivations that make simple storytelling inadequate. Or we believe we understand the motivation for an incident only to discover that there are influences of which we are unaware. Everyday experience is in this way similar to the workings of the mind. Early computational theories of cognition assumed that memories are stored like bytes on a hard drive and can be retrieved by following a trail of neurons. It is now evident that this paradigm is inaccurate. Theories of dynamic—or self-organizing, nonlinear—systems offer an alternative that more adequately addresses the complexity of experience, as well as how scientists are coming to understand the functioning of the brain.

A linear system tends to be closed, in the sense that a stimulus triggers a sequence that moves along a path, to be redirected at certain intersections as it moves toward a final destination, such as an action or the retrieval of memory. This model parallels the structure of a standard logical argument, which moves from point to point to conclusion, taking into consideration challenges presented by alternative points of view only to dismiss them. There is very little room for improvisation or for changing direction midstream. The overall movement in linear systems is from excitation (the disruption of a steady state) to equilibrium. Put another way, linear systems follow the typical narrative structure of beginning, middle, end. DST argues against the tidy formalism of this representation of cognitive processes. Rather than following a prescribed structure, an open system is self-organizing; that is, conclusions or patterns of behavior emerge from a system that is *always* in a state of *disequilibrium*. The influx of stimuli destabilizes the system, leading to a response expressed as actions, images, or concepts relevant to the situation; but it does not return to a static, preexisting state of homeostasis. Other excitations keep the system from returning to equilibrium. The outcome of a perceptual experience may leave a lasting impression (the construction of a long-term memory) or be quickly forgotten. Regardless, this new state is not stable but is disrupted by new excitations that lead to new responses in an ongoing process. As I write, my next thought is already being formulated, leading to the next phrase I write or resulting in uncertainty. What emerges when "words fail me" is the frustration of not yet knowing what comes next. This feeling does not just dissipate, however, but further perturbs the system as I struggle to fashion the words that will communicate what I want to say. Lewis writes of DST: "Broadly defined, self-organization refers to the emergence of novel patterns or structures, the appearance of new levels of integration and organization in existing structures, and the spontaneous transition from states of lower order to states of higher order."[5] At some point my uncertainty is replaced by the words. This higher order, for an actor, might be an understanding of the action that needs to be performed or coming to grips with a character's relationships.

The complexity of DST's interweaving of cognitive functions with social and cultural interactions may be approached indirectly through an analogy with a performance developed by the National Theatre of Great Britain. *Waves,* an adaptation of Virginia Woolf's 1931 novel *The Waves,* was directed by Katie Mitchell in collaboration with eight actors and the video artist Leo Warner in 2006.

Woolf's novel tells of six friends, Susan, Jinny, Rhoda, Louis, Bernard, and Neville, who grow up together, drift apart over time, and come back occasionally to experience anew the relationships they once had. Told as a series of internal monologues, the narrative revolves around Percival, who is known only through their subjective descriptions. Percival is an idealized figure who enters their lives at school and seems to hold the future in his hands but is then sent to India, where he is thrown from a horse and dies. The six grieve the loss of this Adonis, but they think of him less as they enter middle age and become increasingly caught up in their adult lives.

The unintentional influence that Percival has over the characters mirrors the tides: getting to know him is the waves reaching far up the beach at high tide, culminating in the dinner party held in his honor when he sets out for India; his subsequent death and the fading of his memory is the ebbing of the waves toward the ocean. This sequence echoes through other temporal sequences in the book. Each chapter, initiating a different phase in the lives of the six, begins with a description of the change in season and the light that colors the waves as they roll onto the beach. At the same time, the story of their lives is equated with a single day, and the tempo of the storytelling reflects fluctuations in the energy of life: the exuberance of childhood signifies the morning; coming of age, the afternoon; the onset of middle age, the evening. The intensity with which the waves hit the beach in the opening of each section parallels the emotional intensity of the characters, sometimes hitting with passion and at other times rolling gently up the strand.

For Virginia Woolf, the rhythms of life blend with those of the natural world, defining an overarching structure (like the longue durée of history) that persists despite the existential fluctuations—loves, jealousies, losses—that mark the moment-to-moment vacillations of daily life and form the indelible memories that define a sense of self. From the interweaving of these rhythms emerges a series of impressions that belie an inevitability hidden below the tumult of the everyday. For the reader, these patterns emerge slowly, and a comprehensive understanding becomes conscious through the tension between what is repeated and what is new, from the disjunction between human life and natural occurrences. In reading the book, we carry forward what we've read as we encounter what is new, the former providing a frame, the latter modifying our emergent understanding. It is through this recursive process that meaning is achieved and sense can be made of the six lives that unfold in Woolf's book.

At the National Theatre's production of *Waves,* the spectator is confronted by a large screen that covers most of the stage opening and is set back approximately twelve feet from the edge of the stage. In front of the screen is a long table with eight chairs, a few microphones, and adjustable gooseneck desk lamps. Downstage on right and left are four boxes, about three feet square and two inches deep. A standing microphone is placed on one of the boxes on each side of the stage, while the rest contain natural materials, such as stones, grass, and dirt. Flanking the stage are shelves that hold the props to be used during the performance. In the dark, the actors enter and sit in the chairs, while a video shows a shoreline, filmed with a stationary camera, accompanied by the sound of crashing waves. As the lights come up, one of the actors sits at a microphone, cigarette in hand, and recites Woolf's introduction to the first chapter of the book—a pattern repeated throughout the production. This is the only prerecorded video; the rest is created onstage during the performance.

The company selected events from the novel, arranged them in sequences defined by simple everyday activities, and then divided these into the discrete tasks needed to convey the story to the audience. When acted, these tasks are assembled into live video feeds projected onto the central screen. For instance, each new section is identified by time and place, information that is marked on a blackboard placed on left of stage. An actor holds one of the desk lamps to illuminate the blackboard, while a second actor films a third, who writes the information on the board. A fourth actor sits at the table, in front of a microphone, creating the sound of chalk hitting the board and then rubbing a whisk broom across the hand to create the sound of the writing being erased. The audience simultaneously watches the actors create the video and the images they have generated on the large screen. The remainder of the production proceeds in a similar manner, although the images are usually more complex.

Neville and Rhoda walk along a rainy street, while a narrator reads passages about the event from Woolf's novel. The narrating actor stands at the microphone stage right, while other actors spray water on the floor stage left, giving the impression of a wet sidewalk. Another actor holds one of the desk lamps to create the illusion of streetlights shining on wet pavement. A third actor, filming the event, keeps a tight focus on the feet as two others walk, stop, and then continue on their way down the street. Yet another actor, with two lamps, shines light across the scene to suggest a passing car. The spectator has the option of watching the creation of the scene, its projection on the screen at the back of the stage, or shifting attention from one to the other.

In another scene, the actor portraying Jinny looks into a mirror, thinking about an absent Louis. As she looks, he appears in the mirror, a ghostly memory looking over her shoulder. One actor holds a two-way mirror, while another lights it from the front, creating the reflection of the young woman. At the correct moment in the narration, which is being read into a microphone at the table, the actor playing Louis is lit behind the mirror, making visible the memory of which she is speaking. As projected on the screen, the illusion is very precise.

The impressionistic nature of the story and the fragmented structure of the performance may seem alienating and not conducive to strong emotions. However, as the show proceeds and the spectator becomes accustomed to the way in which images are put together, the emotional trajectory of the performance gains in intensity. By the end, the feelings experienced are quite powerful and unexpected. The emotions were always present, but there was no time to appreciate them fully. They are implicit in the action, but it is only through their accretion over time that the full impact is felt. There is a feeling of sadness, less at the death of Percival than at the loss of youth and the distance that weakens the intimacy of the friendships. That there are feelings is in part due to the narrative and the beauty of Woolf's language, but there is also something emotive in the precision and seemingly effortless activity of creating the image sequences that provide a counterpoint to the sadness and sense of loss.

Waves, like Woolf's novel, uses structure and framing devices to examine the changing relationships between the characters. Woolf combines her own memories of changing tides and seasons with her characters' reflections on their fictional lives to create a rich blend of narrative and metaphorical imagery. Katie Mitchell and the National Theatre's company of actors also use juxtaposition as a formal device, but in shifting from a print medium to the video format, they move from the horizontal flow of language to the vertical simultaneity of theatrical representation. Inasmuch as the spectators are aware of the movement of each episode, they are cognizant of how the telling is put together. They see how the company decompresses the narrative moments, breaks them down into constituent activities, and selects from the myriad possibilities the best means of creating an image for conveying the significance of the moment. These devices not only provide insight into how the novel and the performance work on us, but also model the creative processes of the different artists. For our purposes, we will focus on the theatre production because, even if not historically accurate, a discussion of how it was made provides a useful metaphor for the workings of the mind as a dynamic system.

Virginia Woolf's novel can be equated with memory, which can be understood as a limit or horizon that frames the creative process. As such, it provides a perspective on the information that arises from the rehearsals and is incorporated into the performance. However, the book is not a passive object to be read; rather, each sequence taken from *The Waves* provides new information, which challenges the appropriateness of what has been discovered to that point, and limits what is selected, analyzed, and used in the construction of the scenes. Every time the company returns to the book, they must reassess what they have accomplished and determine the direction of the next step the performance takes. This transformation of the text into performance is yet more complex, because a scene from the novel will be distorted in the rehearsal process by the creative impulses of the company and the overall structure of the production. The process inevitably attributes new meanings to Woolf's words, as they are edited and visualized in rehearsal. It transforms and is transformed by the limits inherent in *The Waves*. The book, like memory, is not a monolithic structure but a fluid set of relationships that are formed and reformed as the production takes shape.

Katie Mitchell, Leo Warner, and the company do not enact the book verbatim but choose specific monologues for their particular relevance to the production. Woolf's work nevertheless provides a useful limit by defining which moments can be retrieved (selected), altered, and incorporated during the devising process. It is not the only such limit, however. Other horizons include knowledge of video media, an understanding of theatricality, available resources, and the aesthetic values of the artists involved. There is no hierarchy among these factors, despite a tendency to give *The Waves* a privileged status as the source of the work. The production may have arisen from the desire to explore the use of media in developing a theatrical event, and the novel simply proved a convenient vehicle for such an investigation. In all likelihood, there was a multiplicity of origins, only some of which were known consciously, which coalesced when the *opportunity* presented itself and made it possible for the company to engage in the process.

Similarly, while Katie Mitchell and Leo Warner serve executive functions as the director and video artist, the production is an ensemble that combines the creative and analytical skills of the entire company (including designers, dramaturg, stage manager, etc.). It is extremely doubtful that Mitchell and Warner had everything worked out from the beginning. More likely, the rehearsal process involved reading, discussing, and improvising a segment in an effort to identify the best image for the material, edit the text to support the visual action, determine how to carry out the activities in the most efficient and aesthetically pleasing way, and match the precision in the execution of each task to the tempo of the words. Through repetition and appraisal, the outlines of the performance became clearer, while extraneous material was forgotten. Even what is discarded served the purpose of validating what was ultimately chosen for continued repetition, challenging Warner and Mitchell's vision of the theatrical event and allowing for a clearer understanding of the type of material most useful to the production.

This image of a rehearsal process contains the elements necessary to outline a theory of mind as a dynamic system. The interactions between Mitchell and Warner provide a set of parameters, defined by their readings of Woolf's novel, that direct the creativity of the company in certain directions. However, as much as these limits organize the process, what is discovered through the work on the text modifies—in major and minor ways—the vision of the production, which in turn alters the parameters within which the company works. This is known as *circular causality*:

> *circular causality*...describes bidirectional causation between different *levels* of a system. A coherent, higher-order form or function *causes* a particular pattern of coupling among lower-order elements, while this pattern simultaneously *causes* the higher-order form. The top-down flow of causation may be considered an emergent constraint (by the system as a whole) on the actions of the parts.[6]

The production is what *emerges* from this *recursive, cyclic* interaction. The process is constrained not only by what goes on in rehearsals, but also by the techniques and limits (physical, creative, etc.) of the ensemble. Yet these too will be modified by the experiences in the rehearsal space, as problems are encountered and solved—in some cases encountered and solved all over again, only differently. While some of these constraints are more rigid than others, they are all *fluid* and subject to change. The influences that give rise to the circularity are not contained in the rehearsal space, but are nested in the context in which the process takes place. The project is continually subject to external pressure, most notably from *The Waves*, but also to the demands and limits of technology, the space in which the rehearsals take place, the production budget and available resources, pressures from the producers, as well as aesthetic and everyday experiences that occur during the process. In another example of circular causality, what happens in rehearsal affects the company's interactions outside the rehearsal space as much as what happens "out there" influences what happens in rehearsal. Indeed, without these ongoing interactions with the world, the production could never have taken place.

The relationships among the members of the company themselves form a system in a constant process of modification, as they are perturbed during rehearsal by new perceptions that destabilize or reinforce aspects of the performance. As the production evolves, patterns gain a degree of consistency, giving rise to and responding to ongoing cycles of perception and expression, which gradually give shape to the performance in time and space. This is not a singular event, however, as there are different patterns and rhythms, related to language, movement, emotion, and thought, that interconnect in *phase synchronicity*, creating a consistent pattern subject to variation. Gradually, the patterns that emerge are less susceptible to perturbation. Repetition allows for a greater consistency and specificity, forming patterns that can be reactivated when triggered by a particular set of stimuli. The resulting patterns do not create a *homeostasis,* or performance score that will be precisely repeated every time it is presented. Rather, a *metastability* comes into being, which allows for a predictably stable reenactment of the score through the interactions of the different systems and patterns, yet a score still open to perceptual or proprioceptive information. These learned patterns do not lose flexibility; they are still open to shocks from unexpected sources. Therefore, although the performance becomes set and can be enacted with greater confidence, efficiency, and consistency, there remains potential for innovation and disruption. Consistency allows the attention of the performer to focus on unexpected contingencies and the repetition of set patterns.

This analogy is an imprecise and abstract model for the operations of a dynamic system, but it provides images that make the complexities of DST more accessible. With these points of reference, we can turn our attention to a theory of mind.

DST and the Workings of the Mind

Brain processes are recursive, reentrant, and self-activating, and do not start or stop anywhere.[7]

All systems operate according to a set of rules or conditions that allow its contours to be recognized. Dynamic systems are no exception. J.A. Scott Kelso identifies three conditions that define such an organization: "The central idea is that understanding at any level of organization starts with the knowledge of basically three things: the parameters acting on the system (which are sometimes equated with the term *boundary conditions*), the interacting elements themselves (a set of primitives), and the emerging patterns or mode (cooperativities [*sic*]) to which they give rise."[8] The "boundary conditions" are defined both by neural organization and by past and present interactions with the world. They include habitual patterns that have developed over time (a particular approach to acting); the areas of the brain that are primarily activated (language or sensorimotor centers, for instance); and the context in which we find ourselves (improvising, performing, or analyzing a text). The "primitives" are the stimulations that further destabilize the system—what a fellow actor does, a director's note, a snoring member of the audience. From the interaction between the perturbation and the boundary conditions emerges a pattern of behavior that is responsive to the actor's state of mind, the nature and intensity of the excitations, and the situation.

Systems can be differentiated from the rest of the world, but they do not exist in isolation. Although excitations can be self-generated, they tend to consist of perceptions (from the world at large) and proprioceptions (bodily information communicated to the brain) and therefore the patterns that emerge are responsive to the stimulus and the context that generate it. Lewis writes: "With respect to cognition, self-organization usually refers to the emergence and stabilization of psychological or neural configurations that correspond with (or represent) conditions in the world."[9] For a self-organizing system to maintain itself, it must be adaptive to the changing dynamics of its environment (defined by the continual influx of perceptual information), and its emerging patterns (realized as organizational behavior) must be responsive to those conditions for the organism to prosper. This is different from a linear input-to-output schema because there is a continuous flow of inputs and outputs, providing a seamless experience of the world. Part of the ongoing process is evaluating whether actions correspond to conditions in the world. For these appraisals to be useful, there needs to be a baseline awareness of global conditions. For an actor to be prepared to respond to the unexpected, the performer needs to be in the flow of the scene, yet with a sense of what should come next. When an actor forgets a line or encounters unexpected laughs from the audience, the rehearsed pattern is disrupted, necessitating a different set of responses. The goal is to discover a solution that returns the performance to the established score. Actors are aware of the spatiotemporal experience of being onstage, and this awareness allows them to recognize, evaluate, and respond to unexpected situations. The brain is always at work, in a state of disequilibrium, monitoring the environment as part of an ongoing process of which we are seldom consciously aware.

Keeping in mind that the brain is never either at rest or in a state of static equilibrium, we can begin to construct an image of what happens when a stimulus perturbs the system. The excitation, what Marc Lewis calls a "trigger," creates a disturbance: "The orderly behavior of the system is interrupted by a perturbation, resulting in a rapid loss of orderliness and an increase in sensitivity to the environment."[10] The disruption—a prop is not where it is supposed to be or the actor suddenly feels ill—requires a response. The disequilibrium will be experienced as an emotion—for instance, unease, pain, or a desire for an object. These feelings, based in part on past experiences and in part on the immediate circumstances, require an appraisal of the situation, which may take the form of an overt response—flight, love, or aesthetic enjoyment. The process of reconciling the stimulus-emotion-appraisal triad is, as one might expect, complex. While a direct and orderly sequence might seem desirable, in actuality the reconciliation is an inefficient process, especially if the initial solution proves to be inadequate. The ability of the brain to "multitask" allows for a number of contingencies to emerge more or less simultaneously, leading to an appraisal that determines which is the most appropriate: it is better to flee than to fight, to look than to caress, or to stay and soak in the beauty of the moment even if it makes you late for an appointment. And there are yet other options ready for consideration.

When the trigger is sufficiently strong, it "marks a *phase transition*, characterized by sudden change and temporary disorder as the system switches to a new organization."[11] This new disequilibrium is not global, but limited to the *neural assemblies* associated with the trigger. A neural assembly can be defined as "a distributed subset of neurons with strong reciprocal connections."[12] The sudden detection of a smell will trigger neurons associated with olfactory experiences, creating a disturbance that lasts until a recognizable pattern—perhaps the recognition of a rose—emerges. The identification between the odor and the flower, ending the phase transition, results in a new state, that is, a less perturbed disequilibrium. The resulting configuration will be "new" even if it is not the first time a rose has been smelled, because the mind does not return precisely to a previous state. It is not a stable state, because there continue to be inputs that define our ongoing experience, in this case, with the rose. The new condition remains only as long as the olfactory perturbations continue to excite the neural assemblies involved and reinforce emergent patterns associated with the experience of the flower. The neural assemblies excited by the smell are not only olfactory, but also include memories of previous experiences with similar blossoms. It may also bring to mind visual images of a rose, memories of having been given one, or perhaps the memory of being pricked by a thorn. In addition to those linked to the olfactory cortices, neural assemblies linked to the visual and sensorimotor areas of the brain will be activated.

They do not, however, function without limits. As the concept of boundary conditions implies, there are constraints on what can emerge from the influx of stimuli. Thinking of boundary conditions only as limits is a negative way of formulating the concept. The term Kelso gives to the forces that form the boundaries is *attractors*: "[E]ach mode is constrained by a unique number of attractors.... Such attractors are viewed as goal states that act to constrain the system's internal degrees of freedom. Changes in number and configuration of...attractors result in a change in the field that causes qualitative shifts to new action modes."[13] When perturbations give rise to a phase transition, the attractors influence the process of defining a response by encouraging the adoption of a certain pattern of behavior that has proven effective in the past. Attractors are not rigid but are susceptible to change with experience. Actors trained in a particular technique tend to approach a role according to the tenets of the method, but they are also open to learning tricks of the trade that are different from those they acquired during training. Each way of working exerts an influence in the formulation of a response—some with greater force than others. Ultimately, it is the context in which the event takes place that determines which of the alternatives is selected.

Some of these limits are hardwired. That is, one cannot get a visual image from an olfactory perception, unless the visual cortex is activated as well. Some are limits supplied by experience. For some people, going onstage to perform is almost impossible, while for others it is almost a necessity. These limits are likely not neural necessities, but rather the result of social and cultural interactions, having more to do with identity and self-consciousness than with the organization of the brain. In both the hardwiring and "softwiring" situations, there are boundaries determining what can emerge from a set of perturbations. In the latter instance, environmental constraints can be overcome: it is possible for introverts to perform onstage, regardless of how uncomfortable they may feel. Such an experience changes the boundary condition, if only minutely. There is, in other words, a reciprocal relationship between limit conditions and the introduction of new perturbations, or "circular causality" (see page 17). An actor trained in a particular technique approaches each new play with tools that have worked in the past. Those tools will determine to an extent how the actor reads the play. Method actors read a Brecht play for the emotional and psychological dimensions of the characters and tend to miss Brecht's trenchant critique of Capitalism. This is not because Method actors willfully reject the Marxist critique (although they may), but because their boundary conditions presuppose a realist reading of *any* play. Mother Courage becomes a sympathetic character because she loses her children, rather than a callous entrepreneur who makes choices based on economic realities alone. In another example, an actor will develop different kinds of performances depending on whether she is performing a play by Tennessee

Williams or Arthur Miller. The different texts (here understood as a set of perturbations) demand different qualities from the actor. These necessities will alter the boundary conditions, privileging the use of certain tools over others. An actor cannot play Blanche Dubois in *A Streetcar Named Desire* the same way she portrays Elizabeth Proctor in *The Crucible*. The stimuli provided by the two plays alter the boundary conditions. Change is inevitable, but the response to the disruption will be, in large part, determined by the interaction between perceptual experience and the tendency to respond to situations in habitual ways.

An image that is frequently used to describe circular causality is a loop, suggesting the mutual influence of the higher-level boundaries on the lower-level perturbations and vice versa. From the harmonious and disharmonious frequencies in a number of neural assemblies, certain patterns will emerge that reflect these relationships in what is called *phase synchrony:*

> Large-scale integration happens through some form of temporal coding, in which the precise time at which individual neurons fire determines whether they participate in a given assembly. The most well-studied candidate for this kind of temporal coding is *phase synchrony*. Populations of neurons exhibit oscillatory discharges over a wide range of frequencies and can enter into precise synchrony or phase-locking over a limited period of time (a fraction of a second).[14]

Because most events are not limited to a single neural network but reach across a number of different brain areas and functions, phase synchrony occurs within several neural assemblies, as well as in the area of primary perceptual input. The patterns from the various neural networks coalesce in phase locking, giving rise to a "dynamic gestalt" that coordinates the different responses and implements a course of action that will provide, in theory, a positive outcome.[15] The feedback from this decision will reinforce the choice or suggest course corrections to insure a successful choice. The dynamic gestalt, "a large-scale, coherent oscillatory pattern,"[16] unifies the different harmonics, allowing one to identify the aroma with a rose and, at least potentially, a number of associated outcomes, such as a romantic reverie, the decision to look for the rose, etc.

A cognitive event, from the excitation to the emergence of an image, involves two intertwined but theoretically distinguishable aspects: emotion and appraisal. The ineffable quality of emotions makes it a difficult concept to define, despite the fact that we all know when we experience them. Lewis comes the closest to a definition when he articulates qualities associated with emotions:

> There are several features that are usually considered indispensable to emotion, and these are useful designators for emotion components. They include (1) arousal, (2) action tendencies, (3) attentional orientation, and (4) affective feeling. It is also generally agreed that these functions rely on physiological changes throughout the brain and body.[17]

The physiological aspects tend to be the significant difference between emotion and appraisal. The latter tends to be associated solely with mental activities that precede an emotional response:

> "Cognition" includes perception, attention, evaluation, decision-making, memory, and so on. However, these functions are also lumped under the nomenclature of *appraisal,* defined as the evaluation of significance in a situation that can give rise to an emotional response.... I will often use *appraisal* to mean, roughly, cognitive processes that are directed toward what is important for the self.[18]

However, appraisals do not "give rise to an emotional response" in DST. The "coherent oscillatory pattern" that identifies the odor as emanating from a rose consists of neural activations that already involve emotions as well as appraisal processes. The experience of the fragrance cannot be separated from the feelings aroused through the perceptual experience of smell. Lewis is emphatic on this point

> Even if some neural structures are assigned to appraisal versus emotion categories, the interaction of these structures rapidly gives rise to processes that span both categories. Neural structures perform no function at all until they interact with each other, and even interactions among closely related structures, far below the whole-brain level bind emotion and appraisal processes tightly together. Thus, brain function prohibits any real independence between appraisal and emotion, even at the level of subordinate processes.[19]

Indeed, it has become almost commonplace that, as Damasio has argued, emotion is inseparable from cognition.[20] They are inextricably linked in the cognitive process, occurring simultaneously rather than sequentially.

Thus far the discussion of DST has described how perceptual experience initiates disequilibrium across a number of neural networks, creating a phase transition. The firing of the neurons occurs within boundary conditions, which include the limitations of neurons to be activated by the perceptual stimuli, as well as information from past experiences that are relevant to the present situation. This interaction involves circular causality; that is, top-down structures impose limits on the range of possible responses at the same time that those limits are modified by the intensity and content of the perceptual information expressed by bottom-up activations. Through this reciprocal interaction, harmonic patterns begin to emerge in the form of behavior that takes into account both ends of the process. The emerging gestalt incorporates both emotion and appraisal, leading to a dynamic resolution of the disequilibrium and a response to the changes in the environment that gave rise to the event. The process is not a simple binary, because the information that goes into the emergent response arises from numerous areas of the brain, including the sensorimotor, associational, and conceptual areas. The timeframe for this process is a fraction of a second. The entire process takes place, quite literally, in the blink of an eye.

Given the speed and complexity of this activity, one shouldn't be surprised to learn that almost all of it occurs outside of conscious awareness. Only some of the patterns that emerge reach consciousness; the remainder take place in the *cognitive unconscious*, defined by Evan Thompson as follows: "The cognitive unconscious consists of those processes of embodied and embedded cognition and emotion that cannot be made experientially accessible to the person."[21] We have no awareness of the processes taking place. Because we are not aware of them, we are able to focus our attention on the continual flow of experience that is living in the world—an impossible feat if we were attentive to the minute workings of the system. The unconscious work of the brain indicates that we may make most of our decisions before we are aware of having made them. In an interesting experiment, psychologists give subjects two decks of cards that, unknown to the participants, are stacked so that one provides a high-risk game of wild fluctuations in which the investor eventually loses, the other a less volatile game of small-gain growth at low risk. The subjects are asked to play each game and select the deck with which they feel most comfortable. The researchers find there is an overwhelming preference for the low-risk deck and, more important, that the choice is made *before* the subjects are able to make a conscious selection. The privileging of the low-risk game also occurs when the participant is unable to articulate a reason for the choice. Malcolm Gladwell discusses this phenomenon and others like it in his book *Blink: The*

Power of Thinking Without Thinking. It is disconcerting to realize that most often we make decisions without being aware of having made them, that our logical processes are actually a rehashing of a choice that has already been made. Logic and analysis may merely be ways of checking the appropriateness of the choices made by the cognitive unconscious or a means of consolidating what we have learned in long-term memory.

A weakness in the use of DST is the lack of attention it gives to memory and learning; emphasis is placed on the emergence of dynamic gestalts rather than the consolidation of memory. However, the principles of DST resonate well with Eugene Gendlin's theory of carrying forward. He argues that events inevitably bring about change because, in the terms of DST, phase transitions involve the interaction between perturbations and boundary conditions, that is, between fresh information and the residue of past experiences. Through circular causality, as we have seen, both sides are modified in the emergence of phase synchrony and the "coherent oscillatory pattern" of the response. The modifications are the basis of learning, or the consolidation of experience in memory. As it is currently understood, memory strength depends on the number of synaptic connections between neurons. A synapse, the locus of communication between two neural cells, fires when sodium ions flow across the synaptic cleft, or gap, that separates them. There are weak and strong synaptic connections: the stronger the memory, the greater the number of *gates* that release the sodium and of *receptors* that allow the ions to enter the target cell. There is a proportional relationship between the frequency with which a connection is activated and the number of gate-receptor combinations. The stronger the memory, the higher the number of synaptic connections.

Memories form the boundary conditions, or attractors, that determine which of the incoming percepts will be privileged. The recursive interaction between the inputs and the attractors continues throughout the process of arriving at a phase synchrony in response to the perturbation. Those boundary conditions that exert the greatest influence in arriving at a successful interpretation of the event will be "rewarded" by the growth of more synaptic connections, making it likelier that they will be fired when similar stimuli enter the system in the future. The actors in *Waves* went through a process that gradually resulted in the score they performed for the public. Those actions that were most effective in creating the desired image were reinforced through repetition. When it was time to perform the play, the beginning of a scene triggered the activities learned in rehearsal. The strongest synaptic connections fired in the neural assemblies related to the performance of the action, leading to a phase synchrony that communicated the correct sensorimotor commands to be enacted. The rehearsal process allowed the actors to carry forward, in the form of enhanced memory, the performance score.

In a dynamic system, performing a role is never as simple as pushing a button to play out the action. That is one of the differences between making movies and performing live. When an actor performs, the trigger for an action is picked out from the world of the play—a change in lighting, the words or gestures of another actor—setting in motion neural assemblies, giving rise to circular causality, and leading, through the interaction of the trigger information and the attractors that define the boundary conditions, to the enactment of the score. This is part of the reason why two performances of the same action are never precisely the same. The phase synchrony that arises in a dynamic system, on account of its inherent instability, is based on probability rather than precision. For instance, there is always the possibility that extraneous perceptual material will alter the structure of the phase transition, distracting the performer from the primary objective of the scene. When this happens, the actor may forget a line, do an action with unusual intensity, or, in the case of *Waves*, fail to frame the image precisely when using the camera. Moreover, the absence of distracting inputs will not guarantee that the interactions within the dynamic system lead to an identical outcome every time.

The uncertainties of the dynamic system may seem to be a liability in performance, but they do provide certain comforts. The interactive quality of perceptions and memory increases the possibility that when a breakdown in the performance of the score occurs, a solution will be found quickly, because the reciprocal interactions between the boundary conditions and the inputs need immediate attention. Circular causality also allows for improvisation, discussed more fully in chapter 5. Being in an environment that is conducive to play, the actor can embrace freer interaction between information from the environment and the boundary conditions by deferring the need for decision making and allowing responses to morph into new forms of action, emotion, and interpretation through the continuing processes of the dynamic system. Linear systems do not have as much flexibility. Disequilibrium in the system, an apparent weakness, may in fact be what makes creativity possible, what makes possible our adaptability to new circumstances.

Boundary conditions and the influx of the present perceptual information are central cognitive functions, and they also form the baseline of the sense of self. Awareness of the world and the ability to retrieve memories challenge us to respond appropriately to changing circumstances and reassure us by providing the necessary tools in the form of past experience. Interacting in the world provides sensory (perceptual and proprioceptive) inputs that coalesce as emotional and intellectual experiences. The feelings that arise from sensorimotor activity (providing a continual flow of perceptual information) and their engagement with boundary conditions allow us to be aware that we are living at this moment with a sense of our own history. There are, of course, traumatic experiences for which we are not well equipped and novel circumstances that outstrip our past experiences, leading to complicated if not catastrophic results. Although they might compromise our ability to function, disastrous experiences almost never disrupt our ongoing sense of being in the world. A dynamic system does not exist in isolation, but is thoroughly integrated with the world. Thompson writes: "The central metaphor for this approach is the mind as an embodied dynamic system in the world, rather than the mind as neural network in the head."[22] The perturbations from the flesh, in the phenomenological sense, are indispensable to cognitive functioning—both conscious and unconscious—and to our experiences as sentient beings.

The collaborative and performative nature of theatre makes it an intersubjective experience. Unlike the reclusive artist or the poet in the garret, actors need others, whether those others are fellow performers or the audience. A considerable amount of attention, therefore, must be placed on the actions of the others in the room. Bruce McConachie, in *Engaging Audiences: A Cognitive Approach to Spectating in the Theatre,* cites the work of Pierre Jacob and Marc Jennerod, who have identified two types of vision: visual perceptions (looking at the inanimate world) and visual representations (vision related to intentional acts or watching others).[23] The first is at work when one looks at a landscape; it is frequently spoken of in acting as "soft focus." The latter, a hard focus, comes into play when a specific activity is undertaken. In performance, the actor will shift from one type of vision to the other, aware of the emotional and physical landscape (audience response, for instance, or the location of props on the set) and the specificity of playing out the rehearsed score. Although both types of vision play a significant role, specific attention to the flow of the performance, particularly the work of the other actors, is crucial to success. The speed and timing required to create an image in *Waves* makes it imperative that a performer be cognizant of what her task is, as well as where others are and what they are doing. To spend too much time using soft focus could be disastrous. Such awareness not only takes in the activity being carried out but also the state of mind, if you will, of the other performers. In more realistic forms of acting, this awareness takes the form of attention to affective states and shifting intensities in the other actors (as well as their characters). These phenomena have recently been brought together under the general rubric of mirror neurons.

Although neurons have only recently been identified in human beings, many scientists have come to believe that mirror neurons are a source of empathy. Among primates, when one monkey sees another perform a familiar action, the sensorimotor neurons associated with that activity will fire in the observing monkey *as if* he were performing the same task. While there is no evidence that mirror neurons are also linked to emotional states, the existing evidence has led to theories of empathetic responses and in some areas the belief that mirror neurons are indeed the source of empathy. Whether or not they can be linked to empathic emotions is less important than accounting for empathy or emotional identification with another being.

DST can account for empathy without either discounting or depending on the existence of mirror neurons. Stimulations from the environment are, as we have seen, seldom isolated to one area of the brain but tend to have more global impacts. Gestalts are the result of coordinated, harmonic oscillations; and emotion and appraisals always coincide in cognitive acts. Visual representations, to use Jacob and Jennerod's terminology, are likely to activate areas of the sensorimotor cortex as well as areas of the visual cortex because a physical response to the situation may also require an action to adjust to the movement of another. This would be an evolutionary, adaptive strategy, linked to instinctual behaviors such as fight or flight, because the ability to imaginatively reenact the behavior of another would allow for a more adequate appraisal of and response to the situation. To recognize in the behavior of others actions that I have enacted will encourage me to respond in terms that have proven successful for me. If I am attracted to someone and recognize behavior that parallels my own experiences of being interested in someone, I will respond differently than if I read the body language of the other as indifference. These appraisals are infused with emotion that reflects both present and past experience in the development of a coherent, if dynamic, gestalt. According to social psychologist Brian Parkinson and others, emotions are not individual responses to situations but have a social dimension; that is, we learn to have emotions through two sources: proprioception and social interaction.[24] Therefore, the perturbations to the system during an encounter with another involve sensorimotor areas of the brain interacting with boundary conditions that reflect past experience in relation to the current context. Through appraisal and the shifting form of gestalts, the sensorimotor areas recognize emotional resonances with the behavior of the other, giving rise to empathy. An empathic response, however, does not merely mean that we feel the same as the person with whom we are engaged. It may lead to responses that are quite different from that of the other. For instance, on seeing a person in distress, we might feel anger at the situation rather than the intensity of the other's pain. Thompson makes the argument from the perspective of nonlinear dynamics:

> This experience of yours contributes to the constitution of me for myself, for I experience myself as an intersubjective being by empathetically imagining your empathetic experience of me. Conversely, I imagine myself in your place, and this experience of mine contributes to the constitution of you for yourself. As we communicate in language and gesture, we interpret and understand each other dialogically. This dialogical dynamic is not a linear or additive combination of two preexisting, skull-bound minds. It emerges from and reciprocally shapes the nonlinear coupling of oneself and another in perception and action, emotion and imagination, gesture and speech.[25]

Without depending on mirror neurons and yet acknowledging a mirroring function (see chapter 7), DST can account for empathy without being reductive and while maintaining the coherence of the theory. The actor's ability to respond with sensitivity to the acting of a fellow performer is, in this theory, a result of the recursive interaction of perceptions and boundary conditions across a number of neural assemblies. Emotion and appraisal thus occur in the ongoing flow of cognition and in the blink of an eye.

With these theoretical foundations in mind, we can turn to the focus of this study, the art of the actor. In part II, we will look at technique, improvisation, and the development of the acting score, before bringing all three together to conceptualize the actor in performance. But first we must take a look at the actor's tools, and in the next chapter we move from the consideration of cognitive processes to the structures that define our engagement with the world.

Chapter 3

The Actor's Tools

The claim made in the first chapter is that a general theory of acting is possible because there are a number of concepts held in common that form the foundations of the dominant approaches to actor training. The underlying assumption is that actors take the methods learned in the studio into the practice of theatre. Although actors learn new techniques and develop hybrid forms, the values and beliefs about what constitutes good acting remain relatively consistent throughout a career. Chapter 2 argues for a model of cognition that has the potential to account for the similarities and differences among the various approaches to the art, as well as for the actors' penchant for learning new techniques to enhance their process. Dynamic Systems Theory (DST) provides a structure for exploring the principles on which acting discourse is based and for resisting the tendency to differentiate between qualities that are seen as valuable (emotional availability) and qualities that are denigrated (intellectualism). A dynamic system is different from other systems in that it is not closed, but responsive to changes in the environment (internal and external). What happens in the world affects the actions performed and vice versa. Reciprocal communication between actors mirrors precisely this tenet of DST not only because it reflects qualities inherent in good acting regardless of the form, but also because it is the nature of human interaction. Not everyone can act well, but everyone's cognitive machinery works in the same way. To insist that artists are different from other people is to undervalue what makes them special. What makes actors unique is the way they are able to use the tools they have in common with everyone else to create performances that have the potential to enthrall an audience.

This chapter introduces the tools that an actor employs. The six tools, which they have in common with most other people, are movement, language, gesture, memory, attention, and executive control. The last two require a preliminary introduction, because they are the least immediately definable. They encompass the familiar concepts of need, desire, concentration, and perception. The first three are understandable aspects of executive control, while the last, perception, seems like an outsider. For many years, I assumed that we are bombarded by perceptions and, through a process of discrimination, weed out those that are not necessary, focusing on those that are crucial to the current situation. However, it is now fairly well documented that we choose what we perceive, that perception is an intentional act. If someone is curious about the smell of a flower or the bouquet of a wine, she brackets everything but the sensations relevant to the aroma. Therefore, although perceptions are received from the external environment, the sensations recognized at a particular moment are those that are most useful. An actor onstage needs to focus on her own score and the work of the other actors performing with her. If her attention shifts to an inconsequential concern, trouble is on the horizon. The approach we take to the world determines the world we perceive. The exception to this rule occurs when there is a disruption in the environment that demands our attention, such as when an actor forgets a line or a necessary prop is not where it should be. Shifts in perceptual focus underscore the value of DST.

The discussion of the actor's tools will be divided into two parts: one subset of three that are expressive and used to act in the world (movement, language, and gesture) and another subset that provide the foundations (memory) and impetus (attention and executive control) for that engagement in the world.

The Foundations of Worldly Interactions

An actor enters the rehearsal room intentionally and with a history of experiences that define her subjectivity. In this regard, there is no difference between the person she is on her way to the theatre and the person she is when she arrives. What changes as she crosses the threshold between everyday life and the work of creating a performance is where her attention is directed, the kinds of perceptual information to which she is attuned, the memories of recent events that are set aside, and the expectations about what is going to take place. To abstract this moment, one set of attractors and boundary conditions is replaced by another that is more appropriate to the circumstances. The actor anticipates a different type of perturbation and feels relaxed, anxious, excited, or any number of other emotional states. The change is not sudden but takes place over time as she adjusts to the atmosphere of the room, the actors, director, stage manager, dramaturg, and others in the space. The process can be facilitated by warming up (alone or with others) or going over bits of business that have yet to be perfected or are central to initiating the performance. She retrieves certain memories, suppresses others, and focuses on the sequence of activities that will allow her to attend to the moment. She is not a passive but an active agent, engaged in the world around her. Without this preparation—evoking the correct sets of memories and focusing on what she intends to do— her work will not be effective.

Memory

Memory plays a role in virtually every aspect of our lives, from retrieving information for graphing a mathematical formula, reciting a soliloquy, or brushing our teeth, to providing continuity to what we see and hear when walking down the street. It not only functions consciously but also unconsciously, reminding us how to walk and consolidating experiences for retrieval night and day. As this repertoire suggests, there is a variety of kinds of memory. Psychologists have identified at least seven kinds, and there is little confidence that all have been discovered. Temporality is central to defining three of the seven: perceptual, working (or short-term), and long-term memory. The last is differentiated into semantic (associated with meanings) and episodic (linked to autobiographical experiences). The final two categories occur across the others: implicit (unconscious) and explicit (conscious) memory. Each of these will be defined briefly before a model of how memory works is introduced with special reference to acting.

Perceptual, or sensory, memory provides continuity of experience and has the shortest duration of all types, lasting between one and two seconds. As I turn my head or listen to music, the visual or aural field seems to be unbroken. This is an illusion created by perceptions that are held in memory just long enough to produce the sensation of continuity. Without the continued presence of the perception, listening to music would be less like hearing a melody and more like hearing an atonal composition, in which it is virtually impossible to predict what will be heard next. Even when there is an unexpected disturbance—the sudden blare of a siren—the disturbance is woven into the ongoing thread of existence. The timing prior to the decay is impeccable, because if these contents lingered any longer, the flow of experience would become a jumble. Thus far, two types of memory have been identified—visual and echoic (sound)—but it is assumed that there are perceptual structures for all of the senses, accounting for the continuity of touch, taste, and smell.

The second mode is short-term, or working, memory, and it refers to the information used to appraise and respond to changing circumstances in the present moment. It is not clear exactly how working memory functions, but there are two models that have gained traction in scientific circles. Both assume that there is a central executive, which focuses attention on material relevant to the immediate situation, and a pool (or pools) of data held in readiness should they be needed. Alan Baddeley's model consists of a central executive and "slave" buffers (think of RAM in a computer) called the phonological loop (language), visuospatial sketchpad (vision), and episodic buffer (events or activities). Nelson Cowan's model consists of a central executive, a pool of activated long-term memories available for immediate use, and nonactivated long-term memories.[1] Baddeley's theory assumes different areas of the brain link certain types of remembered information to specific cognitive abilities; while Cowan argues that perceptual input activates neural bundles associated with a wide range of data that can be accessed as needed. The principles underlying each model have much in common. A central executive is attentive to perceptual or proprioceptive information, and through the manipulation of the data and retrieved memories, patterns emerge and the appropriate response to the circumstances is determined, frequently in the form of behavior.

Long-term memory consists of data that has been consolidated; that is, the material is associated with certain neural networks and is retrievable when activated. The name "long-term memory" can be deceiving, because it refers to any data that can be retrieved after being consolidated. Remembering an appointment, even though it happens thirty minutes from now and will be forgotten shortly after it happens, is considered long-term memory because it involves the remembering of stored information. At issue is not the length of time the memory is stored, but how the memory is created and retrieved. On the neural level, this means synaptic connections are strengthened through the growth of multiple points of contact between relevant cells. The more links that neurons generate with receptor cells, the stronger the communication between them and the more likely the information will be retrieved. The more frequently the cells are utilized, the easier it is to remember the data they contain. Conversely, when the connections are used infrequently, the synaptic connections atrophy, and it is more difficult to retrieve the information.[2] When the connectivity gets extremely weak, we say that the information has been forgotten. The incidence of suddenly remembering events after many years supports the conclusion that nothing consolidated in long-term memory is ever completely forgotten, but, like downloaded data on a hard drive, remains difficult to recover. Many of the attractors and boundary conditions that are engaged when a dynamic system responds to a perturbation are long-term memories. They are stimulated because the disturbing event possesses characteristics that relate to a certain category of memory: "Categories are bursts of mutually reinforcing and synchronized activity."[3] As the appropriate neural networks are recalled, the information they contain is made available to consciousness for use in decision making or, in the case of a reflex response, for influencing behavior unconsciously.

Virtually everything we do, from eating to walking to singing to writing, draws on long-term memory. Remembered information that affects how we act but does not reach consciousness is implicit memory. For instance, while I may need to think about which finger needs to hit which letter on the keypad when typing, how to move my fingers to do so happens "automatically." The more frequently an activity takes place, the less conscious the effort that is needed to retrieve it. There are times when I don't need to think about which letter comes next and can rely on implicit memory. The ability to complete a task without conscious attention is a sign of mastery or of expertise. Experienced actors become masters of a number of techniques over the years: how they go about learning lines, control of the voice, stage combat, and so forth. One of the signs of expertise in acting is the ability to perform without thinking about how it is done. Explicit memories are those that must be brought to consciousness to complete a task. While I might wish that these words could be written utilizing only implicit memory, I need to remember what has been learned about memory and organize those thoughts into words that (I hope) communicate the knowledge. As I struggle with the syntax of the sentence, a selection process takes place, and certain words are chosen from all of those that offer alternative ways of expressing the same idea. There is more remembered material available than necessary, because quite often I do not know what is going to be said next until the thought is formulated into language. This is the nature of long-term memory in a dynamic system. A perturbation resonates with a number of possibilities, but only those that (seem to) fit the situation are actually used. This may seem inefficient, but this is not actually the case. If I discover that the sentence is not making sense halfway through, I do not have to return to the beginning of the thought; I can change the wording midstream.

The act of remembering is yet more complicated. When talking about writing, the reference is to semantic memory. At other times, when relating an event—encountering snow in Venice, for instance—I draw on episodic memory. This type of memory has a temporal dimension, while semantic memory uses abstract categories. This does not mean that the two types of memory are completely autonomous neural activities, because as I select the words to write about snow in Venice, images of the time spent there are also retrieved. The complexity of the process of remembering can be glimpsed if you consider that as I employ semantic and episodic memory in writing these last two paragraphs, I am also using implicit memory through the techniques of typing; at the same time, I become aware of feeling thirsty and prepare to reach for my glass to take another sip of water. To fully appreciate how this happens, we need to look at the limits of working memory.

The ability to utilize the retrieved material is constrained by the amount of data that can be attended to and by the length of time information can be held in the working memory. The data contained in working memory is active for no more than thirty seconds before it "decays," or becomes deactivated. The decay of data can be deferred if new perceptual information in the system activates the same or similar information or if patterns emerge during the process that are potentially useful in bringing about a resolution, requiring continued access to the material. The second limitation is the amount of information that can be held in working memory. Although a precise amount has not been determined, there is general agreement that a maximum of between four and seven "bits" of data can be "online" at any one time.[4] It is generally accepted that other mechanisms are activated in order to deal with the amount of information to be handled. To get around this limitation, two things happen. One is called "chunking" and the other "recoding."[5] If you were shown the number 5552748369, you might have trouble remembering all ten digits. However, if the number is written "555-274-8369," as most telephone numbers are, you have a better chance of remembering all the digits, because they have been divided into "chunks." It is believed that this is what happens in working memory. Instead of trying to learn sequences, the brain organizes groups of related material into chunks in order to allow potentially immense amounts of information to become accessible when a chunk is brought to mind. The other mechanism for handling large amounts of data is recoding:

> The input is given in a code that contains many chunks with few bits per chunk. The operator recodes the input into another code that contains fewer chunks with more bits per chunk. There are many ways to do this recoding, but probably the simplest is to group the input events, apply a new name to the group, and then remember the new name rather than the original input events.[6]

Recoding, then, is repacking information from several chunks into larger packages. This allows vast amounts of information to be retrieved more efficiently.

Memory is also plagued by its opposite: forgetting. In the perceptual and working systems, information is lost through decay—the inability of the neural networks to hold information for any length of time. Long-term memory is subject to both unintentional and intentional forgetting. Consolidation, as we have seen, involves the creation of synapses between neurons, which allows for retrieval. If the memory is not exercised, those links will break down, making recollection more difficult. It may be true that once you learn how to ride a bike, you never forget, but if you have not ridden for a while, you quickly realize that you need some practice to recover the skills that were second nature when you were a child. You need to relearn, that is, to reconsolidate the data through the strengthening, once again, of the synaptic connections. Intentional forgetting occurs when learning one mode of behavior means forgetting another. There are two processes involved when the learning of one set of information involves losing another. Actors working with new plays frequently find they are asked to replace one set of text with another. Not only do they need to memorize the new material, but they also have to forget the old. There is an active suppression of the existing memories; at the same time, attention is focused on memorizing the new. This concept will return during the discussion of creating the actor's score, but now we will turn our attention to another element of the cognitive process.

Executive Function

The prefrontal cortex is linked to executive function, which is identified by attention and executive control. Attention, connected to working memory, directs focus on the environment, selecting those stimuli that are necessary for responding to a person's specific circumstances in any given moment. Executive control is associated with decision making, particularly in novel situations, such as determining a course of action, responding to unusual circumstances, or abstract reasoning. This part of the brain has specialized neurons that are bidirectional; that is, these neurons can send and receive activations from the sensorimotor regions of the brain. The executive function also works through inhibition and disinhibition, the suppression or facilitation of behaviors. There is no consensus about how these processes work, but there is general acceptance about what they do.

When the world speaks to us or we have a desire to do something, a cognitive pattern focuses the mind on those aspects of the environment related to the situation. The implication, discussed more fully in chapter 5, is that perception is not a process of winnowing necessary from unnecessary data, but of preselecting and attending to the information that is most useful in the current situation. As cues from the environment accrue, memories of relevant past experiences are retrieved and are either brought into the circle of attention or remain active in case they are needed. Patterns of behavior begin to emerge among the neural networks and suggest responses to be tested for appropriateness or, in another type of situation, to occur as a reflex action. Potential reactions are evaluated by projecting perceptual information onto the patterns of remembered behavior, creating what Gerald Edelman calls a reentrant map.[7] If there is a resonance between the data and the attractors associated with the retrieved behavior, a response will take place. If not, a decision will be delayed until a proper course of action can be determined, by the brain continuing to scan other memories that were activated for their potential relevance but were not immediately brought into the circle of attention. Novel behaviors occur when existing patterns fail to satisfy the current conditions, allowing a resolution to emerge from slotting new or unexpected data into an existing pattern.

This decision-making process is carried out by the executive control. Writing, for instance, involves a struggle to find the right words to express a thought. The words you are reading were chosen because, after scanning the various possibilities brought to consciousness, they most closely satisfy the ideas to be communicated. This does not mean that there is a homunculus in the brain who is sorting through potential words to find the right one. Executive control is subject to the same dynamic properties as the rest of the system. I do not write like a philosopher, a scientist, or a psychologist. Over time I have developed a style of writing that approximates habitual ways of thinking. When I sit down to write, certain templates are activated, and through a process of mapping the ideas to be communicated onto the existing patterns, the act of writing (and rewriting) takes place. It is the same with acting. When developing a performance, the actor brings to the production a set of techniques that lead her to approach the process with a set of expectations. As the work proceeds, an actable score emerges. It is never a simple process, however, because it involves exploring many avenues of expression until one is found to satisfy the demands of the overall production. Through exercising executive control, the actor attends to certain types of information and recalls experiences that bear a resemblance to the current circumstances. As obstacles are encountered, alternative behaviors are tested until a solution is found or a compromise is reached. Whether writing or acting, through attention and executive control, emerging patterns are tested, embraced, or rejected until a sequence of actions is deemed acceptable. This will be developed more fully in the section on language.

Not every disturbance is a novel experience; indeed, most inciting perceptions are familiar. When the input is recognized as calling for a habitual response, a behavioral template is activated, or, in Baddeley's words, "large patterns of information that an expert can retain as a single complex chunk."[8] Those patterns are a set of attractors and boundary conditions that provide the correct responses to enact the appropriate behavior under the right circumstances. For instance, when walking and carrying a full cup of coffee, I don't need to think about how to move or balance—I've learned to move and balance through experiences as a child, when spilling was the rule rather than the exception. When it is put into play, the template adjusts the output of the sensorimotor system, so I do not need to think about it. My attention is placed instead on the variables of the particular situation: how fast I'm moving, the obstacles in my path, the dimensions of the cup, the surface of the floor, and so on. Spilling remains a possibility, particularly if attention is not being paid to the immediate circumstances, but if I am aware of my surroundings, I can generally avoid spillage. As the template is enacted through implicit, or unconscious, memory, consciousness can be focused on the novel details.

Executive control is not merely responding to incoming perceptual information, but it is also overseeing intentional actions. As human beings, we have needs and desires—whether hunger pains or an influx of hormones—that cause us to intervene in the world on our own behalf. In other words, perturbations to the system can be self-generated. In such cases, attention focuses on external conditions, comparing a desire to act to remembered patterns of behavior and engaging an appropriate template, or else creating a relatively novel response that will bring a resolution—satisfactory or not—to the underlying demands of the body. Meisner actors need to identify a reason to enter the stage of sufficient intensity to fuel the interaction between characters. Michael Chekhov uses psychological gestures to give energy to the action. Every acting system has recommended templates, in the form of techniques, that actors use in devising a performance. Each technique has "slots" that allow for the insertion of new data, which result in the performer engaging the world, perturbing other actors into similar engagements. Technique is not only the basis of character interaction, but also the basis of any performance, whether realistic, nonrealistic, or the postdramatic.

Through the exercise of memory, attention, and executive control, the performer engages the world in everyday life and in creating illusory realities. The interactions of these three systems elicit behavior that allows for the communication of intentions and responses in the theatre. We turn now to the other three tools available to the actor: movement, language, and gesture.

Engaging the World and DST

In creating a performance, the actor structures a sequence of actions that are expressed through movement, voice, and gesture. Some may wonder why gesture is being differentiated from movement, especially as they seem to be generated by the same physical mechanisms. Most training programs offer classes in voice and movement, assuming the latter includes the techniques intrinsic to gesturing. However, imaging studies show that gesture uses the areas of the brain associated with language more than those linked to movement. This association will be explored more fully in a moment. First, let us consider all three domains that comprise the actor's tools: movement, voice, and gesture, keeping in mind that although they are discussed individually, they are interconnected, providing triggers that retrieve information relevant to the other domains as well as their own. They interact dynamically, perturbing, prodding, and probing memory, evoking the connections that allow the acting score to unfold (more or less) as rehearsed. The intent here is not to provide an extended exegesis on each, but to discuss how they function, individually and together, as dynamic systems in the evolution of a performance.

Movement

It may seem unnecessary to give movement special attention: we know how to move. It is an innate ability—we move before we are born. However, as movement trainers understand and Stanislavski noted, "The hardest thing for an actor to do on stage, though he had been doing it all his life, is to walk."[9] Or, as those familiar with David Toole's performance in Lloyd Newson's physical-theatre piece *The Cost of Living*, choreographed for the company DV8, the hardest thing may be walking without legs. Disabled or not, the actor will ask, why is it so difficult to move effectively onstage? We can approach an answer by identifying what limits movement and, at least theoretically, how to engage these boundaries. Shaun Gallagher focuses his philosophy on the question of embodiment and how the concept of body schema and body image are useful in understanding our phenomenological engagement with the world. In his recent book, *How the Body Shapes the Mind*, he investigates the two terms as integral parts of mental processes and how they can be used to articulate a theory of embodied cognition.[10]

Body image is the easier of the two to grasp, at least on the surface. It can be reduced to a simple question: how do you feel about what you see when looking in a mirror? It becomes more complicated when trying to define the determinants of your response, whatever that response is. The attitude toward the image in the mirror is going to have internal and external valences. The internal are defined by the term proprioceptive, which refers to the information gathered by internal sensors. For instance, we feel different about our bodies when we are sick. The aches and pains of the flu or cancer alter our understanding of and attitude toward our body. Rigorous exercise makes us feel differently. We may experience exhaustion or exhilaration, or we may become conscious of certain muscles. The frequency with which the body image can change—the onset of illness or exercise—indicates that it is not a stable form but subject to variation according to the internal environment. Body image, however, is not just present in extreme situations, but is part of an ongoing process of proprioceptive awareness through self-monitoring. We only become conscious of the process when there is a significant change, which requires us to make a decision about what actions to take. Body image is also changed by variations in the external world. It changes with the temperature—the cold of winter or the heat of summer. More important, the social environment affects it. Cultural attitudes to the body are reflected in values associated with beauty, age, weight, height, disability, and so on. Normative ideologies of gender and sexuality promulgated by institutions, such as religion or the entertainment media (including sports) exert a significant influence on how bodies are perceived.[11] While these effects are more deep-seated and longer lasting, the experience of them varies with the environment. The sense of her body and degree of comfort are different depending on whether she is attending the ballet or a wrestling match.

The two sides of body image—proprioception and perception—are not mutually exclusive. Rather they are inherently interconnected. Gallagher writes: "[O]ur beliefs and attitudes towards our bodies, even if non-conscious, will have an effect on how we perceive our bodies and the bodies of others. In this sense, the body image is not inert or simply an ideational product of cognitive acts; it plays an active role in shaping our perceptions."[12] Feeling sick affects how an audience member perceives a performance, significantly changing the experience. Similarly, the cold of winter may be a perceptual experience, but the shivers are a proprioceptive one. A circular causality exists between them. Proprioception influences perception. The opposite is equally true. What I perceive walking down a dark, deserted street is affected by how safe I feel. These, along with beliefs and values arising from past experiences, are primary factors in determining the image we have of our bodies.

Body schema is less intuitive because it is less conscious. When I grasp a glass, I do not need to think about how to move my arm or the effort needed to hold on without dropping or shattering it. The *act* is intentional and conscious; *how* it is accomplished is not. The latter is the work of the body schema:

> The body schema...involves certain motor capacities, abilities, and habits that both enable and constrain movement and the maintenance of posture. It continues to operate, and in many cases operates best, when the intentional object of perception is something other than one's own body. Therefore, the difference between body image and body schema is like the difference between a *perception* (or conscious monitoring) of movement and the actual *accomplishment* of movement, respectively.[13]

There are two sides of the body schema: the innate and the learned potentials and constraints. When I need to regain my balance or judge how fast a car is coming down a street, I don't need to think about it. The data needed to respond appropriately is present "instinctively." It is not all instinctive, however. Certain aspects of the body schema *are* physical limitations: the head can turn only so far; it is not possible to fly. But some of it is learned: how to pick up a glass safely, how the performer with DV8 dances without legs. What is learned is always in the context of the body's limitations and can become so ingrained that it is "second nature" and, at least potentially, another set of limitations. Movement technique refines the body schema, building on the catalogue of "I cans" and natural limitations, increasing the range of potentials that can be learned, allowing the body to respond in ways those without a given skill cannot. Performers—actors and athletes—do feats that are seemingly impossible. Derek Jeter has less than a second to decide whether or not to swing at a pitch; the British actor John Wood, playing Sherlock Holmes, would seem to fly from one side of the stage to the other and end up sitting, carefully posed, in a chair. Jeter knows exactly where his bat needs to be to hit an object that is moving approximately ninety miles an hour roughly one out of every three times at bat. Wood's move had been carefully choreographed, but the ability to accomplish it depended on a highly developed physicality. The body schema allows us to orient ourselves in the world and does impose limitations on the possible, but it can also be trained to do the astonishing.

The boundary between the body image and the body schema is not clearly defined. Like perception and proprioception, they are intertwined. The image I have of myself is determined in part by what I am capable of doing; at the same time, the image I (want to) have of myself will determine the effort needed to enhance my body schema. According to Gallagher, "Movements controlled by a body schema can be precisely shaped by the intentional experience or goal-directed behavior of the subject."[14] Body image and body schema are not static concepts, but exist in a dynamic relationship. They form boundary parameters, subject to perturbations, that determine whether or not to swing the bat, how to move across the stage, or how to focus attention so that the creative associations required for improvisation can happen. Developing the interconnections between the image and schema does not guarantee success. Jeter swings and misses more often than his bat connects with the ball; in some performances, Wood crossed the stage with less grace than in others; and improvisations all too often fail. Dynamic systems are not stable, so understanding the complex relationship between body image and body schema is central to coming to terms with movement.

Gallagher identifies four ways of moving: reflex, locomotion, instrumental movements, and expression. Reflex is an involuntary response to a stimulus, involving only the brainstem and cerebellum. Other parts of the brain become involved when the reflex action is experienced proprioceptively. As such, this way of moving does not concern us here. Locomotion, as the name implies, refers to movement through space: walking, climbing, crawling, swimming, and so on. It is generally intentional, although activities such as pacing to and fro can be habitual activities that supplement "higher order" processes. Instrumental movements are used to carry out specific tasks, such as picking up a glass, writing, hammering, or navigating the Internet. These tend to be more complex processes that require multiple muscle systems, areas of the brain associated with different sensory inputs, and concentrated attention. They are not only linked to intentional acts, but may also be employed in response to unconscious needs and desires. The first three kinds of movement are primarily associated with body schema, while the fourth, expression, is linked more directly to body image. It is the movement perhaps most important for the actor, because its function is communication, because it "involves a direct mapping of meaning onto space and motion."[15] Linked to the emotion-reason complex, expression inflects the way we walk and engage with objects, but it is also found in movements that are neither locomotive nor instrumental, such as facial expression.

Stage movement incorporates these six elements—image, schema, reflex action, locomotion, instrumentality, and expression—in intricate patterns that form and support the structure of the performance. A significant difference between theatrical movement and that of everyday life is the relative weight given to these constituent parts in the evolution of the acting score. The expressive qualities of movement are intentional in the theatre, while in the everyday they attend an action without our necessarily being aware of them. It is common to think about a person's body language during an interview; for example, what she is saying may be contradicted by how she is sitting. While an actor may *choose* to create a tension between her posture and what she is saying, it can be a problem onstage and in everyday life to be *unaware* that such a tension exists. A frequent criticism of actors, especially of the inexperienced, is the lack of emotion conveyed by their bodies compared with the intensity of their speech, what might be called "talking-head syndrome." Overcoming this problem requires improving technique and working toward a more flexible body schema; the circular or looped interaction between technique and schema flexibility then modifies the body image. Improved technique enhances the performer's conscious awareness of herself and how she moves in a particular sequence.[16] When the body is sufficiently supple (e.g., through Grotowski's via negativa), expressive communication is more fully integrated into the movement of the performer.

Body image and body schema—concepts we will return to in the next chapter—are complex and dynamic forms that define parameters, threatening to limit the actor's range of possible movements. As relatively flexible structures, they function as attractors that increase the probability that certain movement patterns will be adopted. However, they are not so dominant as to be the determining factor. Perceptual and proprioceptive information register external and internal environments, respectively, and perturb the semi-stable state, demanding a pattern that is responsive to the demands of the immediate circumstances. The more flexible the body—that is, the better the technique—the more likely it is that creative and innovative movements will present themselves. In addition to technique, memories of past experiences intersect with the desired ends and exert pressure on the system, which resolves the perturbation through reflex, locomotion, instrumental movement, and expression. What should be evident is that this process is not a simple stimulus-response model. The sensory information activates a range of neural networks, which offer a number of possible options, out of which one particular route is taken. The others do not then disappear, but remain as potentials should circumstances change and a different movement sequence becomes necessary or desirable. It is not unusual for actors to be asked to provide a range of choices. I remember hearing an anecdote, perhaps apocryphal, about Sir Ralph Richardson, rehearsing Harold Pinter's *No Man's Land* late in his career. The director, fearing for the actor's well-being, was nervous about how to approach the moment in the play when the character had to collapse. Richardson said, "Would you like me to do it like this...or this...or this?" He demonstrated each one in turn, giving the director a number of options and relieving him of a great deal of anxiety. Such choices are not simply movements; they are expressions of a character's emotional life or nonexpressive enactments of an abstract pattern.

Language

Language in the theatre is generally thought of as an object of analysis or in relation to the voice. Play analysis explores metaphors, grammatical idiosyncrasies (e.g., usage of pronouns, adjectives, verbs), given circumstances, actions, objectives, obstacles, and so forth. The emphasis is on understanding the text and the tasks actors are expected to fulfill. Voice training (see chapter 4) focuses on the mechanics of vocal production in order to insure the maximum expressivity in the communication of the desired linguistic nuance. The subtleties of character, the beauty of the language itself, and the complexity of thought and intention depend in part on the actor's understanding of the text and in part on the proficiency of her instrument. While textual interpretation and instrumental proficiency are necessary components in developing an actor's score, they do not sufficiently account for the interrelatedness of linguistic formations and vocal production as part of a dynamic system. The neural theory of language provides a framework for understanding the intertwining of language and experience.

The fundamental tenet of the neural theory of language is that abstract thought, long considered an autonomous function of the mind, is based on embodied experience. This claim has consequences that reach far beyond the refutation of Descartes' mind-body dualism; and it is based on two supporting claims. First, the ability to understand language, both conceptually and grammatically, is possible because (a) members of a culture have similar experiences, particularly as children, and (b) they are taught to organize their experiences according to frames that reflect cultural norms. Frames consist of attractors and boundary conditions, which encourage the use of familiar patterns for understanding, and in language these patterns form the basis of grammar. While other languages present a variety of alternative frames for organizing thought, English-speaking cultures generally use the subject-verb-object frame as an organizing principle. This pattern is central to articulating thoughts in ways that are comprehensible within and across the culture. Common experiences and shared frames are the basis for understanding the structure and flexibility of language.

A second supporting claim of the neural theory of language, with consequences for understanding creativity in general and acting in particular, is the premise that the world does not consist of discrete objects. The division of reality into things occurs, because frames are applied that organize it in a way that makes sense of reality for us. Jerome Feldman, an advocate of the neural theory of language, writes: "[M]y categorization of trees is not at all like that of an arborist."[17] Language, therefore, is based on a way of structuring the world that is formulated through experience and cultural frames, but it is circular in that the form and content of words and their arrangement also determines how we construct our reality.

Experience in its "raw" form is not equivalent to meaningful language; the gestalt image derived from perceptual and proprioceptive information is used to generate more complex thoughts through metaphor. An adequate understanding of the neural theory of language, therefore, demands a further look at metaphor. In this context, Feldman explains, "metaphor in general refers to understanding one domain in terms of another."[18] First steps in gaining control of the body and interacting with objects (such as liquid in a cup) provide meaningful experiences, which form schemas that can be used to communicate very different concepts. Schemas are constructs that are formed through active engagement with the world, consolidating memories that are comprehensible to people with similar histories. Shared, if not identical, histories allow schemas to serve in communicating to others concepts not directly related to a given experience. For instance, an infant moving because she wants to get hold of an object, such as a favorite toy, is the kind of experience that gives rise to the source-path-goal schema; or seeing water poured into a glass can form the foundation of the containment schema. These schemas are useful because they can be employed in a great variety of contexts, creating metaphors. Containment, for instance, can be used positively, in reference to military strategy (to hold off the enemy), medicine (to keep the disease from spreading), architecture (the articulation of space); or negatively, in reference to astronomy (the disarming infinity of space).

Feldman differentiates between primary and complex metaphors: "In each primary metaphor, such as affection is warmth, an experience brings together a subjective judgment (here, affection) and a sensory-motor occurrence (temperature)."[19] Complexity arises from combining primaries, as in this example of a statement using the source-path-goal schema: "The economy is heating up [warmth is good; up is good] suggesting an end to the recession [going backward or down is bad]." The same concept can also be associated with different metaphors, depending on the context. Causation, for instance, can be expressed as "causes are forces," "states are locations," or "change is motion."[20] What may at first seem like a simplistic way of thinking about language mirrors the complexity of abstract thought, which requires flexibility and openness to different permutations and combinations.

A neural theory of language needs to account for the biological processes that make possible the correlation of embodied experience, thought, and language. Languages are linear, as sequences of words (or, in Asian languages, ideographs) provide a structure that makes a thought comprehensible to the listener or reader. Clarity is desirable in most cases, but the danger exists that the strictures of grammar can oversimplify complex ideas. This is the conflict that plagued Artaud, who felt that language lacked the suppleness to capture thought.[21] The associative nature of metaphor, the mapping of a concept from one domain onto another, mitigates against this reductive threat by encouraging resonances that evoke memories from a vast array of experiences in the process of thinking. Poetry depends on the ability of language to evoke multiple responses to words and their combinations: Take Dylan Thomas's famous opening line "Do not go gentle into that good night."[22] A brain that is linear—its trigger activates a sequence of neurons leading to a specific memory—cannot elicit the associations necessary to experience the nuance and richness of Thomas' language. A theory of the brain that recognizes parallel processes, on the other hand, allows for language of greater complexity, involving denotative interpretation, inference, and emotion, while accommodating the need for meaning. In terms of DST, words serve as a perturbation; they have the potential to cause a destabilization that activates a number of attractors (possible meanings) and boundary conditions (cultural frames) across several domains. The return to a near stable condition takes place not because the correct answer is found, but because the "best fit" is found. Feldman writes: "People, including children, are always trying to find the best fit between what they observe and what they know."[23] Because the solution is a best fit, activations that do *not* lead to stability do not simply disappear. They begin to "decay"; that is, they lose force as a possible solution to the perturbation. However, as communication continues and the system is once again disrupted, the search for a best fit can "revive" a decaying meaning if it leads to a best fit in the new situation. The temporal dimension of communication takes advantage of the instability of dynamic processes to "allow" consideration of a number of different patterns to emerge in the coming to understanding (or the lack thereof). The meanings that emerge will be sensible, provided they utilize cultural frames with sufficient precision to allow for a best fit. As long as the structure of the sentence more or less follows the rules of grammar and the listener has the appropriate experiential schemas, meaning will evolve that approximates the intended idea in all its richness of content.

That is a lot of information packed into a single paragraph, and some examples might be useful. When I say "follow," a spatial relationship comes to mind in which something is ahead of another. We have all had experiences of following or being followed ("Stop following me," says one sibling to another). The image, however, is not a complete thought, and we are left anticipating what will come next. If *me* comes next (we are now using a temporal as well as a spatial metaphor), it defines a relationship between the speaker and the listener that is different if *the white rabbit* are the next words uttered (or, for *Matrix* fans, typed on a screen) or, again, if the next words are *the logic of the argument*. To make sense of whichever phrase is actually used, the listener needs to keep all the possibilities (there are many, many more) available until what is said renders a possible interpretation irrelevant. Once I've said, "Follow *me*," the other associations are allowed to decay. They will again become active, however, if I later say, "'Follow me,' said the White Rabbit." Understanding is not a passive process, however, because we are able to *anticipate* what the next best fit is going to be. We have all had the experience of knowing what someone is going to say before it is said. By anticipating what is going to be said and keeping possible associations in working memory, we develop a robust understanding of a communication in milliseconds. It would be inefficient and time consuming if instead of keeping various possibilities alive through parallel processing, the act of interpretation had to begin anew each time an unanticipated element was added to the conversation.

The ability to anticipate does not depend on the words alone. Several other frames affect the interpretation of language. The context in which the utterance is made influences expectations. "Follow the white rabbit" might refer to a line in a script or to a direction given by the director. The environment in which an utterance takes place will, to a large extent, predispose an actor to respond in a particular way, setting the stage for certain patterns to emerge. Should the phrase be introduced during a production of *Hamlet*, it is quite likely that it would confound the actor, because it would be out of place in the context and disrupt her expectations. She would probably look askance at the director until some sense (the best fit) could be made of the comment. Understanding arises from a complex set of circumstances, schemas, and cultural frames evoked by the choice of words.

Thus far I have been talking about hearing. Much the same process is involved in speaking. The intent to say something comes, for whatever reason, from the particular context in which the utterance is to take place. The intention sets the system in motion, evoking a number of different schemas and their associated images. Through the "best fit" scenario, words are selected not only because they fit the idea to be communicated, but also because they are appropriate for the grammatical frames current to the culture. If you listen closely to people talking, you may find that they seldom speak in complete sentences and that their thought patterns suddenly shift in the middle of a phrase, leading to mixed metaphors. Ideas take form as they are spoken. As the speaker hears what is being said, the words are looped back further, perturbing the system and placing additional boundary conditions on the process of discovering the best fit. Changes in expression take place when the words that would be most appropriate for the idea fail to appear or when they suggest an alternative way of saying the same thing. Speech stops as the speaker reevaluates the dynamic between the intent and the words and as other patterns of words present themselves for consideration. The schemas and the grammatical forms finally selected will, however slightly, alter the idea as they allow the communication to take place. For Gilles Fauconnier and Mark Turner, the mapping of ideas onto embodied schemas in the creation of metaphors is "conceptual blending," a process that is ubiquitous in all areas of human thought: "Metaphoric thinking, regarded in the commonsense view as a special instrument of art and rhetoric, operates at every level of cognition and shows uniform structural and dynamic principles, regardless of whether it is spectacular and noticeable or conventional and unremarkable."[24]

This description may seem either a bit messy or overly intellectual. The process is neither. There are strong cultural frames for grammar that impose structure on the word-selection process, and there are terms that are associated with an idea that begin to be identified as the intent to speak the idea is recognized. The choice of words takes place in milliseconds, and we tend to become aware of what we want to say only when the desired word does not appear and we are conscious of the failure. At those moments, we must recall what we intend and the words uttered to that point in order to decide or find the right thing to say. In bringing the words to mind, we are utilizing implicit (long-term) memory. As the patterns form, more than just the embodied schema is brought to mind; emotions and experiences attend it, giving rise to feelings that influence the way things are being said. Roland Barthes has a beautiful phrase for the emotions that attend speech; he calls them "the grain of the voice": "The 'grain' is the body in the voice as it sings, the hand as it writes, the limb as it performs."[25] In addition, as I say what I say, other passions arise, associated with why I am saying what I say and the satisfaction or disappointment of my words' communication or failure to communicate my ideas.

Language is not a function of mind as distinct from the body. It is a complex process that calls on embodied schemas linked to experience The process uses the schemas metaphorically by mapping onto them the intended contents of speech and blending those contents with other aspects of the idea to create complex phrases, sentences, and utterances. Cultural frames that promote particular word orders and grammatical constructions guide the formulation of phrases. These limits on expression deny speech the perfect phrasing, so the speaker uses the best-fit strategy. At its most successful, the strategy can lead to eloquence; when less successful, it may result in stuttering, mixed metaphors, and unfinished phrases as the speaker strives to find a more precise way of communicating the ideas. It is not merely the internal processes that determine what is said. The speaker is also aware (if not conscious) of the external world and the circumstances in which a verbal exchange is taking place. The location of the exchange—classroom, church, dinner for two—influences what is being said and how.

For the actor who is delivering a memorized text, the contours of the speech act are different. Instead of improvising language, she is recalling previously written grammatical structures that have certain content and an emotional through line that has been determined during rehearsals. This does not mean that different parts of the brain are being used; that would be an extremely inefficient use of mental space. Although the degree of each area's influence will differ, areas of the brain can adapt to changing circumstances without needing to evolve new regions. The rehearsed text takes the form of frames, or boundary conditions, which encourage the use of patterns devised during the production process. The degree to which the patterns have been learned determines the predictability of the speech on any given night. Yet each night different perturbations will influence the recall and expression of the patterns, giving each performance unique nuances and enriching and bringing life to the theatre experience, both onstage and in the audience.

Gesture

It is typical for beginning actors to say, "I don't know what to do with my hands." The most effective response tends to be, "Don't worry about it. They will take care of themselves." Researchers, like David MacNeill, who look at the connection between gesture and language are discovering that this is very good advice. We tend to think of gesture as a form of movement ("Where do I *put* my hands?"), and there are gestural forms that take the place of words, such as a salute or pointing to indicate a direction or location. However, the gestures used in everyday conversation do not express complete meanings. They cannot stand alone, but are an integral part of communicating and intimately connected to language. McNeil explains: "Gesture is not input to speech, nor is speech input to gesture; they occur together."[26] Gestures do not serve language; they are part of the generation of meaning, arising from the process of transforming thought into words: "To make a gesture, then, is to iconically materialize a meaning in actional and spatial form."[27] Instead of taking the form of words, gestures are moving images (iconic) that relate to and communicate the thought being formed in space and over time.

Gestures appear to arise spontaneously, and indeed they are frequently unconscious acts. They are, however, part of the cognitive processes of language production and in fact have their origins in the same part of the brain. Broca's area, located in the inferior frontal gyrus, part of the left frontal lobe, is generally associated with speech. More recent imaging technologies confirm that the area is also used to generate physical actions, including gesture. McNeil defines its function in more detail:

> Broca's area is more than a "speech center." It is *the area of the brain orchestrating actions under some significance*—that is, it is the area of the brain that assembles sequences of movements and/or complexes of moving parts into performance packages unified by goals, meanings, and adaptability.[28]

Producing gestures to express a thought occurs simultaneously with the search for the appropriate words. As an idea perturbs the speech centers, activating attractors and boundary conditions in the search for linguistic patterns that best approximate a thought, action centers are also put into phase transition, producing gestures that assist the speaker and enhance communication. Gestures, therefore, are not arbitrary; they are material carriers of meaning, "not a representation but an updating [of] the speaker's momentary state of mind."[29] I gesture because it helps me to formulate the phrases (gestural and linguistic) that will communicate the idea to my listener. As we saw with language, thoughts do not appear in grammatical form; rather, the form arises with the expression of the ideas. Similarly, gestures emanate as part of a process parallel to and intimately intertwined with the articulation of thought in words.

Granpa Joad's last scene before he dies in *The Grapes of Wrath* is one of resistance. Acknowledging his love of the earth that he has tilled throughout his adult life, he is determined to stay on the land that is his home. The family refuses to let him stay; and the last the audience sees of him is his being carried and put down on the bed of the truck. Playing the role, I refused to go, sitting down—in an act that showed weakness more than defiance—and telling my son to leave me behind. With my arm directed at him, palm down, and fingers curled in, I made two quick flicks, implying that he should go on without me. What is important about this particular move is that when it first happened, I did not consciously decide to make the gesture, it simply happened. Yet it was as much a part of communicating the action as the words that went with it. The flicks were iconic (in the sense of being meaningful) but would have generated no meaning without the accompanying words. Making the gesture clarified the action alongside the words. Earlier, when the character is feigning excitement about going to California, he talks about getting in a vat of grapes and "scrooging" around. With knees bent, I wiggled my hips from side to side as if squashing the grapes with my rear end. Without the context, the gesture would have been meaningless, and the word *scrooging* would have been nonsensical. Words and gestures work together to communicate meaning.

To put it another way, the relationship between gesture and speech is dialectical, an interaction between different types of thought in the movement toward a synthesis of image and language. As McNeil explains it

> This imagery language dialectic (materialized in gesture and speech) is an interaction between unlike modes of thinking. The disparity of these modes is the "fuel" that propels thought and language; the dialectic is the point at which the two dimensions intersect.[30]

The sequence is further complicated because the dialectic takes place within the crucible of boundary conditions that reflect subjective intents and pressures exerted by the environment: "The field of oppositions indexes and is constrained by external conditions, both social and material, but an essential fact is that it is also *a mental construction, part of the speaker's effort to construct a meaning.*"[31] The intent to speak provides an impetus to the speech centers and the area associated with movement sequences, creating a three-step process of growth point (GP), unpacking, and stop order:

> The key to the dialectic is that the two modes are simultaneously active in the mental experience of the speaker. Simultaneously representing the same idea unit in opposite modes creates instability, a

"benevolent instability" that is resolved by accessing forms on the state dimension—constructions and lexical choice, states of repose par excellence.[32]

Intent leads to instability, which resolves itself in repose. Unlike the dynamic system itself, which only achieves relative stability, the language-gesture dialectic comes to an end when the thought is complete. This concept will have important ramifications in the discussion of structuring a performance, but first the three parts of the dialectical process need to be defined.

The GP, or psychological predicate, arises from the speaker's intent.[33] It is the perturbation that destabilizes the system, setting in motion the process of transforming thought into language and gesture. The uncertain origins of a GP make it impossible to identify a starting point. Suffice it to say that it arises from subjective desires and environmental constraints. As the name suggests, it is a seed from which a larger process grows, and yet it is not a singular event. The thought contained by the GP that initiates the dialectic between language and gesture does not disappear but persists as the expressive forms develop. The psychological predicate reenters the dialectic, assessing the proximity between what needs to be expressed and the emerging patterns of speech and gesture. Depending on the extent to which the thought is already resolved, the reintroduction of the GP can encourage the path embarked on, lead to a redirection of the process (perhaps leading to mixed metaphors), or in certain situations reformulate the predicate. McNeil writes: "All of this is meant to be a dynamic, continuously updated process in which new fields of oppositions are formed and new GPs or psychological predicates are differentiated in ongoing cycles of thinking or speaking."[34] That is, it becomes evident that a variation of the GP would more adequately address what needs to be communicated.

As noted earlier, the process of perturbation in dynamic systems continues as new perceptions and proprioceptions are introduced, evoking new patterns of behavior; so it is with speech and gesture. A sentence is started but stopped because it is not saying what needs to be said; the speaker begins again. Many have undoubtedly had the experience of talking with someone who cannot finish a sentence but continually starts over, never getting to the end. In exasperation, one finally says, "Just say what you mean!" She would if she could. The problem is that she is unable to "unpack" the thought. The metaphor is somewhat misleading, because unpacking generally implies that all the objects to be moved are already present and are simply moved from one place to another. We have already seen with the dialectic that the emergence of language is a complex process during which the intent to speak is transformed into words and gestures. So it is with unpacking,

> The implication of the unpacking effect is that, before a GP is unpacked, thinking is not complete. It is not that one thinks first, then finds the language to express the thought...rather, thinking, as the source of meaning, emerges throughout the process of utterance formation.[35]

The act of unpacking is the formulation of the thought in material forms. As I write, the thoughts to be communicated start and stop, wrong words are identified, some are replaced, additional phrases are added or deleted; and slowly the ideas gain clarity. The knowledge of what is to be said only comes with the saying. There are some thoughts that come with relative ease. In New York, when someone sneezes, almost invariably someone else will say, "Bless you." The response is habitual, and the perturbation to the system quickly brings the appropriate pattern to mind. It is with thoughts that require reflection in the formulation that the concept of unpacking is useful. It is at these times, according to McNeil, that gesture becomes an integral part of the process: "Unpacking fleshes out the material carrier of the speaker's meaning in its particular context of speaking, with added meanings generated to achieve a well-formed pattern."[36] A pattern that consists of both words and gesture is formed, communicating the ideas as they pertain to the specific environment.

The third and final element of the dialectic is the stop-order. It occurs when a thought is complete. Then words and gestures also cease. The process has no defined limit: some thoughts can be resolved in two words (*bless you*), while others can take several sentences to bring to a satisfactory end:

> This process continues until, eventually, a "stop-order' occurs (it stops only temporarily: a new cycle begins immediately or might overlap the earlier one). A stop order is an intuitively complete (or complete enough) static structure (intuitions of well-formedness being how one experiences the static dimension).[37]

At other times the dialectic does not come to a happy conclusion, and the speaker is stymied, unable to complete the thought. Cycles may begin again; or the person speaking may become a listener in a dialogic process, as an interlocutor begins the transformation of thought into word and gesture.

Movement, language, and gesture are tools the actor uses to communicate the performance. As categories, they can be clearly defined, but as the outcomes of a dynamic system, they are part of an emerging pattern of behavior. As Esther Thelen and Linda Smith write: "There is only process—only activity."[38] Combined with memory, attention, and executive control, movement, language, and gesture form a complex organism that is influenced by its most intimate desires and by the social and cultural complex in which it lives and interacts with others. Nothing happens out of context. Acting, like life, takes place against a background from which it differentiates its singularity and recognizes its mode of participating in the world. The actor does not only respond to stimuli; she also actively engages in life, aware of the state of her body and the reality she constructs, based on the perceptual and proprioceptive experience to which she attends. As a dynamic system, the actor is perturbed by proprioceptive and perceptual information that engages memory and activates templates. Attractors and boundary conditions arise that elicit emergent patterns of behavior, including ways of interacting with others, that are responsive to changes in the environment. This process takes place whether the actor is learning lines on her own or engaging with the chorus as she justifies the murder of Agamemnon. It is a ubiquitous and necessary set of conditions for living an engaged and interactive life onstage and off. Acting is part of an actor's everyday life. The artist does not have mysterious skills that others do not possess; her creative talent is determined by the techniques she has learned and her ability to discover patterns of behavior that communicate and sustain the potential to surprise. It is to the process of creating a performance—how a dynamic system employs these tools and abilities—that we turn next.

Part II

Chapter 4

Technique

No one seriously doubts the importance of technique in acting. However, it is also viewed with ambivalence. As a positive force, technique allows the performer to develop a role efficiently and creatively, providing confidence that a performance is repeatable. The last thing an actor wants to do is work with someone who lacks technique, who wastes precious rehearsal time because she is incapable of making appropriate choices in a timely manner. Yet technique can be perceived as a problem when it becomes an end in itself, leading to performances that are consistent but lack the vitality that, according to Stanislavski, elevates theatre from a craft to an art. In the latter instance, technique is apparent, the performance mechanical. With proper deployment, technique seems to disappear; the acting appears to be effortless while being appropriate to the style of the performance.

There is no single technique. To create the desired effect, each distinct style of acting requires specific modes of training. As a style takes hold, it spawns a number of teachers who believe their approach provides the best education. In the United States, where the predominant type of acting is linked to Stanislavski's system, Strasberg, Meisner, and Hagen are responsible for but three of the many approaches that individuals, acting studios, and university degree programs use to train actors. Each claims to provide the best technical training for creating performances that achieve the level of art. Although there are certainly charlatans, most teachers of acting provide a reasonably good approach for the student with the right disposition. As much as technique is about the utility of the approach, each method also depends on a positive, constructive relationship between the student and her mentor. Performers have different temperaments and sensibilities, causing them to respond positively to certain exercises and forms of engagement and to be unresponsive to others.

There is, of course, no one approach that works for all, and very few actors will claim to follow a single technique. Experience is a great teacher, and as actors encounter new situations, they discover alternative ways of addressing the problems they confront. Some of these involve self-discovery, while some are found through interactions with teachers, directors, or other actors who have faced similar concerns. Therefore, when talking about an actor's technique, it is better to use the plural or to think of technique as a hybrid or a series of adaptations. Even for those few who work with only one mentor throughout their career, it is impossible to think about technique as a singular entity. There are different techniques for the various facets of acting, such as vocal production, physical movement, mask work, stage combat, memorizing lines, and conveying emotions that are not fully felt. Similarly, different styles of acting approach action and character differently. For instance, realistic acting utilizes different techniques than those required for Restoration comedy, Shakespeare, or postdramatic performances.

The underlying assumption of this discussion is that gaining technique requires repetition. Techniques are not innate but learned through practice, and the deftness with which they are used indicates the degree of mastery. Those extremely proficient in their use and who continually seek to improve can be said to be experts.[1] A clear understanding of the different types of mastery depends on a more thorough definition of technique, the subject of the next section, which includes a brief look at some of the cognitive processes central to the acquisition of technique. This will be followed by a genealogy that examines the place of technique in the development of children and the establishment of identity, and by two case studies: one a comparison of different approaches to training the voice, the other an instance of a ballet dancer who decided to learn a new form of dance. The chapter will conclude with a discussion of the significance such crossing of techniques has for a theory of acting. For the purposes of discussion, three major categories of technique can be identified: improvisational (chapter 5), analytical (chapter 6), and physical (the subject of this chapter). The final chapter will examine the coming together of all three.

Defining Technique

The Oxford English Dictionary (OED), in one of its definitions, refers to technique as "mechanical skill in artistic work," or more fully as the "manner of artistic execution or performance in relation to formal or practical details (as distinct from general effect, expression, sentiment, etc.)." Technique is a skill that can be learned and employed to accomplish a task; it is inherently practical and related to form rather than to content. Music and the visual arts, in which it is perhaps easier to differentiate the formal and practical from the expressive, are the forms of art used by the *OED* to refine its definition. Moreover, it may be easier to visualize what is meant by technique when an object is involved, such as the bow that is used to play string instruments or the brush that is used to apply paint. Distinguishing between the formal and the expressive is harder in theatre and dance, because the body is the instrument and "sentiment" is inherent to the performance. Because the purpose of definitions is to differentiate, scant attention is paid to the ways in which the mechanical is integrated with the nontechnical aspects of performance. In this chapter, the focus is on how technique is embodied in everyday life and the theatre.

Actors use techniques every day, from brushing their teeth in the morning to performing *Medea* at night. Their techniques are learned modes of behavior that simplify and influence how they engage the world, affecting everything from eating with a knife and fork to performing the intricacies of Bob Fosse's choreography, and techniques allow them to engage successfully time and time again. "A technique is the standardization of a performance ability—something the actor knows how to do—such that it fulfills expectations reliably enough to be put to the service of some other performance, wherein a new kind of performance ability—a new kind of interplay with phenomena—becomes possible."[2]

A technique, like a building block, can serve as a foundation for developing new abilities. Techniques, adequately learned, can be used as a basis for learning new skills, executing an action effectively and efficiently, and employing it in novel situations. Depending on the degree of mastery, techniques can become almost second nature and we may be virtually unconscious that they are being employed, or they can be used deliberately. But we never lose sight of them completely. "A technique can be thought of as something we use, but whose principles are still perspicuous to us, and thus still under our control. Techniques, unlike technologies, can be thought of as performance abilities that are still "thick," not transparent as a pane of glass is to the viewer of a garden."[3] Learning a technique so it becomes "second nature," allows the performer (in the theatre or everyday life) to shift focus from how a task is done to the goals of the activity.

Learning to ride a bicycle can serve as an example. It is something that most children learn how to do, and, as the saying goes, once you learn, you never forget. Riding depends on a certain number of "I cans." The child needs, among other things, to be able to balance herself while standing or sitting, to have sufficient visual and physical acuity to negotiate obstacles, and to have adequate flexibility and strength in the hip, knee, and ankle to push the pedals. These prerequisites establish the potential to control the distribution of weight, steering, and propulsion of the bike. Caregivers generally prepare a child to learn how to ride by having her practice these skills with certain toys—a tricycle (steering, pedaling, and breaking), a scooter (steering and balance), and so on. Training wheels, while not absolutely necessary, then give the child the experience of riding on two wheels with less concern for the need to maintain balance. These preparatory stages permit incremental learning, the development of confidence, and a refinement of the coordination of the various skills, so that when riding on just two wheels for the first time, a child can place more attention on maintaining balance, the sine qua non of bicycling. In the final stages before she becomes an independent rider, a caregiver generally provides support—both in balancing the bike and in easing anxiety—until that fateful moment when the child is ready to take control. Learning to adjust the distribution of weight appropriately, to turn the handlebars, to direct the bike around curves, and to maintain balance while coming to a stop and starting up again are all refinements necessary to successful riding.

These rudimentary stages need to become second nature, so the rider can pay attention to other issues, such as shifting gears, looking out for other vehicles, signaling turns, adjusting the effort to go uphill (i.e., standing to apply more pressure to the pedals), and maintaining a safe speed when coasting downhill. As the child's confidence in her bike-riding skills increases, new feats may be attempted, such as riding with "no hands," doing "wheelies," taking one or more passengers for a ride, or mounting and dismounting the bike in various ways. Self-assurance can also lead to explorations of different surfaces (gravel), new terrain (mountain biking), and more crowded thoroughfares (city streets). Greater risks can be taken in the belief, if not knowledge, that control can be maintained and injury avoided. At this point, bicycling is mastered. Once learned, the cyclist can add new skills based on her mastery of the ability to ride. She can ride competitively, learn to use a unicycle, or ride on a high wire.

This brief description of the process of mastering a technique allows us to draw some preliminary conclusions. New skills are not learned from scratch but build on existing abilities. The technique of bike riding combines other sets of skills associated with the body schema and body image. As new connections are created and old ones strengthened through practice, the various threads of the activity are woven together into a dynamic gestalt, or template. As the different aspects of the activity become solidified, less conscious attention needs to be paid to each specific task and more may be paid to the circumstances of the overall situation (turning tight corners, braking suddenly, or avoiding another cyclist). That less attention needs to be placed on each task does not mean that it becomes "transparent as a pane of glass is to the viewer of a garden." The rider is still aware of needing to apply pressure to the pedals, shift weight, turn the handlebars, and slow down in a single gesture in order to stop. The difference, once technique has been mastered, is that there is no longer a need to be concerned with how to do it; the concern has become what to do with the knowledge of how to do it. Techniques are not learned in isolation, but involve some degree of interpersonal interaction, at least in the early stages, whether it is through imitation or work with a mentor. At later stages, when some facility has been achieved, experimentation with variations can take place in solitude and may result in the development of new techniques. Once learned, the set of skills that is technique cannot be eliminated from memory, although the connections can atrophy from lack of practice or get mapped onto new techniques. With effort, the connections can be recalled.

Each modification of technique further articulates the template "bicycle riding," is stored in memory as additional boundary conditions and control parameters, and gains more relevance with repetition. The new conditions and parameters never become rigid, however, because each time the bike is taken out, the rider adapts consciously to new variables and implicit memory manages basic skills. The rider is conscious of the choices and the effects of her actions but is unaware of the steps that make the choices and effects possible. Each variation alters how a particular situation is perceived, giving rise to new expectations of the environment. As a cyclist approaches an intersection, she will look for cars and pedestrians, prepared to stop or redirect the bike. The bike is now an extension of herself; part of her flesh, as it were. She can feel the wheels pressing against the road as she squeezes the brakes on the handles to come to a stop. There was a time when it was necessary to look at the brake grips and actively will her body to grasp them; now the act is second nature. A technique has been mastered.

It is difficult to identify a single location in the brain that is central to the learning and activation of a technique. Mastery relies on so many different areas, from the gross motor controls of the cerebellum and brain stem, which interact directly with the spinal cord, to the cerebrum (particularly the primary motor cortex, supplementary motor area, premotor area, the somatosensory cortex, and locations in the various associative cortices). Nonetheless, one crucial locus is the basal ganglia.[4] It is involved in the fine motor control of "willful movement," incorporating memories linked to the amount of force needed to carry out a task, perhaps the gentleness required of dealing with a pet or the differing efforts required in picking up a piece of fine china or a cast-iron skillet.

> These differences suggest that the cerebellum directly regulates execution of movement, whereas the basal ganglia are involved in higher-order, cognitive aspects of motor control: the planning and execution of complex motor strategies. In addition, because of their extensive connections with association cortex and limbic structures, the basal ganglia unlike the cerebellum are involved in many functions other than motor control.[5]
>
> The full range of the basal ganglia's relationships to other parts of the brain is not clear, but it appears to be influenced by the limbic system, suggesting a responsiveness to emotional contents, as well as to memories more directly associated with muscular control.

There are two pathways through the basal ganglia: the direct and the indirect. As Eric Kandel and his coauthors note, the indirect path projects information from the various sensory receptors and the motor systems to the thalamus, whence the data are relayed to the appropriate areas of the cortex. There, memories of previous experiences are engaged, potentially modifying the signals forwarded to the motor neurons. As a result, a child picks up a cat gently and does not squeeze it too hard. A loop is established that permits the constant monitoring of information about the qualities of the movements being made, allowing the direct path to bypass the thalamus and communicate about movements more immediately with the cerebellum and brain stem. Together they assist in the fine motor control needed for sophisticated actions. These pathways are important in the development of new techniques, particularly when a new pattern is in conflict with an existing mode.

Through processes of neural excitation and inhibition, the basal ganglia draw on memories of movements and previous experience with similar contexts to modulate the expression of a technique. The direct connections to the motor areas of the neuromuscular system permit the execution of a technique with a minimal involvement of consciousness. I can walk through a field, for example, and look at the flowers without being concerned about putting one foot in front of the other. Through learning how to move myself, pathways across neural networks are established and facilitated that allow for more than one activity to be carried out simultaneously and with varying degrees of attention. Stepping in a hole draws my attention away from the flowers and to the necessity of regaining my balance or adjusting to the fact that I am falling in order to avoid serious injury. Conscious effort is focused on the information most central to the immediate task, while habitual patterns provide a flow of movement that is inflected by the decisions made in response to changing circumstances. The actor does not need to think about walking or talking. The techniques of everyday life, learned in her *apprenticeship* to her body, allow her to focus on her interaction with the other actors, the actions demanded of the performance, and the multitude of contingencies that may require immediate attention.

The Genealogy of Technique

We learn our mother tongues from our mothers, imitating them, but we forget that. As we forget, we become ourselves; we speak and believe that we're the ones who are speaking.[6]

The prospective actor does not begin learning technique tabula rasa, that is, as a clean slate. She has gained mastery over a large number of complex skills before her first thoughts about training for the stage. Some of these skills will prove useful in learning to act, while others will prove to be detrimental and will need to be transformed. Part of the training process is getting the student to "unlearn" habits, as well as to learn new habits of performing that are appropriate for the stage. As Herbert Blau reminds us in *The Eye of Prey,* Stanislavski believed "that the hardest thing for an actor to do on stage, though he had been doing it all his life, is to walk."[7] The walking of everyday life did not appear "natural" to Stanislavski, requiring that the student gain a technique for walking that would serve the needs of the stage. More extreme attitudes toward the techniques of everyday life can be seen in Grotowski's and Lecoq's respective approaches to training. Grotowski employed via negativa to eliminate cultural forms and free the actor's creative expression, while Lecoq used the neutral mask to release the body from its habitual ways of moving, allowing for developing facility with other mask forms (see chapter 1). The need to "undo" is also present in the theories of Brecht and Artaud. Still others, such as Meisner and Hagen, use an "add on" approach, which alters by incorporating new skills into the roster of existing techniques. The differentiation between the techniques of the everyday and the craft of acting may explain why students of Eastern performance traditions begin training at a very early age. Children are able to master the specific skills required for performing Noh, Kabuki, or the Chinese opera before the techniques of everyday culture are completely ingrained in their bodies.

To better understand how the techniques of acting are learned, it is important to understand how the actor's instrument is already formed when her training begins. How and when these skill sets are learned are subjects of some debate. Those who believe that humans are social beings through and through argue that the acquisition of skills can begin in the womb. Others believe that there are innate abilities that allow an infant to "learn to move" from birth. Yet others give little thought to infants and assume that techniques are acquired later in childhood. The weight of current scientific thought is behind the claim that acquisition begins shortly after birth. This is the approach offered here, which takes the work of Maxine Sheets-Johnstone as a theoretical basis for its argument. The simultaneous process of socialization is addressed through the writing of Marcel Mauss. Both are tempered by the work on emergence of Evan Thompson. Before engaging this discussion, however, we must return to the two terms that deepen our understanding of technique: body schema and body image.

The relevance of body schema to technique may be best established by way of example. Mounting a bike, once learned, seems to be a single motion. If the different elements are parsed, however, the complexity of the action becomes clear. It is not an exhaustive list, but the following steps need to be done: the bicycle must be supported with two hands. Grasping the far-side handlebar requires the arm to be fully extended, and grasping the near one requires the arm to be flexed. Both hands exert pressure to keep the bike vertical and stable during mounting. The body is tilted forward with its weight on the leg that's farthest from the bike, reducing the pressure on the inside leg, so it can be swung over the seat. The outside leg flexes and the hips twist upward, adding more pressure on the outer leg as the inside leg is lifted and swung over the seat. As it passes over the seat, the outer knee straightens and the hips and shoulders return to center. The weight remains on the same leg, but the pressure on the handlebars equalizes as the body's center of gravity shifts. The lifted knee and ankle flex to meet the pedal. The grip on the handlebars adjusts as pressure is applied to the pedal in preparation for putting the bike in motion. All of these adjustments occur without or with minimal conscious awareness. Activations in the sensorimotor cortex respond to a willed action and to changes in proprio- and exteroceptive (external to the body) information. Once the activity is initiated, implicit memory takes over, directing the activity through the implementation of a feedback loop that takes account of the steps of the process in conjunction with variables in the environment. These elements of the action are what Gallagher refers to as the body schema.

The body schema includes activities that are passive as well as active, such as simply standing still or walking. It is involved in any number of everyday postures or habitual practices that are done without our being aware that they are happening. Gallagher defines it explicitly as "a system of sensory-motor capacities that function without awareness or the necessity of perceptual monitoring...[It] involves certain motor capacities, abilities, and habits that both enable and constrain movement and the maintenance of posture."[8] To emphasize the importance of body schema in our lives, he sites the case of Ian Waterman, who at the age of nineteen suffered from infectious mononucleosis that resulted in acute neuropathy, leaving him with "no sense of touch or proprioception below the neck."[9] He is not paralyzed, but he is not aware of his movements either. Through physical therapy, he has learned to lead a "normal" life by means of intense concentration:

> Ian still does not know, without visual perception, where his limbs are or what posture he maintains....His movement requires constant visual and mental concentration. In darkness he is unable to control movement; when he walks he cannot daydream but must concentrate on his movement constantly...Ian learned through trial and error the amount of force needed to pick up and hold an egg without breaking it. If his attention is directed toward a different activity while he holds an egg, his hand either crushes the egg or drops it.[10]

Body schema, therefore, is essential to and a valuable asset for carrying out the large and small activities of everyday life, from the posture of the body as it stands to the movement of the facial musculature in speaking and to the coordination needed to do a cartwheel. All rely on a functioning body schema.

Four additional aspects of body schema need to be mentioned. First, it is not a singular concept. Despite the use of the singular noun, schema refers to a number of such abilities.[11] A different schema is used for kissing and for running. While there may be overlapping musculature sequences (preparing to kiss and gasping for air), each draws on different sequences, learned as body control is gained. Second, a body schema is not limited to an internal loop but can extend into the environment: "The body schema includes information that goes beyond the narrow boundaries defined by body image.... The body schema functions in an integrated way with its environment, even to the extent that it frequently incorporates into itself certain objects."[12] Like the "flesh" described by Merleau-Ponty, the body schema extends beyond the apparent limits of the physical being. In the example used in this chapter, the bike is integrated into the body schema. A very different level of awareness is required to mime the mounting of a bicycle and to actually get on a bike. Third, the body schema increases the efficiency with which an activity is completed. Without engaging consciousness unnecessarily, the willed activity happens fluidly and with minimal effort, allowing the mind to focus on the larger ramifications of the activity while carrying it out. Fourth, body schema tends to remain consistent throughout life, unless it is disrupted by illness (e.g., Waterman) or accident or is modified by age or training.

Body image in Gallagher's terms has less to do with function and more with the sense of self. He defines it as "a (sometimes conscious) system of perceptions, attitudes, beliefs, and dispositions pertaining to one's own body."[13] The tendency, when thinking of "image," is to visualize the object—how I look riding a bicycle. This is certainly part of body image, which also includes how I experience myself as a bike rider. The additional strain on my shoulders as I sway from side to side, taking deeper, more rapid breaths and the additional effort needed to push the pedals coalesce to produce an image of myself riding my bike up a hill. This image is based on proprioceptive rather than visual cues, as well as other aspects. The image changes depending on the steepness of the hill and whether or not I make the summit easily or have to stop part way up and push the bike. The belief that I can make it up the incline and my disposition to bike riding—in general and to riding on a particular day—influence body image. The environment also influences my perception of myself. The temperature, the presence of other riders, being in town or country, the destination, and my motivation for riding are just some of the variables that affect the image I have of my body. Unlike the body schema, which tends to be consistent over time, body image is more dynamic and responds to changing internal and external circumstances.

There are two other important distinctions between body schema and body image. The schema is predominantly unconscious, while the image is more present to the mind, but neither is exclusively one or the other. Baseball pitchers continually work on their mechanics—the amount of force from the back leg in the move toward the plate, the length of stride, and arm angle—which involve a realigning of the body schema. Pitchers do not focus on all aspects of the motion to the plate, but rather on the particular areas in need of improvement. Change in one area will have a trickle-down effect, altering the coordination of the different parts of the body without conscious attention. The objective, in fact, is for mechanics to become habitual or second nature, integrated as a single motion that can be done precisely without thinking. Body image, however, is more easily accessible to consciousness. Pitchers will feel greater confidence in throwing a particular pitch according to how they feel internally (the degree of fatigue, for instance) and the context (the batter, the count, the runners on base, etc.). They respond to a particular set of circumstances, rather than a set of operations. The second difference between body schema and body image is that one is coextensive with the external world while the other is bounded by it. The ball is an extension of the body schema, but it is not part of the pitcher's body image. The image is responsive to but does not include the context. It is self-consciousness.

Although he insists on the difference between the two, Gallagher recognizes that body image and body schema are involved in a complex, reciprocal relationship. The ability to execute an activity is influenced by perceptual monitoring; and the image of the action is heavily influenced by the appropriateness of the body schema. With these two concepts in mind, we can turn our attention to a genealogy of bodily techniques.

The first experiences of learning technique involve a process that philosopher, dancer, and evolutionary biologist Maxine Sheets-Johnstone calls being "apprenticed to our bodies." Rejecting the Cartesian privileging of the mind, Sheets-Johnstone argues that we begin life as mind-full, animate beings and, as infants, experiment with movement, gaining the skills necessary to engage the world in constructive ways: "Infants move in relationally meaningful ways toward the world, developing understandings of others and of objects in the process."[14] From the very first hours of life, infants demonstrate an ability to imitate the movements of caregivers. The child gains knowledge about the body schema through learning how to control movement and the range of biological limitations (e.g., the head can only be moved so far to the left and right). This education is more complex than it may seem, because every action involves parts of the body that may not seem obviously related to the movement. Take turning the head. Gallagher observes "If the head is turned on the vertical axis to the right, extension of the left knee joint is increased, and extension of the right knee joint is decreased."[15] While Gallagher's example assumes a standing adult, the lesson holds for a child: learning to move part of the body involves the development of a sophisticated and nuanced body schema. For example, the move toward the breast to feed engages the head, shoulders, hips, back, and legs. Through practice, these activities become more precise, and the child is able to feed more easily and with less wasted effort. But the impulse to eat, in triggering the set of responses in the sensorimotor system that resolves the need for food, also improves the ability to control movement, enhances an understanding of the body schema, and prepares the infant for learning other skills, such as maintaining balance. Moreover, Sheets-Johnstone argues, in learning these techniques, the infant develops a felt sense of self, which Sheets-Johnstone identifies as the basis of subjectivity.

In exploring how the body moves, the infant demonstrates three seemingly innate abilities: imitation, joint attention, and turn taking.[16] The child, by focusing on the caregiver, perceives that person's movements and attempts to reproduce them. After copying an action, the infant returns to observation, creating a feedback loop that encourages repetition, gradually improving control over movement and developing an understanding of body image and schema. Sheets-Johnstone argues that the process of imitation through joint attention and turn taking is an "apprenticeship." Instead of being apprenticed to a single master, however, the infant is apprenticed first and foremost to her body (proprioception being a primary source of feedback) and second to those with whom she interacts. These formative learning experiences are the foundation of an autobiographical self, arising from a combination of growing bodily awareness and the structuring of movement memory. Through these explorations in movement, an understanding of how to use the body actively and effectively is developed, along with a range of experiences and engagements with objects, whereby the infant gains "an expanding repertoire of 'I cans'."[17] By being attentive to others and the "dynamics of our own movement" along the axes of time and space, she comes to master herself as an animate being and begins to know herself *in* the world as she comes to know the world. She learns to balance herself, to respond to changes in the environment, and to understand the relationship between visual perception and movement, so that she can at a later date negotiate a crowded street with a minimum of difficulty and conscious thought.

This process of learning to move the body initiates a tripartite structure that Martin Heidegger, in *Being and Time*, calls a "hermeneutic circle":

> One moment is the presence of an existing set of involvements and abilities with which we have a grip on the world, which we can bring to each new situation. A second moment is the sense, the suspicion, the expectation, that we can acquire more of a "grip" over the situation....A third moment is the presence of a sense of how to begin to get that better grip with what we already know how to do.[18]

Sheets-Johnstone's triad of imitation, joint attention, and turn taking in the experience of learning to move models Heidegger's hermeneutic circle. Joint attention and turn taking participate in a context that includes the desire to imitate and the implicit recognition of an ability, actual and potential, to accomplish a task. This is accompanied by a *felt* sense of how to improve the performance of the activity, allowing for a more nuanced imagining and execution of it. The infant does not create a gestalt of the activity prior to repeating the movement in the way that I can imagine picking up a cup of coffee prior to reaching for it. That requires a history of moving not yet available to the child. She rather responds to an emergent sense of how the body *can* be moved, that is, to a prelinguistic knowledge that she can control her body. In doing the activity, an implicit comparison is made with the movements being imitated. The experience of moving and the response of the other provide a basis for another iteration and a growing confidence that "I can."

At the same time that control of the body is being learned, emotional connections to specific activities are being formed. Emotions arise under the combined influence of proprioceptive responses to physical activity and perceptions received from the world. Felt experiences—physical activity and emotion—perturb certain neural networks and through repetition facilitate the evolution and consolidation of knowledge. "[Emotions] are first and foremost about the body, that they offer us *the cognition of our visceral and musculoskeletal state* as it becomes affected by pre-organized mechanisms and by the cognitive structures we have developed under their influence."[19] As experience is translated into knowledge (the memory of a physical and emotional experience), it requires less conscious attention, except in novel situations. A new action—or one in a new form—elicits a greater emotional response. The more the act is repeated, however, the more customary the event becomes, until it is habitual and, therefore, less dependent on conscious attention. Emotions linked to an activity that becomes habitual and no longer conscious continue to be part of our experience, becoming a facet of the background—information that lies just outside of and yet accessible to consciousness. It is only in extraordinary circumstances that the action is once again perceived, bringing the emotions and attendant feelings back to consciousness.

Thus far the discussion has been about positive reinforcement. In addition to learning an increasing repertoire of "I cans" however, the infant begins to develop a repertoire of "I should nots." As certain modes of behavior are encouraged, others are not. Infants are encouraged to sleep through the night without the expectation that a caregiver will respond every time she cries. The apprenticeship to the body is an articulation of boundary conditions that support certain ways of behaving, which involves reinforcing actions positively and negatively. In both cases, the construction of appropriate behavior occurs through the facilitation itself—there is, apparently, no repressive act, but rather the articulation of neural connections that support desired behavior—whether habitual behavior that results is considered positive or negative. Bad habits are difficult to overcome because alternative ways of acting do not eliminate those they are designed to replace. Rather, the new pathway is facilitated through positive repetitions, while the connections that are associated with the habit are left to languish. The synaptic connections between neurons atrophy through lack of use, but the potential for returning to an old pattern remains. Being apprenticed to the body is always a process of learning new ways of responding to perceptual information—internal and external—and defining the means of achieving a desired end:

As the child becomes more at ease with her body, she develops confidence in her ability to perform tasks at the same time that she is learning ways of behaving that are acceptable to her culture. Accepted forms of behavior may, however, be at odds with aesthetic practice. Sheets-Johnstone is correct when she says, "Imitation may thus ground not just social but aesthetic practice."[20] Yet some of the learned behaviors need to be replaced in a course of training by practices that alter not only the neural patterns but also the integral relationship between body schema and body image. I will return to the question of aesthetic practice later, but for now it is important to understand that infants have an inherent mimetic ability and that the act of imitation is a mutual, intersubjective activity, structuring the body to move in particular ways and to reproduce behaviors that are valued by society. From the very earliest moments of life outside the womb (perhaps even from the moments prior to birth), the techniques necessary for living in the world are learned.

Gaining a technique through apprenticeship to the body is never simply learning how to move certain sets of muscles. Alan Baddeley identifies five kinds of information that are consolidated in the process of acquiring memory:

> A remembering subject may retrieve five kinds of information, namely: sensory and perceptual detail, contextual information (locating the event in space and time), semantic detail, emotional tone and, finally, information on the cognitive operations performed at the time.[21]

There are two important points to be taken from these categories. First, remembering is not only about facts, but involves a wealth of information, much of which may seem extraneous to the immediate task and which may not be consciously recognized when retrieved. This information includes sensory and emotional memories, in addition to specific details. It is nonetheless present as a resonance in the cognitive act. The second point to remember is that apprenticeship to the body is also an apprenticeship to society. Learning affects body image, and body image is responsive to the contextual information of time and place.

Marcel Mauss, the French sociologist and one of the first practitioners of anthropology, defines technique as "the ways in which from society to society men [sic] know how to use their bodies."[22] Mauss derived his definition by observing differences in how people perform such everyday activities as swimming, walking, and eating. That people use a knife and fork or chopsticks differently in different cultures indicates the variety of learned techniques. From this perspective, technique is not only a set of skills required for achieving mastery in an area of specialization, but also an inevitable part of negotiating everyday life in a particular society. An actor, according to Mauss's definition, employs technique to get to and from the theatre as much as she does to perform a role. We do not think about using silverware or walking to the subway as a technique because it has become second nature or, using Mauss's terminology, a habitus:

Habitus is a term introduced by Mauss as "body techniques' (*techniques du corps*)", he writes

> It does not designate those metaphysical *habitudes,* that mysterious "memory," the subjects of volumes or short and famous theses. These

"habits" do not just vary with individuals and their imitations, they vary especially between societies, educations, proprieties and fashions, prestige. In them we should see the techniques and work of collective and individual practical reason rather than, in the ordinary way, merely the soul and its repetitive faculties.[23]

Habitus needs to be differentiated from habit. Habit refers to a non-addictive action that has become normative, such as reading before going to sleep. Habits frequently incur a social judgment: biting your nails is bad, while getting regular exercise is good. Habitus, on the other hand, refers to ways of performing actions. In the United States, it is standard to hold the fork in the left hand while cutting and to shift it to the right when eating, whereas in Europe, the fork does not change hands. When one tries to mimic the habitus of the other culture, the alternate way of using silverware can seem strange and uncomfortable, because each society is used to its way of using the knife and fork. For those who grew up in England, what seems odd to Americans, seems natural. These techniques of eating become habitual, are learned and solidified in the body through repetition, becoming easier to perform with each iteration until there is no longer need to think about the act of eating. It has become unconscious. Habitus, or technique, is, in other words, less about what we do than how we do it.

Technique is learned through individual experience but is seldom, if ever, completely idiosyncratic. We learn how to use our bodies through observing and interacting with those around us, all of whom have developed *habitus* before us and through similar processes.

> What takes place is a prestigious imitation. The child, the adult, imitates actions which have succeeded and which he has seen successfully performed by people in whom he has confidence and who have authority over him. The action is imposed from without, from above, even if it is an exclusively biological action, involving his body. The individual borrows the series of movements which constitute it from the action executed in front of him or with him by others.[24]

Technique, using Mauss's definition, is the means by which we learn to behave in accord with social norms and is accomplished, through interactions with a social authority, in support of efficiency and tradition.[25] In this context, the learning of a technique need not be a volitional activity but is nevertheless a developed skill.

When actors enter training, they come with technique, with well-established body images and schemas. They arrive with a complex set of "I cans" and are predisposed to behave in ways that reflect social, cultural, and personal experiences. These structures are defined by particular ways of perceiving and are linked to emotions, both of which are central to defining the identity that allows each person to claim, "I am." Techniques are firmly established as attractors and boundary conditions within neural networks that operate with minimal interference by consciousness, entering awareness only when attention is drawn to their presence by novel experiences or when they are challenged by, for instance, an acting teacher. Under normal circumstances, the attractors and boundary conditions form patterns of behavior that are comfortable, efficient, and linked to a robust sense of self, allowing each of us to negotiate the demands placed upon us with confidence. To attempt to eliminate or alter these techniques of identity can be difficult, because they are part of our relationships with family and friends, and they reflect our morals, values, and beliefs.

The task of the acting teacher is to enhance the existing techniques that are most useful for a particular approach to acting and to change those that are at odds with that approach. For the actor, it is necessary to recognize that ways of behaving in everyday life are incommensurate with the demands of the stage. Eugenio Barba stresses this when he differentiates between daily and extra-daily energy:

> The more daily techniques are unconscious, the more functional they are. For this reason, we move, we sit, we carry things, we kiss, we agree, and disagree with gestures which we believe to be natural but which are in fact culturally determined... Daily body techniques generally follow the principles of minimum effort, that is, obtaining a maximum result with a minimum expenditure of energy. Extra-daily techniques are based, on the contrary, on the wasting of energy. At times they even seem to suggest a principle opposite to that which characterizes daily techniques: the principle of maximum commitment of energy for a minimal result.[26]

An actor may enter the studio with a flair for self-presentation, including a penchant for expending the extra-daily. Many others, however, need encouragement to fill the space with their energy. Both may need to learn to focus their respective energies in constructing the dynamics of a performance.

Actors, through the process of training, are reforming their body image, which implies a reformulation of those values and beliefs that run contrary to the demands of the desired technique. At the same time, paths between relevant neural networks are being developed that will enhance the ability to perform in a particular style. Through repetition, the actor undergoes a profound reimagining of the self that enhances a body schema in support of a new way of perceiving with greater attention to a specific kind of detail. Actors are taught to be aware of how people and animals move and behave, for instance, as a means of developing a greater vocabulary of images to be retrieved in the development of a performance. As these changes are made, they inevitably change the actor's body image.

In chapter 1, the different approaches to acting defined styles of acting; it is now clear that each method requires the systematic acquisition of the specific techniques required to perform according to the method's teachings. Actors do not simply learn new skill sets, however; in the process of gaining control over their technique, a new image of the body emerges that has strong ties to the emotional centers and redefines the values and beliefs that structure their identity as performers and human beings.

Acting and Technique

In creating a role, the performer draws on numerous techniques that allow for the expression of a concept through dynamic physical actions. The process results in a temporary body image (character, role, or persona) that intertwines analytical and improvisational discoveries with other techniques. The process forms a complex, emergent matrix that unfolds over the course of the performance. To the degree that it is laid down and consolidated in memory, the playing out is repeatable within parameters sufficiently flexible to permit the actor to respond to variations in the performance of others and to the dynamics of the audience interaction. Without sufficient technique, the whole project is jeopardized, because the performance will be inconsistent and unpredictable. This realization astounded Denis Diderot, the eighteenth-century French writer, who recognized that David Garrick's use of technique provided for consistently moving performances, while the technique of those who depended on real emotion presented powerful portrayals one day and fell flat the next.

Three types of technique will be defined below: analytical, improvisational, and physical. These distinctions are for purposes of argument, and it should not be assumed that they are exercised independently of each other. While one may take priority over another at a particular moment, they are interlaced, mutually reinforcing and influencing as part of the ongoing process of an embodied dynamic system. The analytical techniques are generally associated with textual analysis, including the articulation of actions and objectives, the development of a score, the definition of circumstances, and dramaturgical investigations of the historical, cultural, and social contexts of the play and the playwright. These will be discussed in chapter 6. Improvisation is not generally considered a technique but is viewed as the free play of creative inspiration. These assumptions will be addressed in chapter 5, where we will examine the structure, parameters, and types of questions that are asked in developing the appropriate mind-set for initiating an improvisation. The third type of technique includes training in movement, voice, dialect, stage combat, dance, singing, mime, mask work, gymnastics, and modes of conveying unfelt emotions or physical conditions or states, such as disabilities and pain. It is this physical technique that will be addressed in this section. Given the diversity of its modes, however, not all will be examined. Instead, a comparison between two approaches to vocal training will be discussed, followed by a case study in which a performer, trained in one tradition, decides to learn a related but very different technique.

Two Methods, One End

Acting is different from the other performing arts because of the importance of speech. Vocal production is obviously central to singing—whether opera, oratorio, choral, or popular music—but only in the theatre is the speaking voice the primary vehicle. During the second half of the twentieth century, Arthur Lessac and Kristen Linklater developed distinctive methods for training the voice that continue to inform the curricula in American actor training. While there are other approaches to vocal training, Lessac and Linklater wrote texts to articulate their methodologies. For both, the end is the same—good vocal production on the stage—but their proposed means of developing a quality voice are radically different. Each has adherents who promote the virtues of the particular system. My intent is not to privilege one over the other—both are proven—but to demonstrate that there can be more than one approach to learning the same technique and to raise some of the issues that multiple approaches have for an embodied theory of acting.

The first edition of Lessac's book, *The Use and Training of the Human Voice,* came out in 1960, on the heels of the 1950s, at the dawn of the Cold War, and before the revolutionary fervor of the 1960s. Linklater's book, *Freeing the Natural Voice,* came out in 1976, at the end of the liberatory politics of the previous decade. The milieu of each text may account for some of their differences. Lessac's is analytical and strives to support its methodology with scientific explanations, while Linklater nods to science but ultimately prefers "to describe the voice metaphorically, analogically, and by its perceivable features."[27] Where the older book takes things apart before putting them back together, the later work operates by addition, incorporating new material in an ongoing process.

The language used by each theorist to describe the overall project of developing good vocal technique is surprisingly similar. Both believe that "training must reflect the natural functioning of the human organism, must be based on the development of permanent physical habit patterns, and will, therefore, be training that lasts."[28] They recognize that the habitual patterns that need to be changed are the result of social conditioning and that eliminating them will result in recovering "the natural way in which the body produces vocal sounds."[29] The bad habits that hinder good vocal production are manifest in bodily tensions. Relaxation is, therefore, a necessary first step. The ear is not to be trusted in learning new patterns of vocal production. "The criterion for assessing progress lay in the answer to the question 'how does it feel?' rather than 'how does it sound?'"[30] Experiencing and, through repetition, learning new proprioceptive patterns are central to developing good technique. The differences between Lessac's and Linklater's methods lie in the approaches each uses to obtain the same end.

Lessac defines three energies, "a trinity of actions that produces dynamic voice and speech" and encourages a vocal life powered by "a dual feeling of relaxed energy and energetic relaxation." The well-trained voice is "not merely an instrument for expressing emotions but a creator and controller of emotions, not only in others but in oneself as well."[31] The power of the voice comes from the effective use of the three energies: structural action, tonal action, and consonant action. Structural action refers to preparation and flexibility of those aspects of the voice that can come under conscious control:

> The first concept involves muscular sensations and kinesthetic memory—the tendency of muscles to assume accustomed positions—and leads to physical awareness of the contours and movements of the face and the oral cavity that help produce the most satisfactory vocal tones.[32]

The structures that Lessac focuses on are the lips, teeth, tongue, soft palate, and oral cavity. One of the central images in his approach is that of the inverted megaphone. This metaphor refers to the internal shape of the mouth: it should be open to provide the greatest potential resonance and narrowing at the front in the formation of the words as the voice passes across the lips. The structural action "is not static" but "must be dynamic and flexible—a constant awareness of muscle and membrane moving as they accommodate themselves to the inverted-megaphone shape in action."[33] The actions of the vocal structure must be precise and yet plastic, responsive to the shifting demands, comprehensibility, and emotion associated with the text.

Tonal action focuses on vowel sounds, which are shaped in the oral cavity but expressed as vibrations "through the hard palate, the nasal bone, the sinuses, and the forehead. Some of the sound waves continue on through the frontal sinuses, cranial bone, spine, and ribs, to produce chest resonance, but the conscious action takes place in these four areas of the head." Tone is responsible for "full pitch, range, power, and projection of the voice."[34] It is also connected to the duration of sounds and the communication of emotional content (the difference between "aaaaaaah!" and "ah!"). Lessac relates consonant action to the different instruments in an orchestra and associates it with articulation and clarity of expression: "they make three important contributions to speech: (1) They convey and crystallize the intelligibility of the word; (2) they give rhythm, tonal color, and melody to speech; (3) they furnish contrasts and variations through percussive, melodic, and sound effect qualities."[35] These three energies in concert form the totality of the voice, and it is this triad—along with a preliminary section on breath support and relaxation—that Lessac uses to structure his book and the numerous exercises designed to give the student the opportunity to have a robust vocal life.

The exercises combine the International Phonetic Alphabet (IPA), symbols (N^1, N^2, etc. for neutrals, and concrete images ("Y-Y-Y-Y-Y-Y-Y → (#1) Keep cool, Mimi."))[36] to specify particular sounds, the shape of the oral cavity, and resonations. They frequently consist of lists of words, phrases, and speeches that, if sufficiently and accurately practiced, lead to the development and habituation of good vocal techniques. The diagrams tend to be analytical, showing the precise way to shape the oral cavity and the lips to achieve the correct effect of the "natural" voice.[37] The overall objective is to "develop a built-in physical gauge for proper tempos, quality, and clarity, while adding vitality, vibrancy, and excitement to both voice and speech."[38] If successful, the technique diminishes regionalisms (without specifically setting out to do so) while "eliminating nasality, muffled tones, throatiness, and breathiness," leading to the expression of emotion and thought through a rich and powerful voice.[39]

Lessac's approach utilizes "an inner activity" that combines with "all other inner experience, including emotion," whereas Linklater believes in "working from outside inwards."[40] In the tradition of the later Stanislavski, Grotowski, Lecoq, and Brecht, she focuses on physical actions and responsiveness to external stimuli. In keeping with Grotowski's view of the actor's instrument, Linklater believes that "the natural voice is most perceptibly blocked and distorted by physical tension, but it also suffers from emotional blocks, intellectual blocks, aural blocks, spiritual blocks."[41] These obstacles to freeing the natural voice derive from environmental (including social and cultural) influences and take the form of habits and conditioning. Habits are defined as "secondary impulses...so well developed that they blot out the impact of the primary, or reflex impulse." While habits are needed to function in the world, conditioning develops out of that functioning: "Behavior that is suggested or demanded from outside develops the ability to respond to secondary impulses rather than primary ones."[42] Doubly removed from primary impulses, conditioned behavior creates physical tensions that restrict the natural expressiveness of the voice. The exercises in her book thus provide a means for "undoing" the conditioning, making the voice more responsive to the "animal level of emotional response to stimulus." They "are concerned more with re-*thinking* usage than with re-*doing* sounds."[43] Linklater strives to change the actor's understanding of the relationship between the body and voice, rather than, for instance, insisting on the precise shaping of the tongue in the creation of a particular sound.[44]

Like her counterpart, however, she does believe that "assessing progress [lies] in the answer to the question 'how does it feel?' rather than 'how does it sound?'" Yet while Lessac utilizes intellectual conceptualization, Linklater resists it:

> Although intelligence is needed to understand the exercises, you must abandon intellect when doing them in favor of feelings and sensory impressions. You must not jump to conclusions as to what is right or wrong, because you are already a well-developed censor of self. Nor can you trust your judgment, since it is biased by habitual ideas of good and bad and wary of new experiences.[45]

If rational evaluations reinforce existing habits and inhibit progress, using external cues and being aware of internal changes can help the actor achieve a voice that can "communicate the thoughts and a continuum of feelings of a...human being who is uninhibited, open, sensitive, emotionally mature, intelligent, and uncensored."[46] This ideal vision of an unmediated impulse that finds expression is, ironically, based on mastering a technique of vocal production that strives for a balance of elements. The "[p]erfect communication for the actor implies a balanced quartet of intellect and emotion, body and voice—a quartet in which no one instrument compensates with its strength for the weakness of another."[47] Like Lesssac's three energies, the quartet of Linklater finds its perfection as the integration into an aesthetically powerful and articulate voice.

Her approach to achieving this end is a considerable distance from that of Lessac. Rather than separating the voice into different facets, Linklater begins with basic relaxation exercises and builds on them, gradually adding new elements but always beginning with the basic "touch of sound." Rather than focus on the IPA or descriptive drawings, she uses expressive drawings and musical notation, as well as images—concrete and abstract ("Thought: 'A long horizon of blue sea waves'")—to convey the structure of the exercise and to encourage the full participation of impulse and imagination in the development of the voice.[48] This is not to say that she does not get specific, but she always works from a foundation of breath and relaxation that incorporates the whole body.

That two methods can be used to achieve the same end raises a number of interesting questions for a cognitive theory of acting. Are different approaches to arrive at the same end necessary? The multiplicity of acting methods discussed in chapter 1 suggests that people have different ways of learning and, therefore, a variety of pedagogies are needed to support diverse creative styles. For instance, Lessac and Linklater maintain the debate over whether it is better to work from the "outside in" or from the "inside out." This division is parallel to another argument: do actors respond better to images that invoke emotion or rational analysis? Performers do seem to prefer one approach to the other, which suggests that different types of cues trigger different kinds of responses and that this varies from person to person. Does this individuation suggest genetic variation, or does experience determine the way that people learn how to learn? Does a particular technique define how a person's neural networks are structured, or does it facilitate a particular way of laying down one type of memory while allowing another to atrophy? While these questions cannot yet be answered, a case study of a performer who has mastered one technique and decides to learn another can provide some potential answers.

Crossing Techniques

As Brecht discovered to his dismay, a new approach to acting may not always be apparent to viewers or practitioners. Audiences that included other practitioners, critics, and spectators untrained in theatre were often at a loss to distinguish between realistic acting and that based on the *Verfremdungseffekt*. Differences in styles of dancing are more readily discernable, particularly when comparing ballet with modern dance. It provides a better venue for exploring what happens when a performer decides to master a different style. Mikhail Baryshnikov, toward the end of his career as the premier male dancer in classical ballet, decided to work with Twyla Tharp as she continued to explore her "hybrid style of both ballet and modern dance."[49] One does not need to be a dancer to appreciate Tharp's interest in exploring the "collision" of dance styles and the effect when her work is placed on the body of a supremely trained performer such as Baryshnikov. The result is a disjunction that both enriches and startles because of a perceptible qualitative difference in the way he performs the dances and the movements of those who perform regularly with the choreographer.[50]

A starting point for understanding the contrast between Baryshnikov's performance of Tharp's choreography and that of those who perform her work regularly is the way in which the body moves as the result of a technique. Classical ballet requires a certain quality of movement that, to my untrained eye, focuses on lifts and extensions, a moving upwards and outwards and, for all the graceful curves of the hands, arms, and torso, is based on straight lines. Tharp's "hybrid" style of choreography has a lower "center of gravity" and is based on the sinuousness of the "s-curve" achieved by contrapuntal movement between one part of the body and another, for instance moving the hips to the left and the chest to the right. Achieving Tharp's preferred mode of moving requires a different emphasis in dance training. Both approaches achieve highly skilled and expressive dancers—at least within the chosen mode of expression—yet dancers who move most easily in very different ways. In short, Tharp's dancers cannot perform ballet in the way that Baryshnikov can, while his habitual way of performing is at odds with the movement style of Tharp's dancers.

To dance her dances, Baryshnikov had to reeducate his body to move in ways that ran counter to his ballet training. He had to learn a new technique that interacted with or, to use a concept developed by E. T. Gendlin, "crossed" with his ballet training. Gendlin's concept of crossing, staying within the discourse of dance, is the interaction of two modes of moving: "When experiential intricacies cross, the result can be new, and not logically consistent with how each seemed to be alone. In crossing, neither functions as it was. Rather: *each functions as already cross-affected by the other.* Each is determined by, and also *determines* the other."[51] Crossing operates through an additive process that has subtractive effects. Certain ways of moving are integrated into existing ways of moving the body, leaving some existing patterns unchanged while altering others, resulting in a new form or idiom. The collision that Tharp explores creates a new style of dance out of the constellation of particular aspects of ballet and modern dance. The result, in performance, is a productive combination in which one mode of training encounters the product of another technique, not in a way that is seamless, but in a way that emphasizes certain qualities of the different techniques. The positive effect in the example above is that Baryshnikov alters his body image as a dancer, while Tharp's choreography is enriched through the performance of his ballet-trained body. Baryshnikov's willingness to engage Tharp's choreography resulted in a new idiom, or at least a new dialect of dance, expanding the horizon of potential forms and modes of dancing.

There is a potential downside to the crossing. Learning a new technique does not mean sacrificing one technique in favor of another, but it does result in an adulteration of previously learned techniques. To use another of Gendlin's concepts, when we engage a new technique, we "carry forward." When one technique comes into conflict with another—the body wants to lift when the choreography dictates a lateral swing—either the dance needs to be changed or the body needs to learn a new way of moving. This learning does not negate the old technique; it does not lead to the elimination of existing neural patterns. Rather, the newly learned way of moving requires the development of new patterns that take precedence in this particular dance. "*In crossing each opens the other to a carrying forward which makes new possibilities.*"[52] But the generation of new possibilities makes it difficult, if not impossible, to return to the previous way of moving. Were Baryshnikov to return to dance *Copelia,* for instance, he could return to the techniques of ballet, but they would now be inflected by the pedestrian mode of movement that Tharp uses to create her hybrid. He could not return to a time when the techniques of ballet were his area of expertise—perhaps enriching, perhaps diminishing his ability to dance that technique.

Gendlin's crossing and carrying forward are useful concepts for understanding what happens when two techniques intersect. Within this paradigm, learning a new technique has the potential for being productive, providing a degree of freedom through opening the realm of possible actions; but at the same time it places limits on the body, an inevitable effect of learning a technique. By extension, learning new techniques allows for newly facilitated avenues of expression. On the one hand, this makes it difficult, if not impossible, to return to an earlier mode of performing. On the other, this effect of learning defines a potentially liberating value: we are able to express ourselves differently, exploring the potentials inherent in the values that cling to a particular mode and in the process, at least potentially, discovering a new way of engaging the world.

Actors are *bricoleurs*. They pick up techniques wherever they can and add them to their storehouse of "I cans" if they prove to be productive and supply an efficient means for resolving a problem. Insofar as they continue to be productive, each technique modifies the relations among neural networks, allowing for new resonations and new ways of engaging in performance, as an actor or dancer.

Actors, Technique, and the Embodied Mind

Mastering a technique is a process of consolidating memory among neural networks through establishing attractors and boundary conditions that are "tagged," so that, when triggered, the desired operations will take place. A significant portion of the activity will occur without conscious effort, reflecting the work of the unconscious and implicit memory. As discussed earlier, the activation of a sequence of actions involves the dynamic body, including "sensory and perceptual detail, contextual information (locating the event in space and time), semantic detail, emotional tone and, finally, information on the cognitive operations performed at the time."[53] This information allows the actor to determine how best to deploy techniques under different circumstances based on earlier applications and how to adapt them to insure a successful outcome. This evaluation may result in the activation of skills related to different techniques (voice and movement) and the combination of secondary with primary skills (a dialect and good vocal production) in finding a solution to a problem. Bringing together different abilities defines one of the values of being a bricoleur.

The excitation of the neurons central to a technique will engage other neurons in the same or associated neural bundles, which may or may not be linked to the specific skill set. This is valuable because it brings into play related information that may allow for a more rapid evaluation of a situation and the alternatives for approaching a problem. Subsidiary data will become conscious if the habitual modes of action meet with resistance because of internal or external circumstances. For instance, a bruised shoulder may require an actor to roll differently than originally choreographed during stage combat. By practicing a new move, an adjustment in the body image and body schema will be learned as the maneuver becomes an implicit memory, requiring less conscious thought. Some elements remain conscious—the need to make eye contact and receive permission before entering into stage combat—while other levels of attention are aware of background occurrences, allowing the performer to respond quickly should an unexpected circumstance occur.

The likelihood that a set of neurons will be activated increases the more frequently the set of neurons is used. The process of its becoming consolidated in long-term memory includes an increase in the number of synaptic connections, or "buds," along the axon where dendrites can be activated. The larger the number of such connections, the more likely it is that the set of neurons will be activated and the greater the potential for making connections with other neurons in the same neural bundle. The growth of these buds increases the probability that the neurons will play a larger role in the retrieval of the memory and in the execution of the technique.

When Baryshnikov decided to perform Tharp's choreography, the work required a complex reorganization of attractors and boundary conditions. Learning a new technique is not simply a matter creating new sets of associations among neural connections; it also requires actively resisting the inclination to engage in a previously established mode of behavior. It is similar to fighting an addiction. The will to quit smoking, for instance, requires resisting the demand for nicotine and other substances to the same extent that it requires adopting new behaviors not associated with lighting up. A number of researchers use instruments such as the "stop-go" test and fMRI to explore the temporal dimension of telling a subject who is expecting to do one task to instead undertake another.[54] As one would expect, the "command-to-action" times were shorter for practiced tasks than for new ones. Imaging demonstrates that as the subject is asked to change from an expected activity to an unanticipated one, the brain's processes involve inhibiting neural responses in addition to facilitating new ones. As one technique is crossed with another, the effort it takes to learn a new way of moving, for instance, works in tandem with the effort not to move in the old way. As the frequency of the new movement regime increases, less effort is needed to resist the old regime, freeing consciousness to focus on other aspects of the technique.

The evident tension in Baryshnikov as he performs Tharp's choreography suggests that crossing techniques makes use of existing patterns by blending them with new movement regimes. The way the body is used in her dances is not completely novel to Baryshnikov. They are part of an existing vocabulary that he committed to memory when he learned to move his body in his youth. What is new is the way the dances are put together and how that hybrid choreography alters the body schema and body image as neural networks are reconfigured to combine the verticality of ballet with the sinuousness of Tharp's technique. The more he practices her dance, the more proficient he becomes at performing the steps.[55] Either some neural connections in the network are abandoned in favor of those that facilitate his performance of the hybrid form more efficiently, or, as his facility with the new choreography takes precedence, what were significant resistances decay but do not disappear altogether.

What happens at the neural level is not clear. However, the work of Dr. Peter R. Rapp, chair of Neuroscience at Mount Sinai Medical Center, suggests one possibility. Neural imaging of aging patients indicates that one cause of memory loss is a decrease in the number of buds where synaptic connections occur.[56] It is conceivable, therefore, that the synaptic connections among neurons atrophy through reduced use, particularly as new synapses develop in association with a new technique. The strengthening of one pathway in combination with the inhibition of connections associated with former patterns may explain not only the process of crossing techniques, but also why it is possible to "revive" a technique that has been superseded. In the case of Baryshnikov, he has not lost the ability to dance ballet; but to return to his expertise in that technique would require strengthening once again those neural networks. Yet because he cannot completely abandon his ballet techniques for those demanded by modern dance, his return to ballet will carry forward the new associations developed in learning Tharp's technique.

Actors, like dancers, learn numerous techniques. As they did for Baryshnikov, the different techniques make use of the same neural networks, overlapping at points of similarity rather than creating completely new pathways. Adding new sets of skills increases the actor's ability by more than the sum of individual skills. The activation of one technique brings along associations that arise at the point of intersection with other skills. The image of a rail system is useful. Trains follow set patterns, and different trains use the same tracks before they branch off in various directions. The trains intersect at certain points, allowing passengers to board different trains on their way to different destinations. The metaphor is limited because memories work by associations; changes in track happen as necessary, not at designated terminals. As the actor moves from one project to another, changes in the specific circumstances require variation in the application of technique, utilizing and combining different subsets of a particular skill, such as voice modulation, stage movement, etc. To learn one technique gives the actor mastery; to master a number of techniques enables a much richer palate from which to color a performance, respond to novel situations, and address difficult problems.

For actors, technique is not simply a tool, but a means to an end: the creation of an experience for an audience. Actors recognize that technique is gained through training in voice, movement, dance, and stage combat, but when actors talk about *their* technique, they do so not in terms of distinct abilities but as though it were a single force. One actor declares: "What we need is a body that has the capacity to create."[57] Technique is or should be indistinguishable from the complex, cognitive instrument. Like an athlete who needs to respond with reflex actions, the actor needs to react to the multiple demands of performance. Technique, in its various forms, provides the actor with templates that can be adapted to changing circumstances and enhance the potential for generating a positive, extra-daily energy in the performance. Technique does not rigidly structure the organism but provides parameters for creating a dynamic performance. Actors are able to seek out new ways of solving problems because having an array of techniques allows them to respond more productively to novel situations and to select the approach most effective for keeping their work alive, increasing their control over their art, and enriching the experience of their audience.

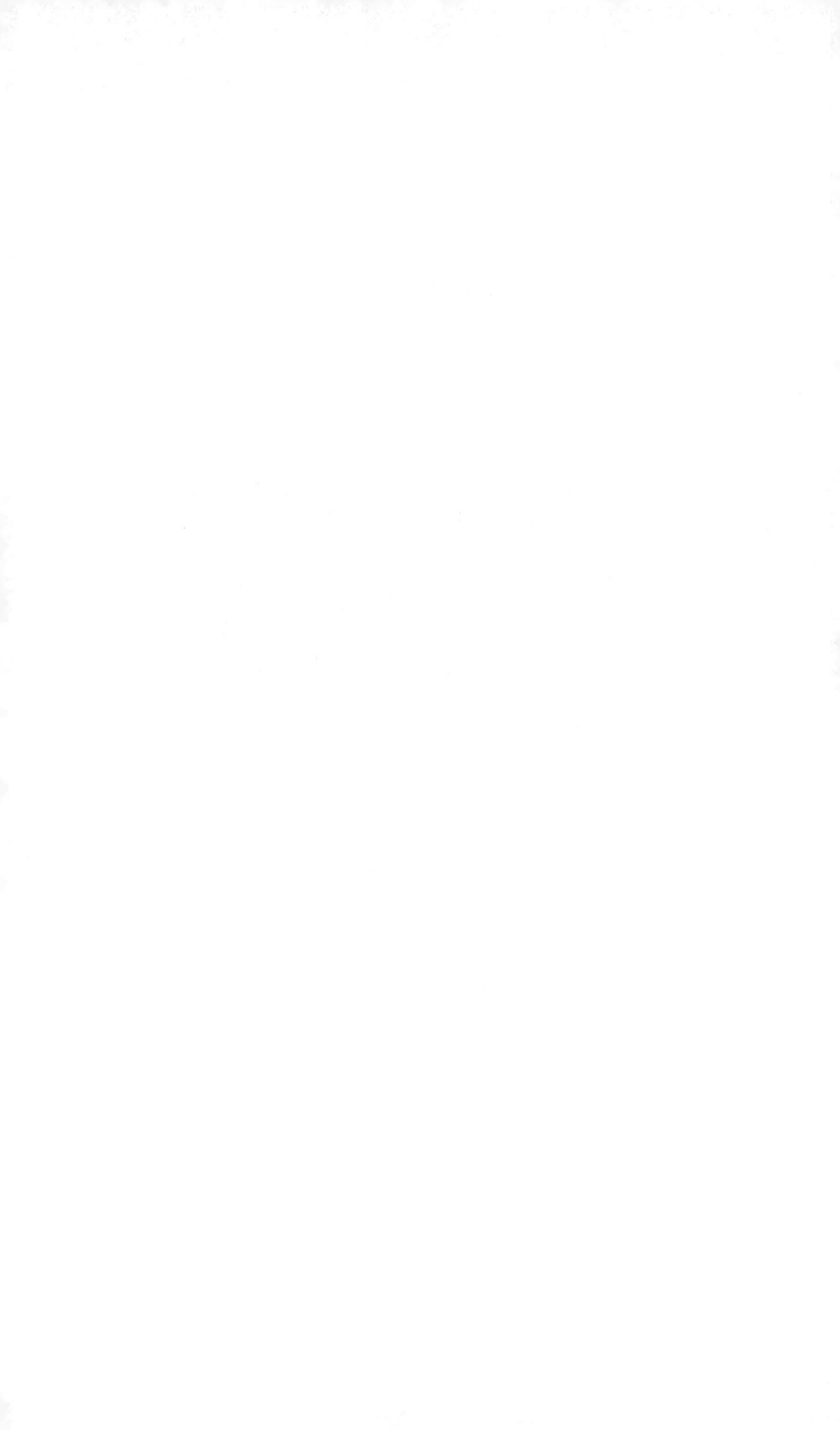

Chapter 5

Improvisation

Play as a state in which meaning is in flux, in which possibility thrives, in which versions multiply in which the confines of what is real are blurred, buckled, broken. Play as endless transformation, transformations without end and never stillness. Would that be pure play?

Tim Etchells[1]

Actors in the rehearsal space are presented with an array of objects and told to choose one, then to explore it, allowing the thing itself to suggest ways to give it life. One performer chooses a gas mask, seemingly dating from World War I. It is made of canvas, with black, tinted-glass circles over the eyes and a metal canister near the nose, holding a poison filter to make the air safe to breathe. Through an exploration of its textures, weight, size, fit, comfort, and limitations, the mask begins to reveal its qualities. The gas mask is rapidly transformed from a facial mask into an alter ego that is friendly and menacing at turns: a bird of prey one minute, canine-like the next. Gradually its war-determined qualities come to dominate, and it becomes an ally.

Another object is chosen to supplement the first: an expanse of red silk is stuffed into the mask, the surplus flowing from its neck. It becomes a cape, a body, blood. Moving with the actor who has donned the gas mask, the silk strides ahead or brings up the rear, threatening and cowering in turns. With the dark, circular glass eyes and canister muzzle, the modified mask is suddenly able to soar like an eagle and then gently caress an object of desire. It gains a voice but speaks no recognizable language.

As the exercise continues, it joins other object-avatars and their actors in short narratives that unfold and then dissipate as quickly as they develop. The objects explore each other, test for their respective strengths and weaknesses, move in concert or diverge. They become entwined, move forward with deliberate menace, and play.

After four days of such work—remembering the dominant qualities, testing out and rejecting other supplementary objects—two actors enact a sequence together in the same space. They remain aware of each other and the way the space is being used, adjusting their performances to accommodate, interact with, or avoid each other. The workshop ends before the studies are ready to be performed. But the memories are there; the work is not forgotten. The relationship between the performers and their objects need not be spoken, remaining an ineffable presence.

An improvisation is an open-ended exercise, set within limits that define a situation but do not determine an outcome. The parameters of an improvisation can be narrow (a specific moment in the relationship between two characters) or open (a tactile investigation of an object or the exploration of real or imagined spaces). Over the last half century, improvisation has become a standard tool in most rehearsal spaces and a source of material for the development of new performances. For actors who believe that there are better and more direct ways to move the rehearsal process forward, improvisation is an inefficient waste of valuable time. For those who embrace improvisation, it is a method of opening the mind to new possibilities or for devising new theatre pieces. Frequently the decision to try an alternative approach to the work is a response to a perceived need to get an actor "out of her head" and in touch with her emotions or to find unexpected material for a production, material that has the potential to surprise. A closer look at improvisation will help us understand why it is such a robust tool and how it serves the creative process.

There are two primary principles in improvisation. One is being open to whatever happens. The first rule of improvising is to always say "yes" to what is given; to refuse what another offers or to judge one's own work prematurely ends the exercise and forecloses the process. The second principle is that improvisation takes patience. What surfaces initially quite often reflects habitual ways of thinking or solutions that work in other situations. The challenge is to recognize and move beyond the mundane, to be open to the experience of the unexpected. It is in moments that are fresh, surprising, or even startling that the performer experiences the creative potential of improvisation. As in all things in the theatre, the technique can fail to elicit anything interesting or to solve the problem that needs to be addressed.

There are a vast number of improvisational forms. Television programs such as *Whose Line Is It Anyway?* and *comedy clubs* ask audience members to suggest absurd situations that test the performers' ability to allow a narrative to develop within the suggested parameters while spontaneously responding to each other, maintaining character, and keeping a straight face (although part of the fun is when they can't). Augusto Boal had participants in workshops interact with actors around issues central to the well-being of the community in an exploration of ways to respond to real-life instances of oppression. Groups such as Forced Entertainment use observations of city life in Sheffield, England, as a basis for the development of performances that come out of group interactions. The material that arises from this work becomes the basis for structuring the production. Margarita Espada begins with a theme and an image and through solo improvisations attends to new images that arise during the exercise; the process provides the basis of her performances. Jerzy Grotowski worked with Ryszard Cieslak to develop an acting score based on a personal memory for his role in *The Constant Prince*. Eugenio Barba asks performers to respond to physical and vocal impulses in the development of a sequence of actions and then juxtaposes the work of several actors to create a performance. Ann Bogart uses viewpoint exercises to generate alternative ways of communicating written plays. In creating *Les Éphémères,* Ariane Mnouchkine worked with actors to devise narratives that addressed what it might mean to face the end of the world. Contact improvisation is used as a basis for choreographing dances, while Butoh dancers incorporate free associations into otherwise structured performances. Deborah Mayo goes into rehearsal for a play having done her homework and focusing on the effect the actions of the other actors have on her and the impact her actions have on them. Miranda Tufnell and Chris Crickmay begin with the exploration of internal perceptions; through a progression of exercises that lead to group explorations, they then use improvisation as a means of freeing the imagination to generate material for performances and overcome the effects of an alienating culture. This representative list gives an idea of the different kinds of improvisations but should not be taken as exhaustive.

Improvisations extend from personal explorations to collective creations. They can take the form of organized events, or they can occur any time an actor opens herself to respond without expectation to what is happening around her. They engage cognitive processes that allow the performer to explore her interactions with the environment and provide experiences that can shape a performance in profound ways. Before exploring this terrain, a brief foray into the poststructuralist philosophy of Gilles Deleuze and Félix Guattari will provide an abstract but useful way of thinking about improvisation.

Lines of Flight

French philosopher Gilles Deleuze and psychotherapist and philosopher Félix Guattari seek ways of understanding the process and benefits of improvisation—although it is not a word they use—as a means of political resistance. They believe society promulgates institutions and ideologies that structure the day-to-day in order to insure a complacent and docile public. The potential for resisting the oppressiveness of social conformity lies in what they call "lines of flight."[2] As the name suggests, it is a movement away from one position and toward another, but it is different from direct actions such as leading protests or going to the store. A shopper has a particular destination and knows what is going to happen once there. Protests, while generally more volatile, tend to be scripted and happen under the watchful eye of the authorities; when they stray from the script, the officials quickly move to restore order. A line of flight is a riskier sort of action, because there is no known destination and no one to restore order. In fact, the end point is not known until the flight is complete, because if it were known, the trajectory would not be a line of flight. There are, then, two types of knowledge to be gained from such a movement: what happens during the flight and where the flight ends.

Deleuze and Guattari understand that it is not an easy task. As there are techniques in the theatre, so there are techniques in everyday life. Marcel Mauss studied how people do the same thing differently depending on the society. For example, how someone uses silverware, if she uses silverware, is largely determined by the culture in which she lives.[3] Deleuze and Guattari believe the same is true of how populations think and behave. Governments are structures that have relatively rigid hierarchies and need their citizenries to believe in their institutions. Louis Althusser calls the values that authorize such organizations ideology and argues that adopting these values forms a "habit of mind," or an unquestioning acceptance of institutional authority and docility.[4] Deleuze and Guattari pick up on this theme when they call their theory "anti-Oedipal." In the Freudian interpretation of the myth, it is the son who seeks to kill the father. The philosophers argue that this assessment overlooks the fact that Oedipus only killed his father after his father tried to kill him. The perpetuation of this oversight causes sons and daughters to feel guilt when they question authority, producing a society that stifles the creativity of its citizens in order to maintain power. Therefore, pursuing a line of flight is not only an overtly political act, but also challenges deeply held personal beliefs. Preserving the uncertain end of a line of flight is necessary, because if the end is predetermined, it will end more or less where it began, so strong is the pull of cultural/personal values. Thus the act takes place in a very narrow space, in the gap between conflicting sets of belief: between the desire to be a good citizen and the desire to experience freedom from the tyranny of the mundane.

Two intertwining binaries employed by Deleuze and Guattari are worth noting: (1) the molar and the molecular, and (2) the arboreal and the rhizome. The molar (based on the mole, or number of particles in a small amount of carbon-12) is equated with any large state apparatus or any system of values that constitutes a habit of mind. The molecular, just the opposite, refers to the individual entity and is the locus from which lines of flight are possible. The second binary uses flora as a metaphor. The arboreal, or tree, is understood as a hierarchical form with distinct divisions between roots, trunk, branches, and canopy, each having a particular function. It is vertical, while the rhizome is horizontal. The latter has nodes that operate independently of the whole, sending down roots and participating in the reproduction of the species, while remaining connected to the rest of the plant. Moss is an example. It grows over the ground or on trees, expanding without having a center. Kill the roots of a tree, and it dies. Destroy the roots in one part of a rhizome, and it regenerates. Deleuze and Guattari's philosophy privileges the molecular and the rhizome because they offer an alternative political structure based on a radical equality. Yet they also recognize that differentiating between the molar and molecular is difficult: "No becoming-molecular escapes from a molar formation without molar components accompanying it, forming passages or perceptible landmarks for the imperceptible processes."[5] Conversely, the molar is made of the molecular. It is impossible to fully escape our cultural heritage, even though the desire is to become free from its limitations. People are deeply implicated in the society in which they live; at the same time, they have the potential to free themselves from its limitations. In the theatre, this glimpse of freedom is facilitated by improvisation.

Improvisation and Its Discontents

When an actor enters into an improvisation, she carries with her a lifetime of experience. Her body is permeated by various techniques and ways of thinking that allow her to act with grace and authority.

With sufficient experience, she has also learned ways of entering into an improvisation with relative ease. The remainder of this chapter explores the techniques and processes of improvisation, but first a few words about why improvisation fails.

Both the success and failure of improvisation depend on the ways in which the work is set up, carried out, and brought to a conclusion. The following is a short list of some obstacles that interfere with the success of improvisation.

- Too much freedom can be a dangerous thing. Improvisations need boundaries to be successful, whether the boundaries are directives as relatively narrow as those for improvisational comedy or as vague as "choose an object and work with it." The performers need a focal point on which to direct their attention.
- Similarly, too many limits can predetermine the direction the investigation takes and the kind, if not the specificity, of the answers found. The interactions between the actors become self-fulfilling prophecies, preempting more creative resolutions, and ending the line of flight.
- The focus of the performers needs to be appropriate to the form of engagement. Inward-oriented work requires a different frame of reference than exploration of the external environment.
- Self-consciousness can limit the range of creative responses or lead to premature evaluations of the work. When this happens, the banal is mistaken for the creative, or the exploration is concluded before the full potential is realized.
- Working with others requires trust. A high degree of openness on the part of the actors is required if they are to reach the point where novel associations are discovered through improvisation. If the trustworthiness of the participants is in question, they can be hesitant to commit fully to the exercise.
- There needs to be a collective sensitivity to how far any given performer can be pushed. Improvisations are designed to extend the limits of what is possible; but if the interaction moves too far outside a comfort zone and there is a feeling of being physically, psychologically, or ideologically at risk, it may be difficult for the group to commit fully, and creative impulses will be blocked.
- Assessing when to stop an improvisation is difficult. Stopping the work too soon, before an issue has been fully explored, precludes the possibility of discovering more interesting solutions; continuing too long can lead to repetition and staleness, diminishing the value of earlier insights.

There are undoubtedly more factors in devising, performing, and evaluating an improvisation. What is interesting about this list is the emergence of a common denominator: boundaries. Limits are necessary, but why, how, and where they are drawn is crucial to the success of the work.

Deleuze and Guattari observe that lines of flight take place in the spaces between ideological or institutional boundaries. Taking the leap can be the first step to observing new vistas, or the structures can be so oppressive that committing to the leap is virtually impossible. Not all repressions are externally imposed. Boal conceptualized "the cop in the head," recognizing that some forms of oppression are internalized; that is, performers police their own borders, making them resistant to new experiences.[6] Cognitively, these constraints—externally or internally imposed—are boundary conditions, parameters that keep the system in as stable a state as possible because the rewards of continuity are more pleasurable than the unknown consequences of transgressing the limits. The "cop in the head" is an investment in a personal identity that enhances a sense of self and is not easily ignored. Sustained within such a system, the ability to improvise does not come naturally but requires the learning of techniques. Whereas most techniques privilege stable modes of responding to recognizable inputs—approaches to developing characters, preparations before going on stage, and so on—improvisation values the unpredictable response. Improvising requires a willingness to allow the flow of experience to move in any direction, while remaining actively engaged in the world of the performance. The phrase most commonly used in the discourse of acting to describe this phenomenon is "being in the moment."

Being in the Moment

As I move, associations, memories, phrases, pictures... may drop into my mind, and I let them in and out again. They are glimpses of imagery for which I am not yet ready, and which, if I follow at this point, will draw me away from the present moment. Later these images may re-emerge in my writing or making.
—Miranda Tufnell and Chris Crickmay[7]

Two actors from very different backgrounds use similar metaphors to describe their work in rehearsal. Each talks about suspending certain aspects of the self so she can be surprised by the discoveries made in improvisational play. For one actor, the work is in silencing the critical voice, in removing the clutter, so that she can be open in her interaction with other actors and the text.[8] The second actor speaks equally of resisting the intrusions of the mind, but also of letting the body suggest images and directions for the work.[9] In each experience, there is a sense of setting aside cognitive functions in favor of experimentation. As we have seen, such compartmentalization is impossible, because the body doesn't allow for it; yet we know what these actors are describing. In everyday life as well as in the theatre, it is a common experience, trying to quiet the voices in our heads, trying to get rid of distractions in order to focus on the work at hand. Nowhere does the need to keep critical voices at bay become more insistent than in improvisation. Actors call this stilling of voices "being in the moment," that is, being present without the intrusions of past memories or predictions about future activities.

For the record, however, we are always "in the moment," continually interacting with the world around us. Thinking about the past or pondering the future, sleeping or waking, we are continually and presently engaged with the environment. In the middle of the night, I feel cold and seek another layer of covers; writing this—deep in thought about how to word this example—I am aware of the sounds in the environment, the cluttered desk on which the computer sits. I may be no more than peripherally cognizant of this extraneous information, because the ability to concentrate privileges certain perceptual experiences, relegating others to the background. But that does not change the fact that I am still, quite literally, "in the moment." This is not what is meant when the phrase is used in acting, however. In acting, it is used as a metaphor to define a *quality* of being: one that privileges an active engagement with others without conscious evaluation of what is taking place, that responds to what happens without premeditation or by recalling what happened previously and that allows the direction of events to shift without comment. These may seem like stringent regulations, but they are no different from how we interact with one another every day. In conversation, if the topic shifts unexpectedly or someone enters the room, we adapt to the change with relative ease and grace. The difference is that in the everyday, these changes happen as a matter of course, while in the theatre, there is a conscious choice to be open to changes in the environment. We are aware that this is what we are going to do.

Mayo and Espada describe the experience of improvisation as being in a neutral state, or a state that is uncluttered. The implication is that they can choose to be aware of certain physical responses while excluding thoughts that distract from the creative process. It may seem paradoxical to decide consciously to suspend cognitive practices when entering the rehearsal space, but both Mayo and Espada are adamant about the need to avoid certain ways of thinking. "If I go in thinking 'I'm going to try this in this moment,' I'm already out of it. What can I do to be in the moment, there in that day, that moment?"[10] "It can never be what you have in your head; your body will go a different way. But the brain keeps trying to push the body."[11] Conscious thought, it seems, establishes expectations that disrupt work that offers a more complex understanding of the situation. This runs counter to the rationalist discourse in the West, where exercising reason is thought to allow deeper insights into a problem. Actors tend to believe the opposite, discounting anything that smacks of logic and embracing emotional responses as keys to understanding. The theory developed here argues that the distance between emotionally based creativity and rational objectivity is minimal. The claim that a choice can be made to avoid thinking is an illusion, as is the claim that reason can be exercised devoid of emotion. Both occur *in the moment* as part of the normal functioning of the body and improvisational interaction with the environment.

We are engaged in the world as animate beings from infancy and, as Maxine Sheets-Johnstone argues, in that engagement we are undivided. It is only in processing experience that we begin to devise a conceptual structure for understanding through categories of differentiation. When we navigate a crowded street, we do not distinguish between thought and movement; we think *in* movement.[12] It is only when we stop to reflect that we divide the "body without organs" into abstractions such as reason and emotion.[13] We accept the divided body because it helps us give meaning to and communicate experience. We are not segmented creatures with separate systems for thinking and feeling; ours is a mind-full body that is able to know the world concretely and abstractly. The natural and cultural environments in which we live by and large determine how we define structures of thought and feeling; we develop constructs that are not natural forms, and whose value lies in our ability to use these concepts and emotions to navigate the world successfully. The knowledge that we glean—what we are able to think about at a particular moment—depends on an integrated body that is continually intertwined with the world to the full extent of its sensory potential. Without this complex interdependency, one simply cannot think or feel. The intensity that arises from an improvisation is experienced because the performer is fully engaged in thinking, feeling, and interacting with the world—*in the moment.* Consciously making sense of the work happens only after the exercise is over.

The Dynamics of Improvisation

Obtaining and maintaining this state of readiness in an improvisation poses a challenge for dynamic systems theory. In everyday life, the repeatable patterns that emerge from dynamic systems maintain relative stability by providing an efficient use of energy and promoting behavior that is appropriate to the environment. Creative states, particularly those involving performance, are not based on the conservation of resources but, as Eugenio Barba points out, on expenditure. "Daily body techniques generally follow the principle of minimum effort, that is, obtaining a maximum result with a minimum expenditure of energy. Extra-daily techniques are based, on the contrary, on the wasting of energy...the principle of maximum commitment of energy for a minimal result."[14] Theatre improvisation, an extra-daily technique, does not identify patterns of attractors and boundary conditions that hasten a resolution. To the contrary, it tends to postpone the return to a stable state in order to sustain a heightened sense of awareness until the work is concluded, whether successful or not.

A parallel can be drawn to a super objective. In realism, the actor identifies a goal the character pursues to the end of the play. It serves as a benchmark for judging the rising and falling intensities of the emotional through line and for identifying beats, the intermediary actions undertaken in pursuit of the desired end. The super objective is a useful tool for structuring a well-defined performance and for creating the illusion that the end of the story has yet to be determined. The actor does not focus on it onstage, but it hovers just outside the circle of attention as an implicit reminder of the logic behind certain choices. In an improvisation, the parameters of the exercise serve as the super objective. "Explore an object" takes the place of "my character wants power over others." Instead of defining a goal that motivates the action, improvisation creates a context in which a line of flight can be undertaken. That context remains at the edges of consciousness, giving focus to but not directing the patterns that emerge. The actor runs her fingers over the shape and textures of the gas mask, explores ways of holding it as it becomes an extension of her arm, and explores different characteristics as the object becomes anthropomorphic. She does not have to remember that the goal is to explore the object, yet that goal still informs her actions. The process of discovery is what takes place within the contours of the space defined by the exercise. The correlation between the super objective and the parameters of an improvisation breaks down when it comes to the activity these boundaries elicit. The former is a determining factor in everything the actor/character does in the telling of the story, while the latter allows what happens to happen without prescribing a particular direction. Although in an improvisation an objective may emerge that influences the sequence of events, the objective derives from the process and is not a structural limit.

Within the frame of the improvisation, the task that sets the exploration in motion perturbs the system, giving rise to a combination of impulses to act (thoughts, emotions, feelings) and memories from situations in the past. The open focus of the improvisation resists the creation of patterns that restore stability in the system because no single answer can provide a resolution, and the evaluation of the gathered material takes place after the work is complete. Instead, one attractor will be chosen and a series of behaviors elicited that permit the actor to interact in new ways with the environment. She touches the mask with her eyes closed, feeling the roughness of the canvas, the hard coolness of the glass eye plates, the slick metal of the canister at the end of the muzzle. The tactile quality of the surfaces brings back memories of similar sensations, which may take the form of a remembered event or merely of like materials. If one of these associations is sufficiently strong, it will evoke thoughts and feelings that cause ripples in the system, ushering in other sets of attractors and the possibility of new actions. Her attitude toward the mask may change as she projects her feelings onto what was once just an object, which is now endowed with those qualities, changing in subtle or not so subtle ways the direction of the exploration. She may find the mask endearing or frightening, may feel the impulse to embrace it or thrust it from her. Regardless of how she responds, the course of the improvisation is redirected, taking into account these new experiences.

A loop is created. The initial action privileges a particular type of perception (for instance, texture), drawn from the environment, that affects the behavior of the performer. This sensation brings a new set of memories and impulses, which modify her actions in turn. Depending on the intensity of the actor's responses, the kinds of perceptual information the actor seeks will change slightly or significantly:

> It is almost always the other actors that are the stimuli. The way they listened or the way their characters were reacting to me somehow bolstered, or affirmed my going out on the limb I was going out on. So much is response and attentiveness.[15]

Because the challenge that begins the investigation is open-ended and the acceptance of new perceptual information is a spur to continue exploring modified behaviors, a pattern that resolves the investigation does not appear or at least is not recognized as *the* solution. And so the improvisation continues until the line of flight exhausts itself, a new focus is found, or the work is brought to an end.

The attentiveness Mayo identifies as central to her work with other actors is a third layer of the improvisational process. The actor seldom if ever gets so immersed in the work that she is not aware of events. Indeed, central to the success of an improvisation is the performer's attention to what is happening. Not to be aware of the events taking place can bring the work to an untimely end. The improviser must not only say "yes" to what another actor gives, but must also offer an action that the other actor can use. At the same time that the performer remains cognizant of the focus of the work and follows the impulses in response to changes in context, she understands the choices being made and the activities undertaken.

Attentiveness plays another role as well. Within the three-tiered construct, patterns of behavior that create a significant impression will be remembered. The actor does not say, "I have to remember this." That would take her too far out of the situation and disrupt her focus. Because she is aware of what is happening by attending to changes in the environment and her responses to them, the elements that make up the patterns will be stored in long-term memory. Reflecting on the experience after the work is finished further consolidates important pathways, making them available long after the event. Those parts of the experience that are not memorable will decay through inactivity. The ability to recall an event is an indication of both the attentiveness of the performer and the significance of the action.

To summarize, depending on the purpose of the improvisation, arriving at creative associations can take time. When a dynamic system is perturbed by a perception, the sensory information will activate a number of attractors and boundary conditions. One chunk will be drawn into the circle of attention, and its potential will be explored until exhausted and no longer reactivated; another will replace the first and so on throughout the improvisation. In other circumstances, new perceptual information arriving in the system can introduce sensations previously unrelated to the current attractor, expanding the chunk, much like an addition to a house increases the structure's footprint. As the process continues, new resonances are experienced—new perceptions or the residue of data from earlier explorations—and drawn into the emerging pattern, creating novel and unexpected associations. The gas mask gains in complexity when a swath of red material is put inside it and allowed to trail behind. At various times in the work, it could be interpreted as a piece of clothing, as a body, or as blood emanating from a decapitation. The elements from one or all of the initial explorations are brought into a relationship with other material, creating a new set of memories from which the performer can later draw.

There are, of course, shorter improvisations that use a considerably more restricted focus. Two actors do not grasp the intensity of the relationship between them during a particular moment. They might explore the situation in a different context, switch roles to understand how the other character views the circumstances or any of a number of other such scenarios. The investigation need only last as long as it takes for them to have an "Aha!" moment that clarifies the relationship. In public performances, such as in comedy clubs, the work lasts only long enough to establish the circumstances, engage in a series of exchanges, and end well before the spectators expect it. The worst thing that can happen is for the audience to lose interest in what is taking place onstage. Whether long or short, the dynamic process of coming to a new understanding through improvisation remains the same. The system is destabilized and kept in a transient state until what is needed is discovered or the inability of the work to complete the task is recognized.

Conceptual Blending[16]

In a large room I am asked to locate where I was born and to move to that spot on an imaginary map on the floor. This relatively simple task involves a complex set of operations. A map, whether global, regional, national, or local, is a representation of an intricate topography. Unlike Jorge Luis Borges, who imagined a map that was so intricate it covered the whole of the land, point for point, I am required to imagine ignoring the multiplicity of details in order to identify a specific location within the larger contours of the map. Geographical boundaries, political divisions, and the location of other major cities or towns become the focus. Similarly, where I was born is reduced to a particular town or city, irrespective of the specifics of the actual birthplace. There is no interest in whether it took place in a hospital, if so, which hospital, let alone which wing, floor, or room. The whole event is reduced metonymically to a city and state—in my case, to Flint, Michigan—and then further reduced to a black dot on a map: "Some information from both spaces is not projected into the third space."[17] The room, too, is compressed, losing its usual function as a meeting room in the hotel and becoming, for all practical purposes, an empty space that no longer has chairs, painted walls, and chandeliers. Instead, in my mind's eye, it is nothing more than a space with a floor. This compression is used as the basis for another mental space, in which I imagine a map of the world across which I can walk. One salient fact is drawn from a mental space that includes all other memories circulating in my family about my birth and is projected into another mental space, the imaginary map.

Information from one mental space—the compressed image of my place of birth as a city and state—is combined with information from another—the virtual cartography in the rehearsal hall. Together they are projected into yet another mental space, that of the conceptual blend, where the information is combined so that when I move to the appropriate spot, it is the equivalent of being in Flint. Amy Cook, Indiana University, who uses conceptual blending to reread the works of Shakespeare from a cognitive perspective, writes: "Information is projected from two or more input spaces to a blended space, such that the blended space contains information and structure from more than one domain. Importantly, the blended space contains emergent structure not available from the inputs; the collision is synergistic."[18] Merging data from the two input spaces in a blended space allows for an image to emerge that provides the information needed to complete the task. It is not a purely mental operation, but an embodied experience that calls on an awareness of where I am in the room, the shape of the floor on which the map is to be projected, and the framing provided by the leaders of the improvisation.

As I move to the spot where I think Flint is to be found, the room itself "disappears" and a reversal of scale takes place: I can cover vast amounts of territory with a single step, instead of taking hours or days to return to my birthplace. The resulting blend compresses two scales: first, the distance between the location of the improvisation and Flint; second, the time that has passed from the day I was born to the present. I am a constant in the equation: in both places, in both times. In a compression, according to Seana Coulson and Todd Oakley, "the representation in the blended space is interpretable because of metonymic relationships between elements in the blended space and elements in the inputs."[19] Because of the network of spaces, compressions, projections, and blends necessary to understand this seemingly simple rehearsal task—where and when my birth took place in relation to the present—a cognitive blend occurs that allows me to move to the appropriate place in the room.

A second task—"How do you feel about that location?"—evokes a similar but more intricate process. Memories of the few years I lived there before moving, of returning to visit my grandparents, of what has happened to Flint since General Motors closed the factories that sustained the city's economy, and of all the other associations that surface as I undertake the task, allow for a greater amount of material to be active in my consciousness. The amount of data influencing the process can create a less stable blend than the amount of information involved in the simpler question "Where were you born?" As the blend, a network of expanding associations, takes shape, other feelings may emerge from the background that interfere with or influence the shape of the blend. As this process of "elaboration," or "running of the blend," takes place, the significance of the event may change, the focus may shift to a different range of feelings or to the intensification of a particular way of thinking, or the emotional contours of my body may be rearranged. Although the emphasis on feeling, thought, or emotion may change, the three remain inextricable.

During the improvisation, the conceptual blending is not static but dynamic, continually going through transitions and transformations. The inputs are not limited to what is remembered and imagined, but can involve the structure of the space in which the exercise is taking place, what other participants are doing, modifications to the directions by the leaders of the work, and so on. New information is continually introduced into the blend as the different steps of the task are engaged. As the blend becomes more elaborate, the number of associations proliferates, giving rise to potentially novel insights through the introduction of diverse inputs—emotions, memories, movements, perceptions, desires, and so on. As I respond to the task of determining how I feel about my place of birth, I experience a variety of emotions, feel the urge to move, to speak, or in some way to express myself in response to the flow of images that occur. The elaboration of the blend is, according to Cook, "not a combination or a blurring of two ideas, it is a complicated network evoked and integrated to create a new idea."[20] What emerges from the process is not an answer, but a flow of possibilities, from which I can select those actions that are most meaningful to me in carrying out the task of the improvisation. It is a creative moment that may give rise to further creativity.

Not every attempt at a blend—whether in language or improvisation—is successful. In everyday life, mixed metaphors and looks of incomprehension can indicate mental spaces that do not fit together. Similarly, in theatre work, improvisations may prove banal;

the objective may not stimulate the imagination or maintain the flow of images necessary to continue the creative process. At other times, upon reflection, the actors may decide that the work is not meeting the needs of the task set for the exercise. A different direction may have the potential for unearthing a richer vein of images. There are no guarantees that what emerges will be of value. The work ends; the task may be scrapped; and a new starting point is sought, to elicit sets of inputs that have the potential to evoke more productive blends.

The Techniques of Improvisation

It is hard to imagine that there is a technique for a process that has creative freedom as its end. For Artaud, it was only by getting rid of all techniques—professional and social—that the creative impulse could find expression. Grotowski realized, consciously or not, that freeing the body of cultural blocks did not rid the body of technique. Rather, ridding the body of habits requires instilling alternative ways of working that are creatively more productive. As Deleuze and Guattari understand, there is no freedom without limits. If there are no boundaries, a line of flight is not possible; also implicit in the concept is the understanding that if there is no risk, there is no flight. The question is, how is a technique of improvisational risk taking defined?

In a dynamic system, a technique is a multimodal pattern of neural pathways that consist of attractor states and boundary conditions. These components bias the body to act in particular ways, giving preference to certain types of perceptual information and behaviors. In experts, these take the form of templates that provide a flexible structure, that is, one capable of incorporating and responding to inputs from internal and external sensorimotor systems. This new material perturbs the system, permitting it to seek modes of acting that will return it to a near stable state. This is now familiar ground. What makes improvisation different is that it is oriented to change rather than to a return to behaviors that were successful in the past.

The technique of bike riding is based on patterns that allow the biker to control the bike's direction and velocity while maintaining her balance and anticipating and adapting to changes in the environment (such as different road surfaces). The focus is on controlling the number of variables within the limits of what constitutes safe bike riding, so that responses focus only on what is different from the norm. Improvisational techniques work very differently. In an improvisation, the actor opens herself to a variety of inputs, focusing on the potential of perceptual information to provide a multiplicity of possibilities, rather than attributing a single meaning to any given perceptions or promoting habitual behaviors in response to the information. By delaying interpretation, the actor is able, without judgment, to invest in the feelings and thoughts that emerge from the experience.

Watching novices engage in improvisation, even something as basic as a mirror exercise, is informative. Their inexperience is apparent when they try to anticipate what the partner is going to do or when the person in front of the mirror does not help her mirror follow her lead. The novice is paying attention to the wrong perceptual information. She is so concerned about what might happen or about the execution of an action that she neglects to help her partner succeed. Through coaching, the actors gradually or rapidly learn the rules of the exercise. When they return to the exercise, they are able to get in tune with each other much more quickly. They begin to learn the technique through complying with the rules and focus of the exercise. Experts, practiced in devising theatre, are able to enter into an improvisational situation quickly and wholeheartedly. The ease of the transition does not mean they are immediately creative. They, too, are subject to repeating learned behaviors, that is, ways of responding to a certain type of input based on previous experience. As with the novice, it takes time to work through the habitual to find a creative space. Their experience, however, gives them the ability to recognize previous behaviors, to let go of comfortable solutions, and to wait for the unexpected to push the boundaries of what is possible.

That it gets easier does not mean it is ever easy. The process requires that the performer be open to possibilities that may be disturbing socially or personally. The actor cannot walk away from such moments but must be willing to be vulnerable and trust in the relationship developed with other actors. The actor must take risks. Tim Etchell writes

> Risk...[appears] in the strangest places, slipping and hiding. Risk is the thing we're striving for in the performance but not a thing we can look for. We look for something else and hope...that risk shows up. We know it when we see it, I'm sure of that. Risk surprises us, always fleeting—we're slightly out of control....I don't care where we see it, but it's all too rare and it's the only thing we should care about.[21]

Risk is being open to experiences that other techniques cannot control. Like inspiration, it may not appear when summoned, but without it, finding a truly creative solution, one that is startlingly novel, is unlikely. This does not mean that every improvisation involves soul-searching revelations. Some can be lighthearted and funny. Regardless, the intensity and dedication need to be the same.

Failure *is* an option. The purpose of improvisation is not to find *the* answer but to explore a range of conceptual blends to determine which choices offer the richest dynamic and produce the most creative resolutions to the task. Improvisations can fail, though, for a number of reasons. The mind can become congested, not leaving room for new images; the imagination can lose its spontaneity and return endlessly to the same sets of associations; or the physical space can lose its plasticity and become claustrophobic. Sometimes, it simply does not provide interesting material. Any number of obstacles can stand in the way of the creative process. The challenge, when things go wrong, is how to return to the work in a more productive state of mind: "Sometimes when we're working we get stuck, and very often when we do that we end up walking around in the city, talking and trying to work out what we could do next."[22] New stimuli are needed to displace the nonproductive images that refuse to open onto exciting and new horizons. Clearing the mind can also put the actor back into the open frame of mind that allows the work to proceed, that allows, in other words, a return to technique.

Improvisation requires an "intentional naiveté"—however illusory—if it is to work. To enter the process cynically, ironically, or doubtfully, unless these are integral to the exercise, creates an air of detachment that is inimical to the process. These attitudes may be useful in maintaining cognitive stability in a turbulent world, but they interfere with a committed engagement in theatre work. To improvise successfully requires inhibiting the existing cognitive processes and distractions that interfere with the task at hand and being open to letting the conceptual blends run. When this frame of mind is achieved, a chain of associations spirals out as image begets image. It is not a free flow of material, however, because the actor is continually making choices that move the improvisation in different directions, based primarily on the attraction immanent in what is happening at that particular moment. Patterns that are not engaged at a particular moment may decay or remain active outside the center of attention, returning when they are more attractive to the improviser. These decisions are based in part on the structure of the exercise, but they also reflect the actor's curiosity about the relationships and interactions that are constructed in the environment. This is the technique of improvisation.

Improvisations, unless they are ends in themselves, provide material that is then shaped into a performance. Through repetition, certain patterns will be reinforced and linked with other actions in the creation of an actor's score. In the next chapter, questions of technique and the process of creative improvisation will be brought together to discuss how a performer uses both to weave the sequence of actions that defines the structure of her performance.

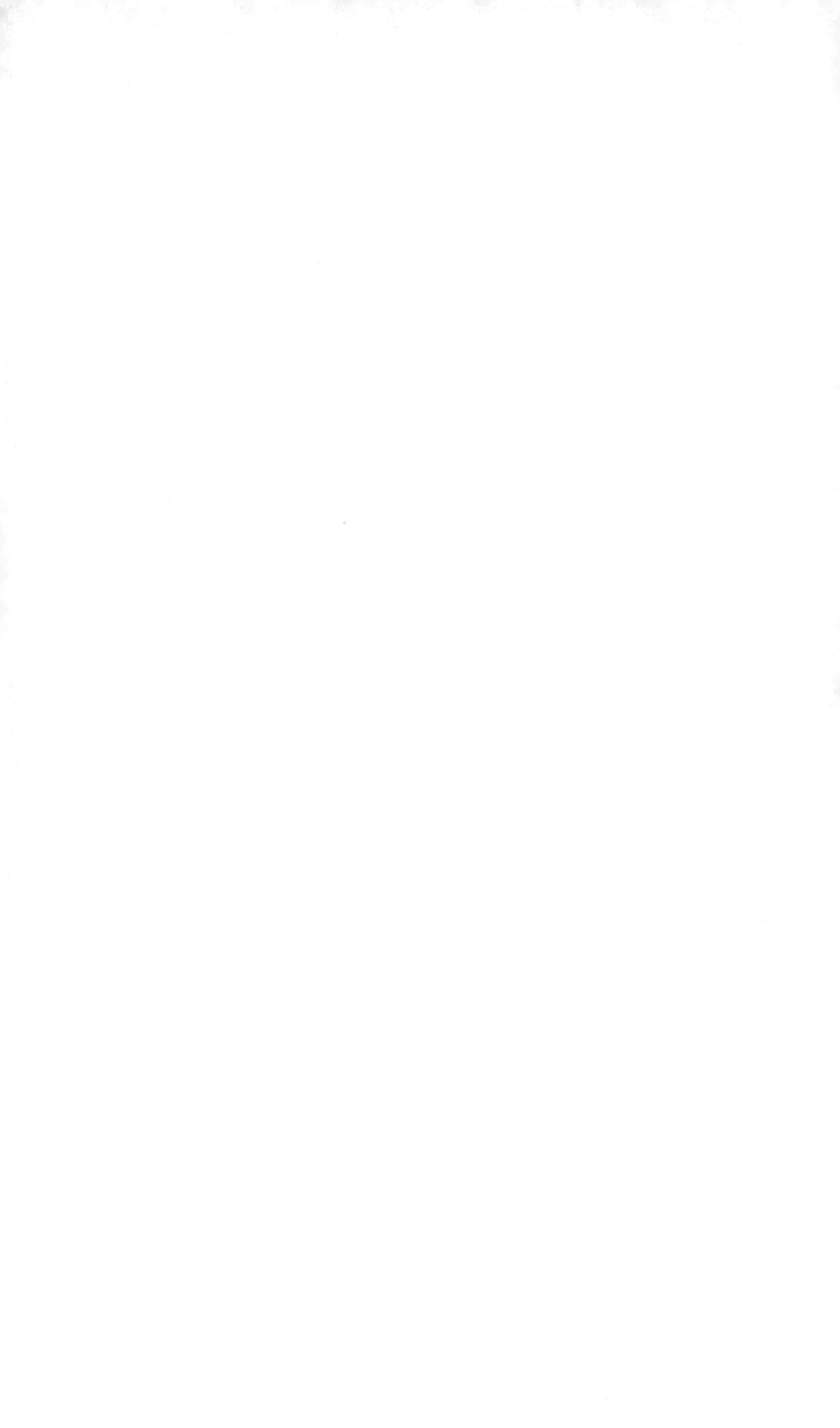

Chapter 6

The Actor's Score

An actor preparing for a performance creates a score, defined as a sequence of actions that is more or less precisely repeatable, depending on the nature of the event. In some instances, such as the Living Theatre's production of *Paradise Now*, the actors have a very loose structure to follow, responding to the impulses of the other actors or members of the audience.[1] At the other end of an imaginary spectrum, the performers in Robert Wilson's *Einstein on the Beach* were drilled in meticulously orchestrated movement and vocal patterns with the expectation that they would be repeated with great precision.[2] However, to think of the score as simply a sequence of activities does a disservice to a very complex structure. This chapter begins with three examples, followed by an examination of the rehearsal process and the cognitive structures that facilitate the creation of a score. The first is a workshop experience in which I participated; the second is Grotowski's discussion of Ryzard Cieslak's performance in *The Constant Prince*; and the third is one of my experiences acting in *The Grapes of Wrath*.

At the 2008 conference of the Association for Theatre in Higher Education, Dijana Milosevic and Sanja Krsmanovic Tasic of the Dah Theatre in Belgrade, Serbia, ran a three-hour workshop on the generation of material for non-text-based performances. The participants were asked to create an imaginary map of the world and to stand in relative proximity to the place on the map where they currently live. They were then asked to locate where they were born, where they had had a memorable experience, where they could provide assistance, and, finally, to imagine an idyllic place. Once identified, all were told to move from one location on the map to another, allowing their emotional connection to the place they were leaving to transform into that associated with the next destination. Each location and movement pattern was to be remembered precisely, to make it repeatable upon request. In each place, the workshop leaders asked the participants to find a sound or phrase that would communicate their attitude toward that particular place. Finally, aware of the others performing with them, the participants explored their interactions with other participants, allowing their movement and vocal patterns to be influenced by the work of others. From the various scores developed, some performers were asked to repeat the work they had done in conjunction with that of others with whom they had not come into contact. If there had been time to continue the process, what evolved from these pairings would have become the material for further development in the creation of a performance.

The workshop not only focused on useful ways of devising a performance, but it also served as a model for the evolution of an actor's score. Each stage of the exercise generated new material, which was then incorporated into what happened previously. The *repetition* of each movement and the *precision* with which it was performed *fixed* it in memory at the same time that new elements were being added. Over the course of the three hours, what began as simple movements gained complexity and depth of feeling. By the end, participants were able to enact their sequences with confidence not only in their own work but also in their ability to respond to the work of others. Not all of the sequences were equal, as one would expect. Some people are simply more creative, and those more experienced in improvisation had techniques that allowed them to experiment, to let their imaginations work with greater freedom. What is missing in this definition of a score—and what is generally missing in a workshop setting—is the focus on a specific concept, idea, or text.

"His long monologues were linked to the actions which belonged to that concrete memory from his life, to the most minute actions and physical and vocal impulses of that remembered moment": Grotowski's description of the origins of Ryzard Cieslak's performance in *The Constant Prince* is remarkable for the insight it gives into the director's understanding of the relationship between the work of the actor and the text.[3] However, by further analyzing this comment, a definition of an actor's score becomes discernable. The text (in this case a play) is linked to physical actions that draw on the past experience and memories of the performer. Each action is linked to the structure of the event (a combination of play and performance) and is created through the physical and vocal impulses that arise from the connections made by the actor in constructing the through line of the (envisioned) theatrical event. The actor's score, as Grotowski intimates, is a subjective form that gains clarity and precision over time yet which is in essence a transformation of a primary text into an embodied form that cannot be adequately notated or replicated by another artist. It is transient, performative, and repeatable, although not with absolute precision.[4]

In the spring of 2008, I was asked to play Granpa Joad in *The Grapes of Wrath* at Stony Brook University, where I teach. It had been many years since I had acted, and I approached this opportunity with some trepidation—memory not being what it used to be and lacking in confidence about how exactly to create the score. The process was traditional: table work, followed by blocking rehearsals, intensive scene work, and run-throughs leading up to performance. This was interspersed with hours spent learning the few lines I had (while walking the dog) and exploring different interpretations of the lines based on my understanding of the character, what the other actors were giving me, and the director's vision. Rehearsals focused on the character's interactions with the other characters, experimenting with defining a physicalization (particularly Joad's limp) and his relationships with his family, as well as the land he is about to leave. As opening night approached, emphasis shifted from articulating specific beats and objectives as they related to the lines and movement patterns to clarifying, physically and vocally, the transition from an energetic "old coot" to a broken and dying man who refuses to be taken from the land to which he has given his life.

I had the embarrassing moment, not having adequately prepared for a final dress rehearsal, of completely going blank. It is a moment indelibly inscribed in my memory, and not only because it was traumatic. As I stood up, breaking with the character's stooped posture, the distance between my everyday self and the Granpa Joad I was creating became apparent. Somewhat surprised that I had actually managed to develop a character, I became aware of the complex processes involved in acting and structuring a score. It is not simply a sequence of actions and objectives, but an intricate pattern that integrates and *embodies* the interaction between memory, physicality, vocal expression, the work with other actors, and the multidimensional space (including volumes of light, costume, and sound) in which the play takes place.

The creation and integration of a score is a function of rehearsals, which are designed to assist the actor through repetition to develop sequences and patterns that run parallel to and intersect with the work of the others onstage. It is an exploration that moves to the clear definition of a score, repeatable from one performance to the next. The process is exceedingly complex, as the actor incorporates information from a number of different sources into the structure of the performance. The inputs range from blocking to interpretation of the text; from a character's identifiable habits and relations with other characters to work with props, costumes, lighting, sound, and other technologies; from working with personal memories to articulating cognitive-emotional trajectories that relate to the perceived arc of action (whether narrative or nonnarrative in form).[5]

If improvisation is about being open to the unexpected, creating a score is about making choices and defining a sequence that can be expected. Through the manipulation of movement, voice, gesture, memory, and attention, the actor crafts a through line of actions that can be unfolded over the time of the performance night after night. It is a prodigious act of memory to which one cannot do justice in the space of a chapter. However, we may glimpse the process by looking at the structure of a single beat—say, Ophelia at the moment she declares, "I was the more deceived"—and developing a model of how a movement or a few words gain the complexity needed to create the illusion of an embodied character.[6] The constituent parts of an action provide clues for understanding how larger sequences can be readily remembered from one performance to the next, leading to the completed score. Anyone who has acted knows that the evolution of a score is a convoluted path, involving many missteps for every step taken. The circuitous route to creating a performance means that an actor has as much forgetting to do as remembering. This chapter concludes with a look at the cognitive processes involved in intentional forgetting. We begin, however, by setting the stage for forgetting, by looking at the variety of demands placed on the actor in three types of theatre and by briefly reviewing Nelson Cowan's theory of memory. The word *score* is not only a noun, but also a transitive verb. "To score" means to etch a mark into a surface. In acting, the scoring is done on the actor's memory.

Acting Scores for Realism, Nonrealism, and the Postdramatic

Theatre comes in many shapes and sizes. Like all arts, it houses under its umbrella traditional forms, challenges to the conventional, and rebellious acts that significantly rethink what constitutes theatre. Sam Mendes's production of *The Cherry Orchard* has little in common with Sarah Kane's *4.48 Psychosis,* the Robert Wilson/Philip Glass collaboration *Einstein on the Beach,* or Forced Entertainment's *Bloody Mess.* But in each, the performers create a score, albeit using very different starting points, rehearsal strategies, and final objectives.

Devising a score is in some ways similar to carving marble, in that a form emerges from the interaction with the material, based on a vision of what the stone might contain. Carving marble is dialectical, involving the ideal object, a structural analysis of the marble, and the artist's expertise with hammer and chisel . Sculpting, however, is a negative process—stone is removed to reveal a shape—while acting is primarily additive, combining emergent material into a final form. In both types of process, the creative act occurs in conversation with its environmental context; it reveals itself against that which it is not. David McNeill elaborates

> The meaning is two things taken jointly, including both the point differentiated and the field of oppositions from which it is differentiated. This concept of meaning as irreducibly a relationship of a point to a background, both of which are constructed in order to make the relationship possible contrasts with the classic view of meaning as "association" or "habit strength" or "content" at a mental address.[7]

An acting score is never definitive, because it depends on a background, which is not consistent but dependent on circumstances. The score is not completely relative, however, because the script, like a block of marble, provides constraints that limit interpretation.

Realism

For reasons of expediency, I define the realism genre well beyond the limits usually associated with it to include most plays that are driven by narrative, constrained by the dialogic structure of the language, and focused on multidimensional characters that seem psychologically motivated and are generally recognizable. Included in this expanded category are the plays of Shakespeare, Molière, Behn, and Rostand, as well as Ibsen, Chekhov, Wilde, O'Neill, Williams, Miller, and Wasserstein. Tori Haring-Smith provides a concise definition of the more traditional understanding of realism:

> At the heart of a modern realist text is character. In realism, we analyze characters in terms of intentions or desires. Realist characters are expected to display some kind of explicit or implicit consistency; their actions and their feelings must be linked in understandable ways.

They conform to the rules of modern psychology. Their past is visible through their present. Their social status shapes their attitudes.[8]

The actor's work is expected to fit within these parameters and is further constrained by the give-and-take dialogue, cause-and-effect action, and the verisimilitude of the relationships between the characters. The primary responsibility of the performer is to develop a consistent character with an emotional and intellectual intensity that is believable within the logic of the plot and which communicates the story. In concert with the other actors, the performer attempts to evoke a world that is an accessible and recognizable reflection of reality for the audience.

The creative work of the actor takes place and within these boundaries, the character takes shape. The traditional approach to rehearsing realism consists of table work, improvisations, blocking rehearsals, scene work, and run-throughs—although there are numerous permutations of the ordering and structure of these elements in the service of the process. The combination of individual (usually done outside rehearsal) and collaborative (usually done during rehearsal) work provides the actor with the material needed to create the role: character history, motivation, objectives, dynamic trajectory, emotional intensity, relationships with others, and so on. The performer uses this information to develop a pattern of behaviors that communicate the character. She does not, however, "become," "step into," or "flesh out" the part. The character does not exist prior to the rehearsal process; the character is "performative," coming into being only when embodied by the actor.[9] The performer uses herself to find the appropriate movements, voice, gestures, emotions, and actions to make an audience believe that she is, for example, Blanche DuBois. Central to this scoring process—particularly in realism as practiced in the United States—is identifying the psychological motivations of the action and the emotional intensity that arises from those motivations. Other genres offer different challenges.

Nonrealism

Nonrealism is difficult to discuss because it tends to be defined in the negative, that is, by the conventions of realism it violates. It is further complicated by plays that are accepted as part of the realist canon without strictly following the conventions. Ibsen had no sooner developed the forms of realism than he began to violate its tenets in such works as *Rosmersholm*. Chekhov is variously linked to realism and impressionism, while canonical plays of American modernism, such as *The Glass Menagerie, Camino Real, Death of a Salesman,* and *After the Fall,* also push the limits of the realist form. This says nothing of the dizzying array of plays that explore dreamscapes and documentary forms, the irrationality of the unconscious and the rationality of political resistance. If realism provides a structure the playwright is expected to inhabit, nonrealism represents the author's struggle to find a form that allows her to speak in her own voice. Haring-Smith writes: "Many writers marginalized by race, gender, sexuality, and socio-economic status turn to this form to highlight ways in which their points of view differ from the conventional."[10] This type of play requires a different kind of analysis and confronts the actor with a different set of challenges in creating a score.

Performing nonrealism creates difficulties for actors, because the absence of a narrative frame and logical interactions among characters makes it difficult to identify the context. Improvisations and discussion can give the actor sufficient material to construct a world for the play that reflects the social criticism, philosophical questions, or intrapersonal conflicts the playwright is addressing. A through line based on emotional continuity and consistent objectives is generally more difficult to develop, however, requiring alternate strategies for remembering the sequences of beats and units. Winnie's lines in *Happy Days* are rife with repetitions, making it very easy for the actress to lose track of where she is at any particular moment. Yet the rhythms inherent in Beckett's use of language demand that the performance follow the ordering of events in the text as precisely as possible. Rather than depending on the logic of cause and effect, the actor must relate sections of dialogue to the tonal changes that correspond to the subtle changes in the writing; the actor must learn to convey the play's progression from morning to noon and then night, despite the fact that no well-defined moments mark the temporal change. To do so, the actor might tie sequences of objects used or changes in visual focus to the next action or part of a monologue. As with realism but even more so, the specificity of the beats and their associated actions are crucial for developing sequences that can be repeated precisely night after night.

In *Waxing West,* Savania Stanescu, a contemporary Romanian playwright, meditates on Western influences in a post-Ceauşescu world. In this short section of the last scene of the play, the principal character is Daniela, a cosmetologist, who appears with her mother, Marcela, brother Elvis, a homeless Yugoslavian Muslim Uros, an

American artist Gloria, and the ghosts of Ceauşescu and his wife, Elena:

> *Gloria, Marcela, and Elvis*: Run!
> *Gloria*: Here.
> *Elvis*: Fire
> **Daniela: Sweat**
> *Ceauşescu*: Blood
> *Marcela*: Money
> *Gloria*: Bodies
> **Daniela: Hair**
> *Gloria*: Hands
> *Elvis*: Legs
> **Daniela: Thighs**
> *Gloria*: Hips
> *Elena*: Buttocks
> *Ceauşescu*: Demolition
> *Elena*: Mutilation
> *Uros*: Death
> **Daniela: Love!**
> *Gloria*: Loss
> *Marcela*: Business!
> *Elvis*: Hope
> *Ceauşescu*: The golden future!
> *Gloria*: The present
> **Daniela: The past, always the past**
> *Ceauşescu, Elena, Marcela, Elvis, Gloria, and Uros*: Guilty!
> **Daniela: Stop this! I've had enough of this! Enough!**[11]

An experienced theatre person will read this passage and understand the intended effect: the tempo, intensity, rhythms, and theatricality, as well as the meaning. But from the actor's point of view, the challenges may be less evident. Daniela has six lines to be delivered in rapid succession but not in a set rhythm. The number of lines between hers varies, so she must focus only on the cues and the voices that deliver the lines preceding hers for the signal to speak. The actress might also notice that the words she says are associated positively or negatively with those that come before: fire/sweat, bodies/hair, legs/thighs, death/love, present/past, and then her final line, which is cued by the collective cry "Guilty." The last line is clearly motivated by what has gone before it and is probably, at least in traditional terms, the easiest to learn. For the earlier lines, she will, in effect, have to learn everyone's words in sequence, on the off chance that someone forgets a line. Her tone of voice, volume, and rhythm will derive from the overall sequence, but she needs to anticipate the next beat with little thought for what the meaning of the association might be. That will happen during rehearsals, not in performance, because there is not the time in performance to improvise with the necessary precision. Thus far I have focused only on the language. It is not clear from the text how the scene is to be staged. The scene could be very still, everyone in place. Alternatively, there could be considerable movement to echo the quick pace of the delivery; or each line could be directed to another cast member or to a particular spot in the audience. These options all *assume* that there are no props to consider, that the costumes will not hinder, and that the lighting does not require the actors to be in a particular place at a precise moment. Some of these concerns apply to working on realistic plays, but nonrealism requires significantly different ways of working and scoring.

A third and final example of the challenges facing actors in nonrealism comes from Heiner Müller's *Hamletmachine*. This short section is from the end of a scene in which the actor playing Hamlet begins: "I'm not Hamlet. I don't take part anymore. My words have nothing to tell me anymore." He then begins the longest monologue in the play, which ends with a combination of verse and prose:

> In the solitude of airports
> I breathe again I am
> A privileged person My nausea
> Is a privilege
> Protected by torture
> Barbed wire Prisons
> *Photograph of the author*
> I don't want to eat drink breathe love a woman a man a child an animal anymore.
> I don't want to die anymore. I don't want to kill anymore.
> *Tearing of the author's photograph*
> I force open my sealed flesh. I want to dwell in my veins, in the marrow of my bones, in the maze of my skull. I retreat into my entrails. I take my seat in my shit, in my blood. Somewhere bodies are torn apart so I can dwell in my shit. Somewhere bodies are opened so I can be alone with my blood. My thoughts are lesions in my brain. My brain is a scar. I want to be a machine. Arms for grabbing Legs to walk on, no pain no thoughts.[12]

The monologue is full of powerful, violent images, giving the actor a wealth of material to investigate. The scene is parallel to Hamlet's "To be, or not to be" soliloquy and concludes by echoing Hamlet's rejection of suicide: the thought of death "does make cowards of us all." In creating a score, the actor in Müller's play may want to look for other parallels between the two speeches, but this approach poses both problems and opportunities. The speech begins with the character destroying the theatrical illusion by rejecting the playing of that character, and the rejection takes place in the name of two people: the actor, who must discover a new role if it is not portraying Hamlet; and the author, Müller, who is saying that he will no longer play the character or, perhaps, no longer write the character. This duality of character is supported by the stage directions to produce and tear a photograph of the author. The actor has, therefore, to be aware of two trajectories: the character's tortured introspection and the author's scathing self-criticism.

This is when the actor turns to the dramaturg, who tells him that the first half of the title of the scene, "Pest in Buda," refers to Budapest and the Hungarian uprising of 1958, which was brutally put down by the Stalinist regime. The dramaturg will also tell him that Müller, an East German at the time of writing, had multiple opportunities to defect but chose to remain in East Berlin. There he received privileges that were denied the average citizen (including better housing and access to Western products), because his plays, though censored in East Germany, were performed in the West, where he had achieved considerable celebrity. His fame also gave him leeway to criticize the government when it would not have been tolerated in others. *Hamletmachine* is, therefore, both a critique of the repressive policies of the German Democratic Republic and of his own complicity with the regime.

The actor who is playing Hamlet needs at this point to mark the change in role. The audience will need to register the difference between actor as Hamlet and actor as Müller, because when the character talks about sitting "in the solitude of airports," he has begun to speak as the author. Moreover, if the actor is going to honor the shift in voice, he must explore not only what it means to be Heiner Müller, but also his own complicity in the repressive policies he critiques for the privileges he enjoys as a citizen of the country that bans his own plays. This is not, for all its introspection, an exercise in emotional recall, but a reflection on national history and the actor's self-reflection on her place in society, leading to a subjective understanding of the depth of Hamlet's—and Müller's—guilt. The actor needs to discover through that investigation a path that leads from the rejection of being Hamlet to the desire to become a machine, to exist without pain and without thought. It requires a high degree of specificity in detailing the movement to invoke the intensity and vividness the images require to communicate to the audience.

Some will argue that this discussion reflects a rather traditional approach to acting, one not in keeping with the postmodern strategies Müller employs. Of course, there are any number of alternative ways of performing the role. There can be more than one Hamlet; the whole cast can be involved in the portrayal; the words can be recorded; the actor or actors can do something parallel to or completely different from the words they are speaking. Each choice requires a different type of score that defines a relationship between the sequences in the language (assuming it is performed as written and not doubled, trebled, or synchronized) and the set of actions carried out by the actor(s). These are decisions that are made by the director and the company in the process of rehearsing, depending on the process chosen for developing the performance. Furthermore, the score developed for this short passage will need to be structured in relation to the rest of the play as it is performed.

These are just three examples of nonrealist plays. Each of them, as well as the many not discussed here, puts different demands on the actor and the production team to come to a collective understanding of how the play works; based on that understanding, a score is developed to be repeatable from performance to performance. The parameters of each play limits at the same time that they open possibilities, taxing the creativity of the performers in ways not required by realism. Before turning to how these differences affect the cognitive processes involved in developing a score, we need first to look at performances created without a script at all.

Postdramatic Theatre

This type of theatre goes by many names: devised, non-text-based, collaborative, experimental, nonmatrixed, avant-garde...I suspect there are many more. The plethora of names indicates the fluidity of the forms and their resistance to categorization. For the present purposes, I will adopt Hans-Thies Lehmann's definition of postdramatic as theatre that rejects the authority of the text and attempts to realize the possibilities of non-text-based theatre:

> The adjective "postdramatic" denotes a theatre that feels bound to operate beyond drama, at a time "after" the authority of the dramatic paradigm in theatre. What it does not mean is an abstract negation and mere looking away from the tradition of drama.[13]

Lehmann defines the dramatic paradigm as "the primacy of the text;" therefore, the postdramatic covers a wide range of forms that frequently overlap with other traditional arts.[14] Some forms of dance, for instance, can fall under this umbrella category, especially recent trends in European Tanz Theater (Dance Theatre), as practiced by Pina Bausch and Sasha Waltz. Robert Wilson calls his theatre pieces "operas," harkening back to the origin of the singular *opus*, which simply means "work," while referencing classic opera as well.[15] In many instances, what evolves is a hybrid that integrates various media (slides, film, digital projections) with movement, song, and the spoken word. Among the more notable practitioners of the postdramatic—in addition to those just mentioned—are the Wooster Group, Richard Foreman, Mabou Mines, Socìetas Raffaello Sanzio, Meredith Monk, Forced Entertainment, The Builders Association, Goat Island, Teatret Gruppe 38, and Martha Clarke. In general these groups begin with a concept, an idea, an image, a concern, or an impulse that can be derived from any number of possible sources, including dramatic texts, literary works, pictures, images, political beliefs, a dream, personal experience, or a combination of the above. The performance is then structured through a process that combines improvisation, directorial vision, and interactions among the members of the company. Rehearsals are often more circuitous than those conducted in traditional approaches to theatre, as investigations can lead to the partial or complete transformation of the initial impulse or the refinement of the impulse as issues of form, content, and aesthetics are addressed. For many practitioners, this approach can seem inefficient and time consuming, while those who work in this manner find it the only viable way of creating art.

Performers in postdramatic work encounter a wide array of working methods, particularly if they are engaged on a show-by-show basis. Yet even those who have an ongoing relationship with a company find that different projects dictate different ways of working, requiring an adaptability on the part of the actor generally not found in practitioners of more conventional approaches to dramatic theatre (of course, productions of traditional texts can use nontraditional approaches, as does Anne Bogart's work with Viewpoints). The range of possible rehearsal techniques makes it difficult, if not impossible, to catalogue methodologies. The rehearsal process can take any number of directions as the modus operandi changes with the reconceptualization of the material, with unexpected discoveries during rehearsals, and with the idiosyncratic creativity of the team. A few examples will serve to give a sense of the flexibility required of the actors in the development of a postdramatic score.

The singers performing in *Einstein on the Beach* were initially frustrated by the changing rhythms of Philip Glass's music. Through rigorous repetition, they came to understand the logic of the changes, not only finding it then easier to sing but also discovering a space for personal expression.[16] Mikhail Baryshnikov, dancing with Twyla Tharp's company, had to learn new techniques of moving that required an alteration of his body image and an enhanced body schema in order to perform the choreography (see chapter 4). Margarita Espada entered the rehearsal space with an image of blood on her feet and let the desire to rub off the blood become a source of images that determined the direction of the work. Forced Entertainment, when they encounter a creative block in rehearsals, will frequently take a walk through their hometown, Sheffield, England, to gain inspiration from the everyday life there:

> Sometimes when we're working we get stuck, and very often when we do that we end up walking around in the city, talking and trying to work out what we could do next. And very often in that situation we end up looking around and asking why all the things that we see there in the city aren't in the performance: a drunk running out of a pub, a tree with a cassette tape caught in the branches, or a crossroads where there's three night clubs, and the music spinning out of them mixes up to make a noise. Or maybe it's just a kid walking slowly on the parapet of a bridge.[17]

Tragedia Endogonidia by Socìetas Raffaello Sanzio was developed in eleven stages, each taking place in a different location.[18] The changing spaces and continued investigation of the relationship between tragedy and self-generation led to strikingly different variations on the theme, requiring an adaptability on the part of the actors as they were expected to retain some elements of preceding performances while learning new patterns as well. The Wooster Group has actors wear in-ear devices, through which they hear their lines as they speak them, and respond to video displays not visible to the audience.[19] The actors need to respond instantaneously to what they hear on the tape at the same time that they are carrying out complex and rapid movement patterns.

This array of working methods helps to explain the complex variety of performances that take place in contemporary cultures around the world and the difficulty of trying to find a suitable term to encompass the field. Fortunately, the task at hand does not focus on these issues but on how actors, involved in whatever form of theatre, create a score that is repeatable with varying degrees of precision. Completing this task, regardless of the starting and ending points, uses the same cognitive equipment and involves the same processes for committing a reliably retrievable score to memory. In turning to the cognitive process of performance, I present a brief recap of Cowan's theory of memory, a hypothetical example of the creation of a score, and the issues relevant to learning, retrieving, and, finally, forgetting. It is important to keep in mind that although I may seem to privilege one way of working, the argument is applicable to realism, nonrealism, and the postdramatic.

The Vicissitudes of Process

An actor's score is a series of intentional acts that interweaves creative associations discovered through analysis and improvisation with the dynamics of technique. These acts are performed through movement, language, and gesture. They combine memories—those retrieved from the past as well as those derived from working on the current production—with data from external perceptions and internal proprioceptions. This complex is generated by the desire to perform with (or without) other actors and for an audience. When all works, the result is a thoughtful, precise, intelligent, and effective series of actions that sustains the performer throughout the performance. The actor derives the material that goes into the structuring of the performance from a number of sources, including the text (script, scenario, images, etc.) and work inside and outside rehearsal.

A play is a source of information and clues that direct a performer in developing a character and a sequence of actions that respond to the circumstances and the behavior of other characters. Plays belonging to the genre of realism work by indirection. The actor grapples with the ebb and flow of conflict among the characters in order to discover a subtext or underlying motivation for the action. Through an analytical process, the realistic performer comes to understand the intricacies of the dialogue, the movement of time, the dynamics of the action, and the consistent system of values by which the characters live (even if their choices are sometimes surprising). Nonrealistic plays require a very different kind of exploration. Whereas realism creates a chronological narrative and follows it through time to a conclusion, abstract plays resist the Aristotelian form of beginning, middle, and end. They produce instead sequences and images that require a different form of analysis. Sense is found by juxtaposing parallel structures, identifying resonances within and between complementary, contrasting or contradictory images. Charles Mee's *bobrauschenbergamerica* uses the visual artist's concept of "combines" to present an array of images of American life—its variety, its richness, its shallowness. Constructing a psychological through line for Mee's characters is impossible, because each scene explores a different aspect of American life and can only be understood on its own terms. Rhythms and physical activities replace linear logic as signposts for changes in the performance.

The absence of a script in devised theatre requires alternative methods for gathering material. While it is possible to say that conventional theatre begins with a text, it is considerably more difficult to pinpoint the origins of devised performances. The Wooster Group's production of *House/Lights* evolved out of a curiosity about juxtaposing the semipornographic movie *Olga's House of Shame* with Gertrude Stein's *Doctor Faustus: Lights the Lights*. A devised piece called *Spirit X*, created at the University of Puget Sound, in Washington, focused on monologues written by students on the topic of "spirit," while *The Unclean*, a clown show I developed with students at Stony Brook University, was generated from personal experiences with feeling or making others feel unclean. Richard Foreman develops plays based on journals he writes on the cusp between wakefulness and sleep, when the unconscious is relatively unaffected by the censors of consciousness. It is not uncommon for actors to enter the rehearsal space without any preconceived notion or intention other than to generate material through improvisation. In a workshop with Margarita Espada, unpremeditated interactions with objects lead to the evolution of personae and action sequences. Sòcietas Raffaello Sanzio's production *Tragedia Endogonidia* evolved from Claudia Castellucci's interest in "what the theatrical arts of mime can amount to in a contemporary world that is in thrall to the technologies of spectacle."[20] The beginning point for such investigations and the directions they take depend on the people in the room and the chemistry between them. Rather than allowing a preexisting structure to define the process, they create the process in the moment.

Just as there are diverse forms of theatre, there are diverse ways of structuring rehearsals. Rehearsing traditional forms of theatre—whether realism or nonrealism—tends to be more economic in terms of time, energy, and money than rehearsing devised work. At the opposite end of the spectrum, rehearsals use improvisations to generate material, and the structure of the performance evolves in step with this process. Nontraditional processes are idiosyncratic, because the process of gathering material depends on the creativity of the participants and the tendency of material to spin off in unexpected directions. Regardless of their approach, companies will find themselves pursuing unfruitful tangents that at first look promising, confronting congested thinking (similar to writer's block), or beginning to define a structure from insufficient material. These and other obstacles impede the process and require time as the actors seek a form of expression that gives voice to their creative needs. With patience and openness to the process, a form will begin to emerge that reflects the actors' creative desires, eventually becoming more or less set.

Hierarchies of authority apply pressure to the process, ranging from the autocratic, associated (rightly or wrongly) with Harold Prince and Robert Wilson, to the democratic or even anarchic configurations of power identified with Forced Entertainment and The Living Theatre, respectively. In addition to the formal structuring of the creative process, actors have idiosyncratic ways of working that add layers of complexity to rehearsals. Some actors memorize their lines before rehearsal begins, preferring to get that task out of the way, while others wait until they are deep into rehearsals before learning them, needing first to understand the director's vision and to develop relationships with the other actors and their characters.

Between rehearsals, the actor strives to consolidate her previous work. This can consist of the mundane learning of lines, remembering blocking patterns, or detailing the vocal and physical characteristics required for the performance. The actor also goes over a scene in detail, remembering what happened in rehearsal, thinking through notes given by other members of the company, and evaluating what worked and what did not. Through this process of repetition, the specifics of the character's motivation are linked to words and movements, increasing the likelihood that the patterns will be repeated with greater precision in the next rehearsal. In the process of committing work to memory, the actor will also be attentive to those sequences that are not clear or that feel overly general. These uncertainties will be tagged in her memory, to be recalled in rehearsal, either in taking an acting partner aside or in working with the ensemble. The goal in either case is to link a specific objective to a particular action and a precise cue, so that the interwoven elements can be retrieved with equal, if not greater, specificity on demand. Going over and over a section increases the likelihood that the work will be consolidated in long-term memory, so that when the cue is perceived, the appropriate pattern of behavior is initiated and the emotion/thought/physicalization/movement/language/gesture complex communicated with the necessary intensity and clarity.

The time between rehearsals is also used to prepare the material to be explored in the next rehearsal. The work is conditional, however, because what is envisioned might not work when the other actors are encountered, or it might not fit into the overall scheme of the production. In early rehearsals, the preparations are generally not detailed with specificity, because the actor needs to respond in the moment to the actions of the others onstage. If the action is too firmly predetermined, playing the score may lack the required spontaneity, and the actor may lack the flexibility to respond to any unanticipated exigencies of the moment. After the rehearsal, the actor can reflect on the usefulness of the imagined form, modifying it or discarding it as necessary and beginning again.

Homework also includes forgetting. Rehearsals are frequently inefficient, because what is imagined in advance is rethought upon encountering the work of others and what seemed to work one day may no longer work the next. As one pattern of behavior is modified or replaced by another, the actor needs to suppress what was learned and commit to memory a new line of thought. Seldom is a choice completely wrong, but the performer needs to be selective, maintaining some aspects of previous work while eliminating others. Unfortunately, the task is not like replacing one light bulb with another. The cue and certain movement patterns might be retained, for instance, while the motivation or emotional intensity are changed. The actor needs to unlearn as she learns.

Creating a score is an intricate process of embodying the source material through analysis and rehearsal. In the terms of dynamic systems theory (DST), generating the sequence of actions involves allowing patterns of behavior to emerge in response to a variety of perturbations. Through repetition, attractors and boundary conditions that encompass a wide range of perceptual data are defined and consolidated, making the precise retrieval of a series of behaviors more likely, also reducing the amount of time and energy expended. As new directions are taken, the patterns are adjusted, activating some aspects of the score and suppressing others. Gradually, within the parameters of the rehearsal time available and the actor's level of expertise, perturbations are transformed into cues that trigger the desired movements, gestures, and vocalizations. Performed with sufficient energy, the sequential playing of the patterns will express the emotional and intellectual intensity required to communicate the score to the audience while interacting with other actors. Remembering that a dynamic system is never perfectly stable, a score is never reproduced precisely; it is subject to the vagaries of the retrieval process and the influx of new perceptual and proprioceptive information. If the patterns are sufficiently specific and learned, new information will not disrupt the process of performing, although a forgotten line, a missing prop, or any number of unexpected eventualities may require adjustment. It even has the potential of enriching the performance, giving it the spontaneity and vitality that one ought to associate with good acting.

Chunking and the Actor's Score

A repeatable performance by an actor depends on all four elements in Cowan's theory of memory. The performer uses long-term memory to retrieve the sequence of actions established through rehearsals. She uses perceptual (particularly the visual and echoic) memory systems and short-term, or working, memory to cue herself throughout the unfolding score and respond to variations from night to night. She uses attention, the fourth element according to Cowan's theory, to focus on those aspects of performance that activate the relevant data pathways and allow her to anticipate the next action. As stated in chapter 3, the capacity of attention is more or less four chunks of information, while each chunk contains—in theory—an unlimited amount of information. The capacity of each chunk is limited by time rather than quantity, since thirty seconds is the upper limit of time that material can remain inactive in the field of attention.[21] With the data from this small number of chunks, an actor can elicit information about the next line, movement patterns, gestures, intonations, emotional intensity, and relationships with other characters. In addition, peripheral memories and perceptual data are retrieved as the performer accesses the score and can be brought into attention if the situation demands. This simple model provides an outline of the cognitive abilities an actor uses in performance and is the topic of the next chapter. The focus of this chapter is not retrieval but how the actor *creates* the score. To address this process, we need to combine Cowan's approach to memory and DST, along with the phenomenon of intentional forgetting.

When the actor enters the rehearsal room, she does so intentionally, ready to bring her understanding of the project, openness to working with others, techniques, and wealth of experience to bear on the process. Borrowing from reception theory, she brings a "horizon of expectations," or boundary conditions, to the foundation of her work.[22] Depending on how much she knows prior to rehearsals (the script, previous experience with other members of the company, discussions at the time of casting, etc.), the performer enters alert, with an idea of the process that will be used in creating the role. In short, she does not enter as a clean slate, ready to be written upon; she enters fully engaged intellectually and emotionally, continually attentive to what is happening around her and ready to put her talents to work.

As the rehearsal begins, her attention is drawn to the work, and she becomes less aware of the general ambience of the room, focusing instead on the specifics of the task and being open to insights into the project and those with whom she is working. The initial horizon of expectations undergoes change as the process retrieves past experiences and elicits epiphanies, large and small, resulting in discoveries that are stored in memory. From the first rehearsal, if not earlier, the score begins to take shape. It is, of course, a complicated journey, involving unanticipated obstacles, dead ends, and new insights, all of which continually alter the structure of the performance. In some instances, getting an overall sense of the production structure allows the actor to proceed in breaking it down into actable beats, while in others the actor may benefit from beginning with work on specific actions, allowing the overall arc of the performance to emerge. In nontraditional forms of theatre, the evolution of form can arise from associations made between disparate and seemingly unrelated improvisations. Regardless of the approach, the end result is the same: a sequence of actions that moves according to the logic of the theatrical event. Depending on the nature of the project, as the work gradually becomes more and more specific and the general outlines are filled in with greater detail, the discoveries tend to become smaller. As the work becomes more precise and individual actions collectively define the overall trajectory of the performance, the actor gains a clearer understanding of how the pieces fit together and of her individual function in the overall production.

This is, of course, an idealized image of the process. Actors do not always get along; the director's vision may be at odds with that of the performers; weaknesses in the structure of the text or arc of the performance may require difficult compromises. Many are the potential pitfalls in creating theatre. These aberrations, as unpleasant as they may be, do not concern us here, because they do not affect the cognitive processes involved in defining the performance. The mechanics remain the same regardless of how unhappy the actors may be with the process, their own work, or the final form.

It also bears repeating that the actor's score is a very complex structure. A short list of the numerous things to which the actor must attend includes her lines, blocking, planned gestures, work with props, costumes, light, and sound; cues, rhythms (including moments of silence), tempos, arcs of intensity, phrasing, and intonation; and the intricate relationships developed with other actors, both in creating the world of the performance and in working together onstage. These relationships require attention, especially to variations in the established patterns. The cumuluative structure is accomplished with an attention capacity of four chunks of information in any given moment of the performance.

Actors know that a score is not a continuous stream of actions but that, like the multiple flashes that make up a bolt of lightning, it consists of a chain of events made up of individual beats. The actor needs a clear, well-defined, incremental sequence of actions that allows the audience to grasp the trajectory of the performance. Although the process for accomplishing this goal varies with the style of production, the development of the score needs to take place one step at a time and, as the French word for rehearsal reminds us, through repetition. The process of creating a repeatable score demands patience. An early lesson of theatre is not overloading the actor with too much information at once. She is already grappling with an immense amount of perceptual data from a number of different sources and needs to be able to focus her attention on the information relevant to the stage of the process that is immediately before her. To use Cowan's model metaphorically, a performer can only pay attention to four chunks of information at a time. In a highly dynamic situation, without a clear focus, information overload can create confusion that delays the process of learning the score. The actor needs time to understand key elements—the meaning of the play, movement phrases, what emerges from the improvisation—to make associations between them and commit that information to memory. Once the fundamental structure is understood, additional information and new connections can be made that give complexity to the action.

Sandy Meisner was known for having an actor begin a scene over and over until an entrance was made "truthfully" and with the right intensity. Beginning with an objective, a reason for going onstage, the performer identifies thoughts, emotions, and motivations that justify the action. Each repetition of the preparation, each improvisation, not only makes the act more specific, but also adds new information. What started as a single bit of data ("I enter the room because...") becomes a complex memory, inducing specific behaviors in the actor: movements, words, emotional intensities, focus, attitudes to the space and person(s) onstage. When the correct equation is found and the entrance is perceived to be truthful, the actor is expected to commit each individual element to memory. This does not, of course, guarantee that the actor will perform the equation perfectly at the next rehearsal. More likely, the action will retain some of the elements from the earlier rehearsal but lack the specificity and nuance of the previous work. The actor has to step back and renew the process of finding the elements and associations that will achieve the objective, recovering past discoveries and gaining new insights to weave into the score, eventually arriving at the point where the entrance has the desired truthfulness and is repeatable.

In committing the rehearsed action to memory, the actor takes small bits of information and consolidates them into a larger, more complex form that neuropsychologists call a "chunk." Cowan, for example, writes: "I will define the term *chunk* as a collection of concepts that have strong associations to one another."[23] It is a condensed set of memories that contain the data needed to provide focus in the present, to allow the retrieval of units of action with considerable precision, to anticipate what happens next, and to understand where she is in the overall trajectory of the performance. A chunk operates at the levels of both implicit and explicit memory; that is, it works below the level of awareness, as well as consciously. But a chunk is not a rigid set of memories. It remains dynamic: open to the integration of new material and the elimination of the old, subject to disruption by distraction. To unfold, it needs to be triggered by a perturbation that elicits the appropriate patterns of thought, emotion, and behavior at the correct moment in the performance.

A chunk is formed through processes of encoding and recoding. As we saw in the discussion on technique in the last chapter, learning involves the strengthening of connections between neurons, which is accomplished by increasing the number of synaptic clefts that allow the current to pass from one cell to the other. The stronger the neural bonds, the easier it is to retrieve the behavior they elicit. Learning a piece of an action does not mean creating a new route through the brain; it means drawing on neural associations from earlier experiences and discovering the rhythm that allows the neurons to fire in the correct sequence to repeat the action. This is *encoding,* and it is central to the creation of a score. Each approach to acting has its own starting point. For Meisner, it is the reason to enter the stage; for Michael Chekhov, it is the psychological gesture; for the early Stanislavski, it is emotional recall and for the later Stanislavski, a physical action. Initially, the starting point is relatively simple (a cross, a phrase, a motivation) and requires a considerable amount of attention.

As rehearsals proceed, connections are made between the smaller bits of action—words and movement—as they become associated with each other and *recoded*, so that a single activation will initiate the sequence of neural firings for each. Cowan describes this process as follows: "In *recoding*, information is transformed in a way that can allow improved associations...the gathering of items...into larger chunks than existed previously."[24] Recoding allows a lot more to be done with considerably less conscious effort. The process continues as more discoveries are made: through rehearsals, relationships between characters and between actors are grasped; the role of the action in the overall scheme of the production becomes clearer. These, too, are integrated, increasing the size of the chunk until what was a simple action becomes a very complex and wide-ranging conglomeration of neural patterns that allows the actor to execute a specific moment in the production.

The encoding and recoding of a chunk utilizes already existing patterns of neural networks, or techniques. Richman et al. call these configurations a *template:* "The latter patterns, gradually acquired in the course of study and play, can be called *templates* to distinguish them from the deliberately acquired retrieval structures.... Templates contain information about a familiar situation, as well as slots for new information."[25] The ability to ride a bike constitutes a template, while the particular bike, the terrain, and other environmental conditions provide the information that is inserted into the slots. Utilizing templates is not only an efficient use of neural space, but it also saves time by drawing on past experiences, allowing the actor to reuse patterns consolidated in neural networks. The value of a template is limited by its suppleness, that is, by whether or not it has sufficient flexibility to allow for the permutations required by the particular action and for the integration of different kinds of information. If the template is too rigid, the performance can appear stilted or lifeless. When open to the input of new data, the template allows that data to be fully interleaved into the action. When that happens, technique seems to disappear and the performance seems effortless, vibrant, and nuanced.

Howard Richman, James Strazewski, and Herbert Simon use the metaphor of veins in a leaf to describe how a chunk operates.[26] The nutrients enter the leaf through a single conduit that branches out across the breadth of the leaf through a series of nodes, allowing the food to reach the extreme edges. In their model of chunking (see Figure 6.1), as the unfolding of the chunk proceeds, patterns emerge that have become associated with one another through consolidation in memory. Once the process begins, a series of activations across a

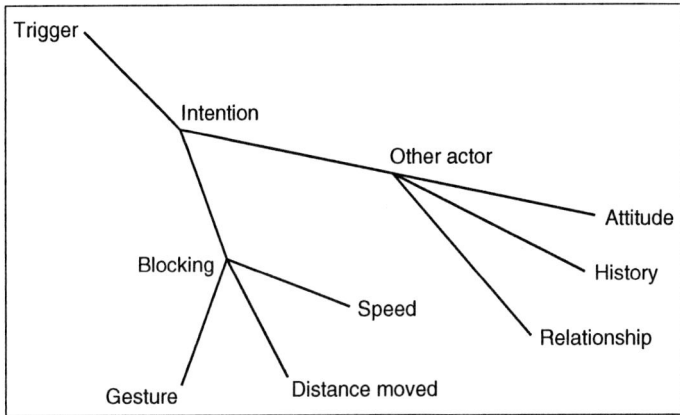

Figure 6.1 A simple model for the structuring of information in a chunk.

range of neural networks occurs more or less automatically and more or less simultaneously. Keep in mind that this diagram is extremely simple, and the number of nodes affected by the initiation of the actor's beat can be significantly greater than two. Moreover, rather than separate lines going to a single location, they can resonate with one another across more than one network and aid in the retrieval of memories that lead to specific behaviors.

The performance of a chunk of the score depends on its being triggered or, to use a word favored by psychologists, *primed*. There are many different kinds of primes, but they all function to start the process by which memories—in this instance a piece of the score—are brought to mind and the associated activities performed. An action can be triggered by cues that are external (what another actor says or does) or self-generated ("As I cross to x, I say y"). Each trigger will unpack the chunk, bringing into the actor's attention smaller bits of information that perform the action. As one bit is expressed, it will move out of attention, to be replaced by another.[27] As the chunk is played out, one bit of information will cue the next bit, leading to the unpacking of the next chunk of the score.

In the course of developing the score, the actor may supplant one trigger with another for the same action. Every approach to acting provides different methods for identifying the initial prime. Michael Chekhov uses the psychological gesture. Sandy Meisner focuses on the motivation to enter the scene. Brecht, the gestus; Grotowski, the physical action; and so forth. This does not mean that when an actor comes to that moment in the performance, that specific trigger will be used. A prime that is effective at an early stage of rehearsal can be replaced by one or more primes better suited to the complexity of the recoded chunk. For example, an initial chunk may consist of a crouching actor standing up. Through rehearsal, this elementary action can become an act of defiance as a motivation is assigned to the movement and linked to a specific dynamic (perhaps strong and quick, perhaps slow and forceful), associating it with what another character is doing and linking it to specific words. The act that initiates the unfolding (i.e., standing up) may continue to be that trigger, or it could be replaced by a specific word, the movement of another actor, or any number of possible alternatives. Chekhov's psychological gesture might be replaced as a prime by more immediate demands of the scene. This does not mean the gesture is forgotten; it will continue to be a significant part of the chunk, but it will no longer be the primary key to the unfolding of that beat. Triggers that are externally motivated may include another actor's words, movements, or gesture; they may also include a change in the environment, such as a change in lighting, sound, or set, or the length of the audience's laughter. Self-cuing can come from the lines or blocking or from a sense of how long a pause or the duration of silence should be prior to beginning a new beat (as in the works of Samuel Beckett, Harold Pinter, Sarah Kane, or Franz Xaver Kroetz, as well as in many forms of postdramatic theatre).

It is also conceivable that a chunk has multiple primes, most of which may occur without conscious awareness. In fact, it is probable that when the actor hears the appropriate cue, of which she is conscious, the chunk is already unfolding. This is the basis of Eugenio Barba's concept of "sats." Like many of Barba's terms, the concept does not have a precise definition. On the one hand, it appears to denote a moment of stasis: "to be ready for action, on the verge of producing work." On the other, it seems to denote a dynamic state: "It is a small charge of energy which causes the action to change its course and intensity or suddenly suspends it. It is a moment of transition which leads to a new, precise posture, and thus to a change in the tonus of the entire body."[28] He does not locate the sats at the beginning of a line or when a cross is initiated, but at the moment when the next action is motivated. Barba's point in developing the concept of sats is that an actor needs to begin her preparation for an action before the cue arrives; that is, she must be aware of the dynamics, so that the body is ready when the beat begins to unfold. Implicit is the recognition that the actor never stops, even when immobile, but is continually and dynamically engaged in the process of acting. In everyday life, we usually know what we are going to say before we have an opportunity to say it. We wait, however, until it is our turn to speak; or when we interrupt our interlocutor, we act intentionally based on an idea of what we want to say, even though the precise words have not yet been formulated. It begins with a "change in the tonus of the entire body." An actor waiting for the precise moment to begin to move is already behind. Actually beginning to speak or move has more to do with the rhythm of the performance (the pattern of pauses, silences, and their absence) than with the initiation of an action, because when it is time to act, the unfolding has already begun.

A final dynamic of a chunk is that it carries the seeds of the next beat. A key to a repeatable performance is the actor's ability to have a peripheral awareness of what happens next at the same time that she is focused on the present action. It is possible that this anticipation occurs when another chunk is brought into the circle of attention, but it would be more efficient if the identity of the next trigger—if not the trigger itself—were included in the patterns that arise when a prime initiates the action.

Continuity in the unfolding of a chunk is maintained through two different processes. One directs the attention of the actor to the focal point for receiving the next cue; the other process is reactivation or looping. In the performance of a beat, there is, one might say, an absence or a space that has to be filled. The actor knows what is needed—the line, movement, gesture, or other cue—and prepares for the moment by activating the next chunk(s) of memory without bringing them to conscious attention until the trigger is pulled. The prime then brings the appropriate unit into focus and initiates a playing out of the remembered action. The second mode involves the continuation of certain patterns from one chunk to the next. Once the task associated with a particular beat is completed and another is triggered, certain resonances from the first action will be reactivated in the second, providing a sense of continuity. The first entrance of a character will be broken into specific activities that change from beat to beat, but the overall action, the reason for entering, will be looped from chunk to chunk until the unit of action is completed. Once brought into the circle of attention, Cowan explains, "it stays activated for a short period of time (e.g. 2 to 30 sec), decaying from activation unless it is reactivated during that period through additional, related stimulus presentations or thought processes."[29] In the production I was in, Granpa Joad's first entrance with Granma begins with an offstage shout, a rush onto the stage, nudging Granma out of the way and moving toward center stage until stopping when he sees his grandson. While my attention needed to be on the specific bits of performance, I nevertheless continued to be aware of the why of the movements. Pulling up abruptly and seeing Tommy "for the first time" triggers the next sequence of actions; it draws the next chunk into the circle of attention.

In this way, the beats are combined into units of action. As the rehearsals proceed, these larger structures become more complex through the addition of information about the scene and through recoding. As the opening approaches, if all is going well, the actor gains a sense of how the pieces fit together, forming the overall trajectory of the performance. This understanding of the event serves as an ideal, against which the performer evaluates how each piece fits into the arc of action and through which she sees how effectively each segment communicates. This is where good directors are invaluable. When looking at the larger picture, the actor loses the details of each beat; while performing small bits of action, she cannot possibly see accurately how each moment fits into the production. The director identifies areas that need further development and provides positive feedback when the work is going well. Through the process of reinforcing and disrupting patterns, the beats become more precise, and the actor incorporates into the structure benchmarks that allow her to self-evaluate and know when the unfolding of the action is working. When a chunk is brought into attention, it brings with it memories of past performances of the action that serve as boundary conditions, framing the patterns that emerge and therefore the precision with which the behavior needs to be enacted onstage. It is because of the vagaries of dynamic systems and acting that the emerging patterns are seldom if ever identical in form or quality from one performance to the next.

To summarize, a prime brings a chunk into attention, setting in motion a process that activates attractors and boundary conditions associated with a specific action. The more frequently the behavior is rehearsed (both in theatrical terms and in memory consolidation), the greater the number of synaptic connections among the affected neurons and the more easily the behavior is retrieved. What began as a significant phase transition in the early stages of work becomes increasingly habitual and more precise, and therefore less energy is required to bring it into the performance. This process necessitates continual encoding and recoding, consolidating bits of information into larger chunks as a single action is mapped across a number of different neural networks. As the action unfolds, some of the data are directed toward new behaviors, and some reactivate information that is still needed to provide the performer with continuity. Finally, the patterns that emerge from the unfolding prepare the actor for the next action, either by providing a trigger that brings the next chunk into attention or by warning her to be on the lookout for a prime from the environment.

The elements that make up a chunk can be held in attention for a relatively short period of time (roughly two to thirty seconds), after which the chunk decays and is replaced by another. Actors know that very few, if any, beats will last for thirty seconds. Scores consist of much shorter acts, because the change between one action and the next helps to sustain the performer's attention, requires her to remember less at any one moment, and keeps her focused on the action yet aware of what is happening onstage. The more concise each action is, the more likely it is to be repeated precisely, rendering the overall performance effective. Through the reactivation of information, the actor is able to cluster beats (a few bits of memory) into longer sequences or units of action. The rhythms between clustered chunks varies, but the movement from one to the next stresses continuity, and changes between units mark breaks in the score. The process of unfolding is the same regardless, but the audience will experience considerable variation according to the changes in behavior. The singers performing Glass's music in *Einstein on the Beach,* focusing on the rhythms in one section, experienced a decided change when the counts per measure shifted. The audience also felt the shift, although less dramatically because the ear registered only an incremental change. In most narrative performances, the spectators' experience of the movement from one unit to another is going to be equally subtle; at moments of higher tension, the breaks are more clearly marked. These differences are all encoded in the chunk, which directs the focus of the actor and defines the dynamics of her physical expression.

Intentional Forgetting

The development of an acting score is a winding path, entailing many wrong turns and dead ends before a "final" version is adopted. It is not always evident from the outset which set of actions is going to best suit the final performance. An actor may orient the work in a particular direction for a number of rehearsals before deciding or being told that a specific choice is not working. Prior to the shift in direction (e.g., motivation, physical action, line reading), the preliminary pattern is going to be consolidated in long-term memory. The more frequently it is rehearsed, the stronger the synaptic connections that associate a specific behavior to a given prime and, as you might expect, the more difficult it is to change the score. Actors working on new plays, for instance, are generally not pleased when they are given significant amounts of new material during previews. They not only have to learn the new text, but they also have to make adjustments to the score, changing the patterns of cues, motivations, character relationships, etc. Learning a new way of limping, as Granpa Joad, required significant adjustments beyond the physical movement, as it gave the character a very different energy and influenced his attitudes across a number of dimensions.

Scientists initially thought that "reversal learning" (replacing one set of memories with another) involved remembering new patterns while allowing existing memories to decay. They thought it was "use it or lose it." Recent work by faculty at University of California, Los Angeles (UCLA) indicates that intentional forgetting involves two distinct processes: the suppression of one pattern and the learning of another.[30] The work further indicates that these processes depend on a cooperative interaction between specific parts of the brain, on the one hand facilitating the recognition and repetition required for learning new information and on the other stopping the retrieval of certain memories.[31] Thus there are two active processes, rather than just one. It seems, in short, that decay is too slow a process, and without suppression, there would be interference with any attempt to retrieve the new material. While new patterns are being committed to memory, those they replace are being inhibited.

If it were merely a semiconscious process, the act of suppressing one action while learning another would not seem particularly difficult. A chunk, however, is a pattern of attractors and boundary conditions that are interwoven into complex forms. There is a ripple effect when new material is introduced into a score. On the surface, changing Granpa Joad's limp merely involved a new way of moving the body, but it had ramifications that reached far beyond a different application of physical technique. The change affected the energy with which the character engaged the rest of the family, setting new tempos and rhythms, and the way he interacted with them. It did not, however, change everything. Some of the work done earlier continued to be useful and was maintained in the restructured score; only some of the patterns encoded and recoded during earlier rehearsals were suppressed. The process of learning new actions involves discriminating between what needs to be inhibited and what continues to be facilitated. This includes defining the data to be reactivated when moving from one chunk to another to provide continuity.

A recent study indicates that where an actor places her attention can have a positive effect on changing memory patterns. Subjects were able to retrieve already learned material by "directing attention toward internally represented associations."[32] In more familiar terms, the actor attends to the "interior monologue," the sequence of primes, chunks, and reactivated material that "re-mind" her of the next words, gestures, movements, and emotional links in the score. In reversal learning, subjects "deliberately focus attention on the external environment."[33] The shift in focus seems to interrupt existing patterns, allowing specific aspects to be inhibited and, with time, leading to the atrophy of existing synaptic connections. Focusing outside herself forces the actor to concentrate on changes and the effect they have on other actors while identifying those aspects of a chunk that need to be preserved. The patterns of behavior that need to be forgotten may be "pushed out" of the circle of attention. As new triggers are identified and linked to actions that are consolidated in memory, the need to inhibit the discarded pieces of the score decreases, allowing the actor to return her attention to the newly modified internal monologue. This does not mean, of course, that the actor ever loses sight of what is happening around her. The score provides cues to direct her attention to specific locations in the environment that contain the prime for the next unfolding of the action. This is the subject of the next and final chapter, where we look at the actor in performance.

The Actor's Score—Redux

An actor's score is a dynamic system within a dynamic system. It is never set in concrete but is always open to the integration of new material and the potential for forgetting, intentional or not. In the primes that retrieve memorized bits of business, reactivate material that provides continuity, and direct attention to the next chunk in the sequence are the triggers that bring into play attractors and boundary conditions, giving rise to emerging patterns of behavior. The novelty that once gave rise to the instability of a phase transition is transformed through repetition into a retrievable, recognizable pattern that can be performed, for all practical purposes, in a stable field. The actor can expect with relative certainty that if the triggers are attended to and attention is focused on the specific steps in the sequence, the performance will unfold as rehearsed.

Nevertheless, performing the score is surrounded by uncertainty. Each beat can elicit emotions and thoughts not encoded in the action, because influences in the environment—proprioceptive and perceptual—define the state of play at any particular moment. Performing the score is also affected by data that unexpectedly manifests despite being suppressed or peripheral to the primary focus of the action. There are moments when attention fails, an unhappy compromise rears its ugly head, or distraction breaks the smooth flow of the score. At those moments, the performer needs to redouble her attention to the specific demands of the next beat to ensure that the unfolding maintains the integrity of the rehearsed sequence. She needs to call on the techniques, which are boundary conditions, learned through years of training and practice to allow her to relax into the moment and regain the composure that comes from confidence in the validity of the work that has been done.

If this discussion has been too narrowly focused on the internal processes of creating a score, it is because the score forms a system of signposts that the actor depends on to navigate the trajectory of the performance no matter what arises. It should be clear by now, however, that there is no score without the performer's embodied interaction with the environment—other actors, directors and dramaturgs, the dynamics of space, and the technologies of theatre. The sequence of events is developed through an active engagement with the dynamic system of rehearsed patterns and perturbations from the rehearsal environment. With this understanding of the actor's preparation, we may turn at last to the performance itself.

Chapter 7

In Performance

> *In this we can recognize a recipe for a dialectic: sign and image are inseparable and jointly form a context to dwell in; the two combine to create the possibility of shared states of cognitive being.... The communication process is then getting the Other to dwell there too.*
> —David McNeill[1]

Public performance is not the sine qua non of theatre. Grotowski, in the last stage of his research, was only interested in work that delved continually deeper into the creative process. While he may never have reached the moment that Artaud calls the "one unique expression which must have been the equivalent of spiritualized gold," the quest was sufficiently compelling for Grotowski that he made it the focus of his life's work without the expectation of performance.[2] Nevertheless, it is safe to say that most actors want to perform before an audience. I directed Peter Nichols' *A Day in the Life of Joe Egg* in San Antonio, Texas, only to have the theatre close its doors the night before opening. We all felt an immense loss at not being able to take our work to the final step. The presence of an audience adds a dimension that makes the experience feel complete.

There are, of course, personal reasons for wanting someone outside the company to see the performance. Actors desire validation, the recognition that their work is good and the overall production effective. The gratification of audience applause justifies the time and effort spent in rehearsal; and for professional companies, a positive critical response provides hope that bread will continue to appear on the table and a pension will be available in later years. For some actors, this may be sufficient, but to sustain a life in the theatre through fertile and fallow periods, something more is needed. The statement from David McNeill that opens this chapter speaks to this other need, which is to create a world in which the spectators and performers dwell together. This chapter explores how actors, by engaging other performers onstage, create an event that allows the audience to participate actively in the creation of a possible world that potentially transcends its expectations.

This line of argument is not meant as an addition to or distraction from the work on reception and theorizing the spectator, such as that undertaken so provocatively by Herbert Blau in *The Audience*. The focus here remains, as it has throughout the book, on the experience of the actor. While, for the sake of argument, it is possible to differentiate technique from improvisation and creating a score, it is virtually impossible to make such distinctions at the moment of performance. In fact, this chapter argues that the performer, as a dynamic system, continually uses technique and improvisation in the unfolding of the score during the act of performing; and that acting is the interaction among different dynamic systems, including the other performers and the audience. The discussion begins with the performer in space, followed by the interaction between actors, and concludes with engaging the spectator.

The Actor in Space

The pictorial stage draws lines through space, while the simple stage is drawn in breath through time.
—Hollis Huston[3]

Warm-ups

The traditional theatre is spatially divided for the actors and the audience. Each space is divided into three parallel areas. First, the entryway—the theatre door or stage door—marks the difference between the everyday and the theatrical experience. Second, the space of performance divides the house, for the spectators, from the stage, for the actors. In addition there are transitional areas, the lobby and surrounds where the audience unconsciously prepares to see the show and the dressing rooms and backstage where the actors prepare to perform the show. Entering the theatre provides the opportunity to forget the tribulations of the day and anticipate the evening's events. Conversations about what has happened intermingle with thoughts about the performance. Audiences discuss what is known about the play, and read the program; actors apply makeup, check props, do physical and vocal warm-ups. The collective focus becomes sharper as the lights dim, cell phones are turned off, and the stage manager calls everyone to their places. One side of the footlights prepares to receive, while the other readies to deliver. In nontraditional performances, the three spaces will vary depending on the scenario, whether, for example, the spectator happens to be viewing a mime in Battery Park or diners have their meals disrupted, unaware that Boal is serving them invisible theatre when a loud discussion erupts in the restaurant. The spaces remain the same, however, for the performer who puts aside the concerns of the day, prepares for what is to happen, and makes it work. The difference is significant. For the audience, the theatre is a special event, something out of the ordinary; for the actor, it is a continuation of everyday life. The audience hopes to see something that transcends their expectations; the performer prepares to equal or improve the previous night's presentation.

Actors score their preparations almost as precisely as they do their performance. They establish a routine that unfolds as they move from space to space: signing in, changing into warm-up clothes, stretching, vocalizing, checking props, putting on makeup, getting notes, donning the costume, and taking places are all linked to specific locations. The space itself provides the perceptual information needed to retrieve the patterns of behavior that allow the performer to feel at ease and work through her preparations. The unfolding can become almost sacrosanct, and an actor can become irritated if she isn't able to follow her routine. The irritation is not necessarily a sign of being temperamental; it may be a recognition that each step must be accomplished if the actor is to be physically and psychologically ready to perform. The preparation mirrors the performance. Going step by step through the warm-up is roughly parallel to the unfolding onstage. In so preparing, the actor follows a set sequence of activities that implicitly initiates the performance of the score.

When places are called and the beginning of the performance approaches, the actor's frame of mind shifts from getting ready to the specific demands of the first beats and units of the score. Whether it is on a Meisner preparation or a Chekhovian psychological gesture or simply on thinking through the blocking, the focus is narrowed, the cue to enter anticipated, the energy heightened. This is a transitional psychological space that separates the generic stages of getting ready from the specific unfolding of the score. Noh actors prepare to enter the stage by contemplating the mask, or character, they are playing that day. At the appropriate time, they walk across the Hashigakari—a bridge between offstage and the main stage—to begin the performance. The Western theatre does not have this defined liminal space between offstage and on, marking the move from one world to the next. But an experienced actor understands the change that takes place between preparing to enter the space of performance and beginning to act. The difference is actually little more than a shift in perspective—the focus on getting ready is redirected to being in the moment of the score—but the alteration is significant. Entering the stage requires Barba's extra-daily energy, because the intensity with which the performer enters the theatre is not adequate either in focus or force to the intensity onstage.

As there are techniques for performing the score, so there are techniques that prepare the actor to enter the stage. By undertaking exercises that focus on movement, language (text and voice), gesture, memory, attention, and executive control (the tools discussed in chapter 3), the actor creates within herself the appropriate balance between the contradictory elements of relaxation and tension, producing the focus and intensity necessary to communicate the role to the audience. If the preparation has been successful, the actor is already engaged in the performance when the cue comes and she crosses the boundary onto the stage.

The performer, readying herself for the evening, engages two spaces: the physical and the metaphysical. The first refers to the rooms in which the preparations take place. The latter defines the movement from an introspective process of getting the instrument ready to externally directed full engagement in performing. Once onstage, this phenomenological bifurcation of space continues.

Negotiating the Mise-en-Scène

Stepping onto the stage involves a split in the dynamics of attention between what can be called image mapping and world making. The space—defined by the landscape of ramps, stairs, and platforms, objects, light, and sound—is a map the actor negotiates. Provided the rehearsal process was successful, the actor follows set cues to move to a relatively precise place onstage at a defined tempo and with a set physicality (Granpa Joad has a limp). Moving to the designated location is further subdivided. The performer is aware not only of the spot on the stage to which she must move, but also of her relationship to other characters and objects; she attends to the spatial relationship between performers in order to create the desired image, such as being in the light, standing, or kneeling, etc. The actor is cognizant of the picture being presented to the audience and of her function in creating it.

Adjustments need to be made if an object is in the wrong place—the chair is farther upstage than it should be—or another actor is moving farther downstage left than usual. These subtle and not-so-subtle shifts disrupt the patterns that compose the chunk of the score being acted, requiring the performer to decide how best to adjust to the changes. Does she get the chair and move it to the correct location? Does she move farther onstage to maintain the relationship defined during rehearsals, or does she stay in the designated spot until her partner returns to the agreed-upon blocking? These disruptions attract new data, whether from environmental perceptions and proprioceptions or from memories of previous experiences, into the circle of attention. As this information is integrated into working memory, the patterns elicited by the blocking template are adjusted. Depending on the authority the actor has to alter the score in the flow of the performance, she may respond conservatively, following the agreed-upon movements, as in Robert Wilson's *Einstein on the Beach,* or go with the changes, allowing the direction of the performance to vary widely. Comedy improvisations depend on this degree of freedom, as do performances such as The Living Theatre's *Paradise Now.*

Whereas image mapping is technical in nature, world making takes place in an interactive environment that is brought into being by the performance of the character or role through actions and activities. It involves creating a mood through emotional intensity, delivery of lines, gesture, and quality of movement. It also evokes a line of thought in the audience that allows its members to generate meaning. The actor is aware of internal states, facial expression, physical urgency (or lack thereof), and how these qualities define the empathetic and ideological dimensions of the space as the world of the production. If mapping is the drawing of lines in pictorial space, world making is what causes the space to breathe, giving vibrancy to the event. Whereas creating images stops time so that the audience can gain insight into the relations that exist in the stage picture, the evocation of the world of the play is temporal, using rhythm to modify the dynamics of the production. Vanessa Redgrave, playing Mary Tyrone in Eugene O'Neill's *Long Day's Journey into Night,* reaches up the wall bringing time to a halt, and through the intensity of extending the arm to reach yet further up, she creates an image of the physical agony of drug addiction in the stifling confines of a family's summer home. The arm comes down, and time begins again as she moves toward the staircase in search of another fix.

This dual focus in the actor is not an absolute split. It is rather the unfolding of a chunk of the score that intertwines memories of spatial location with the quality of movement in order to create a space that is at once material and metaphysical, a materiality that is at once real and illusory. For the actor, the creation of the illusion is the effect of performing the sequence of events with technical expertise and an intensity that mirrors that of everyday life, but at a pitch that communicates beyond the limits of the stage space.

Beyond the Footlights

The space of performance varies considerably from the traditional proscenium to thrust and round, from thousand-seat auditoriums to forty-seat ones. Performances can take place in gymnasiums, art galleries, churches, abandoned factories, unused hospitals, or any number of outside locations. The lighting may obscure the recesses of the hall, or the space might be completely illuminated. The actor may be confined to the limits of the stage, or she may be able to utilize the house for entrances and exits or to engage the audience. On those occasions when the actor ventures into the house, she is, of course, aware of the dimensions of the theatre; but even when confined to the stage, she is always aware, at least peripherally, of the volume in which the production is taking place.

Strasberg's introspective approach to acting had some of its greatest successes in film. The camera's capacity to focus the spectator on the face of the character, along with the size of the projected image, frees the performer from having to enhance emotions. As the saying goes: If you feel it, the camera will pick it up. Performing in the theater is a very different experience. Depending on the volume of the space, the effort needed to communicate with spectators in the furthest reaches of the upper balcony varies greatly. It takes an experienced actor to evaluate how large a gesture needs to be, particularly in realism. In a large theatre, a simple movement needs to be readable from a distance and yet still appear natural. Mary Tyrone reaching up the wall or, in *The Three Sisters,* Tusenbach standing for seconds with arms fully extended, reaching out to Irina on the other side of the stage needs to be justified psychologically and sustained long enough to create the desired impact. An early lesson in the technique of gesture is that every hand movement needs to extend beyond the fingertips, as if the energy were being released into the farthest reaches of the spectator's space. The larger the theatre, the bigger the gesture and the fuller the energy expended in making it need to be.

Audibility is also an issue, particularly in an age when architects of theatres (as opposed to theatre architects) seem incapable of taking acoustics into consideration. Unless the actors are wearing hidden microphones—an increasingly common and unfortunate development—the techniques of vocal projection are crucial to the success of the performance, with respect not only to filling large spaces but also to not overpowering smaller venues. A different range of problems is encountered in outdoor performances, where there are competing sounds and varying acoustic circumstances, from the excellence of ancient Greek theatres to the streets of major cities or public parks. If actors are not aware of the subtle and not-so-subtle differences, the effectiveness of the performance can be diminished, if not lost altogether.

Every space has different dynamics, which inevitably require adjustments by the performers. This is particularly evident in the move from the rehearsal room to the theatre. Although actors are aware of the differences they will experience, they develop patterns in the course of rehearsing that are inevitably influenced by the size, lighting, and acoustics of the room. Relationships with other characters and their performers, intimate explorations, movements, and gestures that make sense in one space will get lost in another. When entering the theatre in which they will perform for the first time, actors take time to look out into the house, testing the acoustic qualities and exploring the different sensations of the movement patterns as experienced in the new space. Similar effects are investigated during technical rehearsals. With new input, it is difficult to focus attention on the patterns that have been developed during rehearsals, because different lights, sounds, and spatial relations are being incorporated into the score. The better the technical staff is at supplying the correct cues at the right time and the greater the theatre experience of the actor, the more likely the transition will be painless. Regardless, it is a period of adjustment, and it always takes time at a moment in the process when time is a precious commodity.

If space is the container, whether speaking of volumes of light or sound or the architecture of the theatre, it is the interactions between the actors that fill it.

Actors Acting

Context makes, selects, and adapts knowledge in our dynamic systems theory because knowledge is only made manifest in a real-time task.
—Esther Thelan and Linda Smith[4]

The actor's score is codified in memory and retrieved in chunks that are playable during the course of the performance and whose qualities are layered. The fundamental stratum is the sequence of actions manifest in movement, language, and gesture that, if well enacted, evoke thoughts and emotions in the spectator. Eliciting these effects is the desired end of acting, but it is a subsidiary concern at the moment of performance. The focus then is on the unfolding of the beats and units, whether as a character in realism or a performer in a postdramatic piece. A performance that consists simply of carrying out a series of commands is seldom interesting or engaging. As we saw in chapter 6, the creation of a score involves a linking of actions that is tied to an internal logic, however unreasoned. This logic defines an intensity and focus that require a considerable expenditure of energy and a precision in the unfolding of beats. Each step in the playing of the score draws on feelings and thoughts associated with a specific action and on communication with other performers, objects, or the self (in the case of a mime, for instance). These different strata of performance are all part of the score and occur in a cued sequence with a prime that activates the retrieval process. There is a mutual dependence between the layers. Attractors and boundary conditions are brought into working memory; they drive the patterns of behavior in all their richness and complexity.

The actor knows, however, that there is no guarantee that once retrieved, the units will unfold in the intended manner. The score, regardless of the precision with which it has been committed to memory, remains dynamic. The potential for disruptions requires a split focus on the part of the performer. To avoid deviations in the performance, a significant portion of the performer's attention is paid to the specific and overall movement of the score, that is, on the benchmarks set in rehearsal to evaluate her relative position to others in the space, to recall the next series of words and movements, and to measure the trajectory of shifting intensities that make up the rhythms of the performance. Attention also needs to be paid to the external environment, wherefrom the performer anticipates cues—such as another actor's lines, a change in lighting, or a sound effect—and follows the work of the other actors in the unfolding of the score.

When the pattern is disturbed, whether by a failure in attention or an error outside the performer's control, the actor's focus shifts to resolving the conflict and returning to the sequences that form the score. Provided that the disruption is not catastrophic so as to destroy the actor's concentration, she seeks to bridge the gap between the chunk of the score currently active in working memory and the elements in that network of memories that anticipate the next in the sequence. If the actor is open to the possibilities of the moment, a number of associations, active but outside the circle of attention, will be present, from which an alternative can be found to restore order. If the event forces the score out of the actor's circle of attention, it will be more difficult to find the associations that will resolve the problem, because the frame of reference for evaluating options is missing. The performer needs to refocus her attention on the appropriate section of the score, so a decision can be made that allows the show to continue. The more expert the actor, the less likely her focus and concentration will be lost and, when a disturbance is experienced, the more easily her performance is returned to the right track.

The actor, attending to the external environment, is not waiting for mistakes to happen; rather, she is open to variations, however subtle, in the work of the actors with whom she interacts. Attention to the work of others is not naive, but comes with boundary conditions; the history of work on a particular section and attractors are cues a performer looks for in preparation for the next beat in the score. Within this structure, there is time for the performer to attend to the intangible qualities of overall performance. This is, to a certain extent, what makes acting the same role night after night interesting and keeps the performance from becoming monotonous. Variations can give rise to fresh associations, which add nuance to the acting. The use of the word *fresh* is intentional. Not every difference is going to be new, but each may implicitly remind the actor of a previous moment in the process of preparing and presenting the show, thereby sparking a slightly different intensity or modulation of the action. Such variations may not happen every evening; the challenge is to be ready for them when they do.

Thus far the discussion has revolved around the single actor as a dynamic system. She contains in memory the patterns of performance that have been established through the rehearsal process. These are complex structures of attractors and boundary conditions that include lines, movement, gestures, links to emotions, cues for future actions, relationships with the space, objects, and other actors, and connections that draw on a history of personal experiences, techniques, and value systems. The unfolding of this structure is fueled by a will to perform, which depends on the intricate web of psychological and material reasons that cause a person to want to act. It is not a closed system, however, and the possibility of performing depends on a number of signals from the external environment that it is time to prepare for the show and then to undertake its performance. This process may begin with the ringing of the alarm clock and the recognition that today the show goes on. Hovering in the background for most of the day, it becomes more and more the focus of attention as curtain time approaches and the routine preparations are engaged that ready the actor to go onstage. None of these are done in isolation. The actor is continually responding to changes in the environment caused by herself and other forces (the air-conditioning is broken and the warm-up room is like an oven; another actor is sick and his understudy is going on, etc.). Each set of perceptual data reinforces or disrupts the process of getting ready and requires different kinds of responses (some habitual, some drawing on different sets of memories, others novel). Regardless, patterns of behavior emerge that allow the actor to resolve the intrusion on the preparations with greater or lesser angst and to be ready when the next cue arrives.

Actors generally perform with other actors, and as the number of people onstage increases, the performance becomes more complex. Each member of the cast is a dynamic system, undertaking the unfolding of a score and responding to changes in the environment. The challenge for the performers and the director is to intertwine the various energies, for lack of a better word, into an ensemble, wherein each person contributes to the whole by playing her part and being attuned to changes in the environment. Achieving this objective depends in part on the level of trust that exists between the members of the cast. The following discussion about creating a harmonious conjunction among dynamic systems begins with an example in which the need for trust seems less important, then progresses to more complex interactions between performers.

Ensemble Acting

> *Because for the first time, through the other body, I see that, in its coupling with the flesh of the world, the body contributes more than it receives, adding to the world that I see the treasure necessary for what the other body sees.*
>
> —Maurice Merleau-Ponty[5]

The actors who work with Eugenio Barba develop the score for an action in relative isolation. He encourages performers to create work out of impulses that arise from "the actor's personal and professional history."[6] Performances consist of the director (Barba) juxtaposing and manipulating the work of several actors based on an intuition and curiosity about the images the combination will create:

> The actor's form is a material with which the director can work according to a dramaturgical need: he can enlarge, minimize, frame, mount various materials, and rotate them like in the editing of a film montage. He can add scenography, costumes, light, and sound as the occasion requires. This presupposes that the actor is able to preserve his original form...[7]

The actors focus on the precise unfolding of their sequences, but are also aware of the work of others. Sensitivity to what is taking place in the space alters the performances in subtle and not so subtle ways as they respond to changing spatial and physical relationships and to different vocalizations (words, songs, vocal rhythms). Distances between actors cause changes in movement patterns; pitches and rhythms are modified to create harmonies or disharmonies in response to the work of the other performers. Recognition of coincidental relationships between performances can develop briefly and disappear, continue for an extended period of time, or not happen at all.

The established patterns in the performances of the other actors may cause disturbances that the actor is not consciously aware of, subliminally catching her attention. Responding to these changes introduces new information that is reflected in the feelings of the performer. Changes in the dynamics of one artist affect the others, creating cycles of mutual influence throughout the performance, and an interconnectedness emerges that was not initially present. The unfolding of the score is altered despite the fact that the primary focus is on the precise performance of the preestablished sequence. The score, the equivalent of a template in working memory, can accommodate new data, allowing for the emergence of new patterns or associations. As the bicycle rider responds to changes in surface (pavement to gravel, for instance) with minimal consciousness, the performer adjusts to changes in the performance environment. This is the defining quality of an expert: to adapt to changing circumstances through improvisations that draw on implicit memories of past experience. The expert performer is able to adjust to changes in the field without deliberation, intuitively.

Barba is a good example, because his work depends on the distinction between a rigorously defined sequence of actions and the improvisation that occurs simultaneously. The clarity of the differentiation between the two aspects of the performance does not mean it is a simple form. It is perhaps more difficult, because the score created does not have the anticipation of another's actions woven into it until late in the process. The split focus between the unfolding of the sequence and an awareness of what is happening in the performance space is more acute than in traditional theatre performances. (Although, in light of the experimental nature of the work, there may be greater tolerance for missteps than there is in work that is tightly choreographed.) These qualities exist in all types of theatre performances, whether realistic, nonrealistic or postdramatic, although the balance between them will change.

When Deborah Mayo opens herself to the performance of other actors (see chapter 5), she is sensitive to the effect her actions have on them and which theirs have on her. She is aware, though not in these terms, that her behavior has the potential for provoking the creative process: for example, causing a phase transition that alters others' patterns of behavior and opening herself to new associations that reinforce or change her acting score. In other words, by accommodating the efforts of others, her work can be enriched and more clearly defined. This is the nature of reciprocation. Being open to the environment and what happens in it, she can exert an influence over it, however benign. In time and through repetition, the information gleaned from working with others is woven into the fabric of the score. These memories allow her and the other actors to anticipate what happens next in the performance.

The actors become interdependent, counting on consistency in the attention to detail and the belief that what they do onstage supports one another, at least for the moment. After the rehearsal, there may be a discussion about what happened, or they may work on a particular section. Running a scene again allows them to make the score specific and to consolidate it in memory. The interaction also improves communication, as they discuss what works or what could work if something were done differently. If the conversation is constructive, a bond of trust will develop among the performers: the focus on the sequence of events includes the mutual understanding that all are aware and open to the unfolding of the score and that each has the right to express the emotions and thoughts that attend it.

For performers, *how* it is done is as important as what is done. The score consists of complex actions and is not simply a list of cues, movement patterns, lines, and objectives. The score contains triggers that elicit emotions, defining the intensity of feeling with which the actions are carried out, including implicit memories that enrich without the performer needing to be consciously aware that they are taking place. Some triggers will be self-generated, as in a soliloquy or solo performance; others will be felt in response to what another actor does, whether it is an intensity, a movement, a gesture, or an expression. Without these keys, the action in a sequence can happen, but the underlying complexity may be lost. The success of the work depends on the mutual belief between actors that they will perform well. In a worst-case scenario, going onstage and encountering the same unyielding expression night after night makes it difficult to generate the necessary energy. A spark that gives life to the relationship is missing, and the actor is limited to her own resources to create the necessary intensity. The show will continue, but the connection between the characters and actors is lost. When, alternatively, there is attentive reciprocity—openness to the nuances of the performance and the affective state of the others onstage—a mutually reinforcing relationship between performers becomes possible, and it gives vitality to the acting of the scores. It is in such moments that the power of the performance, Stanislavski's "living human spirit," becomes evident.

Creating the "living human spirit" is not, of course, the end of all performances. It is anathema for Brecht, who felt that the concept of spirit is what gets in the way of the audience using their critical intelligence; absurdist plays, such as Eugene Ionesco's *The Bald Soprano*, show how everyday life is devoid of spirit; the communication between the Stones in Sarah Ruhl's *Eurydice* depends on the *lack* of emotional connection, and the same can be said of Sara Kane's *4:48 Psychosis*. Oscar Wilde's *The Importance of Being Earnest* loses its humor if the focus is placed on creating emotional connections between the actors. The same is true of the postdramatic, from Robert Wilson's cool neoexpressionism to the rage of Reza Abdoh and the clowning of Bill Irwin in *The Regard of Flight*. These performances are by no means devoid of emotion or life, as some critics of nonrealistic forms assert. If there is a living actor onstage, there is going to be emotion. Performing, regardless of form, elicits all sorts of emotional responses in the actor, from anxiety to joy. It is part of who we are as animate beings to be continually and inextricably responsive to the environment in which we live and breathe.

Performances that do not focus on the emotional connection between characters and actors nevertheless rely on reciprocal interaction. Two performers in Wilson's *Einstein on the Beach* go through a sequence of movements punctuated by short, sharp sounds. The scene is set behind bars, and the costumes are stereotypical, cartoon-worthy prison clothes. There is, however, no narrative, nothing to affirm that the two are prisoners. Instead the characters go through a series of gestures and semigymnastic movements, keeping to a precise timing: "one-and-two-and..." A hand comes up on six; on the "and" after seven, the head turns to the right. In *The Making of Einstein on the Beach,* the actors discuss with one another the most efficient way for the woman to move her body from a sitting position to lying rigidly across the lap of the man, her body wrapped around his.[8] Each of these elements is part of a score that is repeated during each performance. It requires total concentration on the part of the actors, both in the counting of beats and in the timing of movements, to insure precision and the illusion of effortlessness.

In *Book of the Dead (2nd Avenue)* by John Moran, two actors are alone onstage, one portraying the manager of a McDonald's franchise who is giving orders to Jamal, an unseen employee, and the other a waitress taking an order from an unseen customer. The speeches and movements are repeated precisely, again and again. As the sequences—speech and movement—recur, another actor enters, filling in the dialogue as he orders his breakfast. Gradually more performers enter, providing additional layers of interaction, and the phrases heard at the opening of the scene blend into and become lost in the cacophony of a realistic depiction of breakfast at McDonald's.[9] The actors are not speaking the lines, but lip-synching recorded dialogue while repeating movement phrases with absolute precision. The cyclic repetition of movements and conversations, in this and other scenes that form the second act, create a dynamic image out of the minutiae of everyday life. Actors rely on one another to carry out the exact movement at the exact moment, cuing another to initiate the movement pattern in precise time with the recorded dialogue. In all of these performances, the concentration on doing the physical actions synchronously with others puts exceptional demands on the actors to work in perfect harmony, but with little concern for emotional content. Indeed, any focus on emotion would make the repetition impossible, because of the unreliability of effect. Any emotion that does appear arises unconsciously and unintentionally.

All the elements of performing a score in traditional realism, except dialogue, are present in these theatre works. There are memorized chunks of action that are repeated in a precise sequence. There is concentration on the unfolding of events and close attention to and awareness of the work of the other actors. The movements generate emotions and feelings in the performers that inflect each performance, regardless of whether they are an intended part of the performance or not. The difference from other forms of theatre is the emphasis on precision of movement and the limited focus on the emotional content of the scene.

In the movie *The Matrix*, Neo comes to understand his powers when he is able to translate the virtual reality into streams of binary code. It may be useful to think of actors working together in a similar vein, not as lines of code but as intersecting lines of force. In their abstract invocations of the desiring body, Deleuze and Guattari use the image of an egg: "It is crisscrossed with axes and thresholds, with latitudes and longitudes and geodesic lines, traversed by *gradients* marking the transitions and the becomings, the destinations of the subject developing along these particular vectors."[10] When acting works, there is a reciprocal movement of vectors of perceptual data. Focusing on another performer, the actor radiates energy, receiving similar forces in return. The energy of the performers becomes intertwined in a continuous and focused exchange—what leaves one is taken by the other in a cyclic process. Incoming perceptions interact with the gradients of the system, giving rise to resonant associations shaped by the attractors and boundary conditions of the score and performing techniques. What passes between them are not random vectors of energy, but actions that weave together the scores of the performers. The connections are maintained, even though the dynamics vary according to the intensity of the interactions between the actors. These are complex communications that contain primarily expected contents, but the unexpected is also in evidence, evoking responses that modify the scores in minor but interesting ways. M.C. Escher's *Drawing Hands* provides a useful image. In the picture, rising out of the same piece of paper, two hands are holding pencils and drawing each other. Similarly, as the actors' scores synchronously unfold, each actor's performance gains complexity and clarity in accordance with the style of the performance.

Each performer onstage is a dynamic system that responds to changing information in the environment. The primary focus is on the unfolding of the score. For this to happen, however, a secondary focus is placed on the work of the other actors, who are going through a similar process. The actor is looking for the cues that retrieve the appropriate chunks, which contain the trigger for the next sequence of actions. While most of the perceptual data is similar, if not identical, to that rehearsed, there is also unexpected information; the actor may also need to behave *as if* there is new information, so that the full range of responses to the acting of the others can be performed. A third focal point is on the stage space—both the placement of objects and the spatial relationships with other performers. Which of these focal points predominates at any one moment depends on the demands of the score and unexpected events in the space of the stage. Those focal points that are not important at a certain time do not cease to exist but are attended to unconsciously as the template of the score retrieves and enacts learned behaviors, allowing things to happen without apparent intent. There is one other focal point to which the actor responds: the audience. It is to this last but far from least aspect of the actor's performance to which we turn our attention.

Catching the Conscience of the King

In *Hamlet,* the play is not ultimately what forces Claudius to reveal his guilt. It is the acting: no actors, no mousetrap, however clever the plot. The audience is there to experience the acting; and actors are always aware that the audience is there. The last and farthest reaching of Stanislavski's circles of attention includes the spectators; and there are numerous ways to keep the spectator engaged. A basic rule in comic acting is holding for laughs. The laughter begins, peaks, and as it recedes, the actor begins the next line. If the line comes too soon, it will not be heard; if it's too late, the intensity of attention to the action begins to wane and it is that much more difficult to get the next laugh. In a similar vein, a general rule requires that the punch line be delivered when the actor is facing the audience. These elements are techniques that are worked into the score, as are decisions such as when to face upstage and when to "cheat" out, how to whisper so they can hear you in the last row of the balcony. One of the functions of physical and vocal techniques is to draw and maintain the attention of the audience; there is no guarantee, however, that it is going to happen.

Precisely why audiences respond the way they do remains a mystery, despite numerous theories of reception. The most recent concept revolves around the discovery of mirror neurons in macaque monkeys. According to Jean Decety, a psychologist at the University of Georgia, "This model suggests that perception of emotion activates in the observer the neural mechanisms that are responsible for the generation of similar emotion."[11] An action onstage activates in the spectator the same neural patterns that are active when the actor performs it, thus the idea of mirroring. The theory argues that activation is what allows people to feel empathy. The primary problem with this model is the lack of direct evidence for a connection between emotions and the mirroring of motor activity. However, if physical activity elicits emotion, there may be some justification to this claim. A secondary issue is that not all emotions are empathic. Even if there is a bond between mirror neurons and feelings, there is no proof they are linked to empathy. Decety concludes: "While the MNS [Mirror Neuron System] provides a physiological mechanism for motor resonance and plays a role in mimicry, current neurophysiological and neurological evidence does not clearly support the idea that such a mechanism accounts for emotion understanding, empathy or sympathy."[12] Whether or not mirror neurons will be shown to play a role in empathy does not discount the fact that audiences do empathize and sympathize with what happens onstage and that actors elicit these responses. There are neural patterns that give rise to these feelings of identification between the actor and the spectator that can be called a mirror neuron *function*,, but it is not clear that there are specific neurons responsible for this effect.

Regardless of the cause, actors can tell if an audience is engaged in the performance in ways other than their laughter or shifting, rustling pages, and snores. Moreover, the response they get from the spectators affects the performance. One of the stage manager's responsibilities is to warn actors if they are allowing what takes place in the house to affect the performance. Performers can add a lift of the eyebrow to prolong laughter or lengthen a pause to intensify their rapt attention. This may work for the actor but perhaps not for the show. Nevertheless, if they feel audience concentration drifting, they can subtly alter their work to bring the audience back into the show. In addition to the space and work with other actors, perceptual information from the audience affects the unfolding of the actor's score.

If the work between performers can be understood through the idea of intertwining fields of force, the same image can be used for the relationship between the actors and the audience. However, the nature of the interaction is different. The connection between actors is primary and immediate, because the accurate unfolding of the score depends on mutual concentration. Focus on the audience is peripheral and intermittent, usually taking place when the actor is not actively involved in the scene or when there is a pause before the next action begins. As the number of performances accumulates, there develop moments when actors anticipate an audience response, and those moments become, rightly or wrongly, a benchmark for judging the quality of the show that evening. This data affects the system, leading either to change in the dynamics of the performance—a shift in the extra-daily energy—or simply to continuing along the same path. Regardless of the response, it is part of the acting process, only becoming detrimental if focus on the interaction onstage is lost or energy flags.

The curtain call is where the actor has the opportunity to drop all pretence and acknowledge the connection that has developed with the spectator. Attitudes to the final bow can vary from the cursory nod ("This is an obligation I would rather avoid") to a combination of acknowledging the work of the audience—their attentiveness and emotional and intellectual involvement in the play—and receiving their gratitude for the energy they've spent in creating the evening's illusion.

The curtain call is a microcosm of the art of theatre. The simple act is part of an unfolding score, staged in the final dress rehearsals, that involves technique (where are the hands, how deep is the bow, where do the eyes go) and the uncertain freedom of improvisation (how long is a bow held, how long do the eyes wander over the spectators, who is seen, is an extra bow taken). It happens in the most fleeting of moments and is quickly forgotten, but it is nonetheless a dynamic system in operation. The actor, allowing the performance of the score to fade from the center of attention, moves from internalized cuing to a free interchange with the people in the house. The audience is allowed to perturb the system, creating within the boundaries of the ritual a rippling of sensations that evoke memories and define the contours of immediate behavior. This is, of course, an idealized image. In other circumstances, the bow is something to be gotten through so the stage can be vacated and the evening forgotten as quickly as possible. More technique and less improvisation are required in response to the polite clapping of the audience. The creation of illusion continues in thanking the audience for its attention, though it was intermittent at best. Yet even in the most perfunctory of curtain calls, the actor displays the attributes of a dynamic system, responding to changes in the environment, perhaps with fewer associations, less fond memories, and more dependence on technique.

Whether the response is tepid or enthusiastic, the curtain call is part of an actor's everyday life, as well as the audience's, although the audience is likely to view going to the theatre as a special experience that provides a welcome relief from the routines of the day. Whatever the resources the actor musters for performance or the focus the audience invests in watching the event, both are using the same cognitive machinery, though deploying its resources differently. On both sides of the footlights, alternative mind-sets—each requiring a different focus and different qualities of energy and attentiveness—enter the circle of attention, bringing to mind past experiences that establish a fresh set of expectations in anticipation of what is to come. Both have a role to play and, depending on the number of previous experiences, embrace habitual practices that ready them for the stage manager giving the cues (directly to the actors, indirectly to the audience) that begin the performance. As the production unfolds, there is an exchange of energy; a loop is created that involves perturbations to the system, which find resolution in sensorimotor behavior, whether it is sitting forward in the seat or leaning on an armrest, whether ruing the lack of cucumbers—"even for ready money"—or "sitting astride of a grave." Altering or responding to changes in the environment, the body—from its most metaphysical reflections to the fullest extent of the perceiving flesh—is continually engaged in the moment, allowing or directing the focus of attention to move in response to perceptual and proprioceptive shifts to the system. When the stage manager gives the final cues marking the end of the performance, the systems—on both sides—shift gears, allowing new attractors and boundary conditions to come into play and respond to further changes in the environment. Whether it is a release of tension or an upsurge of feeling, the system continues to function according to the same principles when the house lights come up and actors and audience alike move into other aspects of the everyday.

Actors and Dynamic Systems

The premise of this book is that acting utilizes a set of tools—movement, language, gesture, memory, attention, and executive control—to develop techniques that allow for creative improvisation and the consolidation in memory of a repeatable score. The outcome of this process is the performance; an interaction between actors that includes engaging an audience in a particular space. The overarching claim is that these things are possible because each of us is a dynamic system. Some would argue that even prior to birth we are learning to move our bodies and, in the process, developing techniques around attractors that gain preeminence because of their usefulness in achieving an end (even if that end is not known until it is achieved). Boundary conditions also limit certain types of behavior, of performance. These processes are *always* in response to changes in the environment, caused by outside forces or personal actions. As we mature, templates form that can be defined as habits that privilege certain types of behavior but are not rigid, providing space for improvisational responses to changing dynamics in the world. When these techniques are linked to a profession, such as acting, and are honed to the extent that they operate implicitly, or intuitively, they lead to expertise, the ability to respond quickly and appropriately to shifting circumstances without self-conscious reflection.

When the actor crosses onto the stage, she does not become a different person or a machine that automatically performs a sequence of actions. She continues to employ techniques, improvises according to changing circumstances as the score unfolds and a sequence of discrete acts are connected to the overall logic of the performance. However, the actor is always using all three—technique, improvisation, and score—throughout the rehearsal process, whether in the space or at home. That is the nature of a dynamic system.

There are a lot of myths about acting and the training of actors, many of them extremely productive. They are nevertheless reductive and therefore biased toward certain values that define boundaries of inclusion and exclusion, promoting what constitutes good acting according to the principles of that domain. The limits of a method become the limits of the actors, becoming a force of preservation by insisting that the results of the training are aligned with the aesthetics of what acting should be. By cementing the foundations in past accomplishments, training regimes seek to determine the future of the theatre. However, as now more than one hundred years have shown—ever since Père Ubu trod the boards—theatre is, despite the resilience of realism, an expanding field, making increasingly varied demands on actors. The theatre, like the actor, is a dynamic system that must transform itself with changes in the environment if it is to continue to be a vital cultural force. The question is, as it has been since Alfred Jarry: How do we prepare actors in a polyvalent world, which demands—despite or perhaps because of the conservatism of mainstream theatre—equally polyvalent art forms?

This is not a condemnation of realism in its many guises. Seeing Vanessa Redgrave, Brian Dennehy, Philip Seymour Hoffman, and Robert Sean Leonard in *A Long Day's Journey into Night* was an unforgettable experience, as was seeing Alfred Molina and Eddie Redmayne in *Red* or Cate Blanchett and company in *A Streetcar Named Desire*. Witnessing *Einstein on the Beach* or *Book of the Dead (2nd Avenue)* was an *equally* memorable experience. An actor committed to only one style is ill equipped to cross from one domain to the other. Mikhail Baryshnikov engaged a new technique when he committed to working with Twyla Tharp, an implicit acknowledgment that ballet, for all its prominence and beauty, is but one form of dance. The theatre cries for this same kind of adaptability. To answer that call, there needs to be a new language in the training of actors, one that acknowledges the disservice to the playwright, the theatre, and their audiences of treating Brecht as if he were a realist. Michael Chekhov, Jacques Lecoq, and Eugenio Barba are a few of the intellects that seek to train actors to move more easily between different types of theatre. These approaches need to be validated rather than marginalized, as the tendency currently seems to be.

Is dynamic systems theory the answer to understanding acting? Ha! Wouldn't that be wonderful! I have no such illusions. Tomorrow or the next day, experiments may be undertaken that falsify all the claims in support of this model. Such is the nature of science and of theories in general. But for all its frailties, DST does have the virtue of allowing us to rethink the art of acting in a way that, despite the use of science, does not destroy its mystery. It opens up the complexities of the art form in a way that is comprehensible, accessible, and productive for theatre artists. Such provocation is all that any critical theory can hope to achieve: a respectful understanding of the art form and a resistance of the unscientific urge to reduce acting to the least common denominator. The hope is that this alternative language for acting will cause a sufficiently strong perturbation of the system to newly integrate and enrich our understanding of the art. Actors deserve nothing less.

Notes

Editors' Preface

1. Carey, Susan. *The Origin of Concepts.* Oxford: Oxford University Press, 2009, 4.
2. See Zunshine, Lisa. "What is Cognitive Cultural Studies?" *Introduction to Cognitive Cultural Studies.* Ed. Lisa Zunshine. Baltimore: Johns Hopkins University Press, 1.

Introduction

1. Deborah Mayo, Interview with John Lutterbie, Stony Brook University, tape recording, July 3, 2003.
2. Ibid.
3. Margarita Espada, Interview with John Lutterbie, Stony Brook University, tape recording, June 30, 2003.
4. Ibid.
5. Ibid.
6. Margarita Espada, Interview with John Lutterbie, Stony Brook University, tape recording, February 4, 2002.
7. Ibid.
8. Deborah Mayo, Interview with John Lutterbie, Stony Brook University, tape recording, December 5, 2001.
9. Ibid.
10. Ibid.
11. Deborah Mayo, Interview with John Lutterbie, Stony Brook University, tape recording, November 7, 2001.
12. See Patrice Pavis, *Theatre at the Crossroads of Culture* (London and New York: Routledge, 1991), 178–209.
13. Hubert L. Dreyfus and Stuart E. Dreyfus. *Mind Over Machine: The Power of Human Intuition and Expertise in the Era of the Computer* (New York: Free Press, 1986), 50.
14. Ibid., 30.
15. Ibid., 30–31.
16. Neil Young, "Harvest Moon." http://www.lyricsfreak.com/n/neil+young/harvest+moon_20099104.html. March 14, 2011

1 The Language of Acting

1. I saw an Irish dance performance in which a fiddler was given a standing ovation despite the obvious fact that the instrument had no strings .
2. See Helga Noice and Tony Noice. "Two Approaches to Learning a Theatrical Script." *Memory.* 4, no. 1 (1996): 1–17; and Helga Noice and Tony Noice. "Long Term Retention of Theatrical Roles." *Memory.* 7, no. 3 (1997): 357–382.
3. Stuart Jefferies. "Inside the Mind of an Actor (Literally)." *The Guardian.* www.guardian.co.uk/science/2009/nov/24/fiona-shaw-neuroscience. November 24, 2009
4. Maxine Sheets-Johnstone, personal communication with author, April 17, 2007.
5. Maurice Merleau-Ponty. *The Visible and the Invisible* (Evanston: Northwestern University Press, 1968), 148–149.
6. Many of the works here mentioned fit into more than one of the divisions, and in some cases people might argue for a completely different descriptor for a given work. The classification of these playwrights is not meant to be definitive, but simply descriptive of the category of nonrealism.
7. Hans-Thies Lehmann. *Postdramatic Theatre,* Trans. Karen Jürs-Munby (London: Routledge, 2006), 27.
8. Esther Thelen and Linda B. Smith. *A Dynamic Systems Approach to the Development of Cognition and Action* (Cambridge: MIT Press, 1996), 136–140. For more on the way the brain compensates for the loss of certain functions see V.S. Ramachandran and Sandra Blakeslee, *Phantoms in the Brain: Probing the Mysteries of the Human Mind* (New York: Harper Perennial, 1999).
9. Metaphor, as conceived here, is grounded in the work of George Lakoff and Mark Johnson. They argue that metaphors are based on physical experiences and therefore are embodied. For a full discussion of this theory, see Johnson, *The Body in the Mind: The Bodily Basis of Meaning, Imagination and Reason* (Chicago: The University of Chicago Press, 1987); and Lakoff and Johnson. *Philosophy in the Flesh: The Embodied Mind and Its Challenge to Western Philosophy* and *Metaphors We Live By* (New York: Basic Books, 1999).
10. Unfortunately this decision excludes a number of teachers, such as Stella Adler, who did not feel compelled to write about their work. Yet, this choice rests on two factors: (1) Despite the vagaries of ghost writers and translations, the ideas more clearly reflect the practice of the practitioner when he or she is involved in the writing than when theories are written by students once (or more) removed from the tradition's founder. (2) If these additional theories were considered, their respective premises would not substantively alter the conclusions drawn here.

11. Oksana Karneva ed. *Kontstantin Stanislavsky: Selected Works* (Moscow: Raduga Publishers, 1984), 133–134.
12. Ibid., 134, 166.
13. Ibid., 167-174.
14. Ibid., 169.
15. Konstantin Stanislavski. *An Actor's Work on a Role.* Trans. Jean Bendetti (London and New York: Routledge, 2010), 47.
16. Ibid., 57.
17. Ibid., 74.
18. Ibid., 49.
19. Ibid., 54, 74.
20. Ibid., 73.
21. Edward Braun ed. and trans. *Meyerhold on Theatre* (New York: Hill and Wang, 1969), 52.
22. Ibid., 198.
23. Ibid., 63, 56.
24. Ibid., 52.
25. Ibid., 56.
26. Ibid., 55.
27. Ibid., 54.
28. Ibid., 54.
29. Ibid., 54.
30. Barthes, Roland. *Image, Music, Text,* Trans. Stephen Hearh (Hammersmith: Fontana Press, 1977), 181.
31. Ibid., 59.
32. Ibid., 60.
33. Ibid., 55 n.
34. Ibid., 198.
35. Ibid., 205.
36. Ibid., 201.
37. Ibid., 201.
38. Ibid., 198–199.
39. Ibid., 198.
40. For examples of the exercises Meyerhold developed to train Biomechanical actors see *Meyerhold, Theatre and the Russian Avant-garde*, Prod. and directed by Michael Craig (Copernicus Films, 2004).
41. Ibid., 199.
42. Ibid., 199.
43. Ibid., 199.
44. Ibid., 205.
45. Ibid., 205.
46. Bertolt Brecht. *Brecht on Theatre*. Trans. John Willett (New York: Hill and Wang, 1964), 247.
47. Ibid., 44; emphasis added.

48. Ibid., 44.
49. Ibid., 122.
50. Ibid., 138.
51. See John Lutterbie, "Gestus and Acting Style in *The Good Person of Szechwan:* A Case Study." *Gestus.* June 1986.
52. *Brecht on Theatre,* 204.
53. Ibid., 196.
54. Ibid., 277.
55. The photo by Eli Lotar entitled "Abattoir," can be found in *Documents* 6 (1929): 328; or on some browsers by searching: "eli lotar" abbatoir images.
56. A recording can be heard at http://www.ubu.com/sound/artaud.html. March 13, 2011.
57. For a discussion of Artaud's concerns about language, see John Lutterbie. *Hearing Voices: Modern Drama and the Problem of Subjectivity* (Ann Arbor: University of Michigan Press, 1996), 33–37.
58. Antonin Artaud. *The Theatre and Its Double.* Trans. Mary Caroline Richards (New York: Grove Press, 1958), 51
59. Ibid., 54.
60. For a discussion of the correspondence between Artaud and Rivière see *Hearing Voices.*
61. *Theatre and Its Double,* 53.
62. There has been a critique of Artaud's reading of Balinese performance. His cultural biases—his Western predilections and his ignorance of Balinese culture—lead to serious misunderstandings of the dances he saw. This does not, however, undermine the conclusions he draws about Western acting or the significance of his vision of theatre. See Tsu-Chung Su, "The Occidental Theatre and Its Other: The Use and Abuse of the Oriental Theatre in Antonin Artaud." *NTU Studies in Language and Literature.* 1, No. 22 (December 2009): 1–30.
63. *The Theatre and Its Double,* 61.
64. Ibid., 62.
65. Ibid., 62.
66. Ibid., 133.
67. Ibid., 134.
68. Ibid., 141.
69. Ibid., 138.
70. Thomas Richards. *At Work with Grotowski on Physical Actions,* (London and New York: Routledge, 1995), 123.
71. Ibid., 130.
72. Jerzy Grotowski. *Toward a Poor Theatre.* Ed. Eugenio Barba (New York: Simon and Schuster, 1968), 119.
73. Ibid., 16.

74. Ibid., 17.
75. *The Theatre and Its Double*, 51.
76. *Toward a Poor Theatre*, 16.
77. Ibid., 17.
78. Ibid., 18.
79. *At Work with Grotowski*, 122–123.
80. Ibid., 122.
81. Ibid., 125.
82. Ibid., 126.
83. Jacques Lecoq, Jean-Gabriel Carasso and Jean-Claude Lallias. *The Moving Body: Teaching Creative Theatre*. Trans. David Bradby (London and New York: Routledge, 2001), 46; Jacques Lecoq, *Theatre of Movement and Gesture*. Ed. David Bradby (London and New York: Routledge, 2006), 5.
84. *The Moving Body*, 46.
85. *Theatre of Movement*, 5.
86. *The Moving Body*, 36.
87. Ibid., 37.
88. Ibid., 39.
89. Ibid., 37.
90. Ibid., 37.
91. Ibid., 46.
92. Ibid., 46.
93. Ibid., 102.
94. *Theatre of Movement*, 80.
95. Ibid., 86.
96. Ibid., 82.
97. *The Moving Body*, 59.
98. Ibid., 31.
99. Ibid., 30.
100. Michael Chekhov. *To the Actor* (New York, Evanston and London: Harper and Row, 1953), 94.
101. Ibid., 63.
102. Ibid., 63.
103. Ibid., 65.
104. Michael Chekhov. *On the Technique of Acting* (New York: Harper Collins, 1991), 59.
105. *To the Actor*, 71.
106. Ibid., 65.
107. Ibid., 68.
108. Ibid., 71, 73.
109. Robert H. Hethmon ed. *Strasberg at The Actors Studio* (New York: Theatre Communications Group, Inc., 1995), 48.
110. Ibid., 200.
111. Ibid., 218.

112. Ibid., 89.
113. Ibid., 91.
114. Ibid., 34.
115. Ibid., 152.
116. Ibid., 154.
117. Ibid., 67.
118. Ibid., 73.
119. Ibid., 165.
120. Ibid., 42.
121. Ibid., 41.
122. Ibid., 41–42.
123. Ibid., 49.
124. Ibid., 50.
125. Ibid., 53.
126. Ibid., 60–61.
127. Ibid., 37.
128. Ibid., 41.
129. Ibid., 98.
130. Ibid., 77.
131. Ibid., 75.
132. Ibid., 98.
133. Ibid., 53–54.
134. Ibid., 76.
135. For Meisner's opinions on Strasberg, Stella Adler and the Group Theatre see Sanford Meisner and Dennis Longwell. *Sanford Meisner on Acting* (New York: Random House, 1987), 182–184.
136. *Sanford Meisner on Acting*, xviii.
137. Ibid., xviii-xix.
138. Ibid., 115.
139. Ibid., 121.
140. Ibid., 16.
141. Ibid., 141.
142. Ibid., 140.
143. Ibid., 22.
144. Ibid., 34.
145. Ibid., 68–69.
146. Ibid., 102–103.
147. Ibid., 31.
148. Ibid., 36.
149. Ibid., 62.
150. Ibid., 138.
151. Ibid., 138.
152. Ibid., 140.
153. Ibid., 86.
154. Ibid., 28–29.
155. Ibid., 210.

156. Ibid., 97.
157. Ibid., 146.
158. Antonio R. Damasio. *The Feeling of What Happens: Body and Emotion in the Making of Consciousness* (New York, San Diego and London: Harcourt Brace & Company, 1999), 282.
159. Ibid., 42.

2 Theatre and Dynamic Systems Theory

1. J. A. Scott Kelso. *Dynamic Patterns: The Self-Organization of Brain and Behavior* (Cambridge, Mass., and London, UK: The MIT Press, 1995), 28.
2. Sandra Blaskeslee. "Cells that Read Minds", New York Times, 10 January, 2006.
3. Giacomo Rizzolatti, Leonardo Fogassi, and Vittorio Gallese. "Mirrors in the Mind." *Scientific American*. Vol. 295, No. 5 (November 2006): 54–61.; Jean Decety. "To What Extent Is the Experience of Empathy Mediated by Shared Neural Circuits?" *Emotion Review* (2010): 1–4.
4. Bernard J. Baars. *In the Theater of Consciousness: The Workspace of the Mind* (Oxford: Oxford University Press, 1997), 43.
5. Marc D. Lewis. "Bridging Emotion Theory and Neurobiology through Dynamic Systems Modeling." *Behavioral and Brain Sciences*. 28 (2005), 173.
6. "Bridging Emotion Theory," 174.
7. Evan Thompson. *Mind in Life: Biology, Phenomenology, and the Sciences of Mind* (Cambridge, Mass., and London, UK: Harvard University Press, 2007), 366.
8. *Dynamic Patterns*, 18.
9. "Bridging Emotion Theory," 173.
10. Ibid., 173.
11. Ibid., 176; emphasis added.
12. Ibid., 331.
13. *Dynamic Patterns*, 154.
14. Ibid., 332.
15. Gestalts tend to be understood as stable, self-contained images. A "dynamic gestalt" is one that is subject to constant reformulation based on new information across a number of neural networks and, therefore, never achieves a stable, unified state.
16. *Mind in Life*, 368.
17. "Bridging Emotion Theory," 178.
18. Ibid., 170.
19. Ibid., 182.
20. Antonio Damasio, *Descartes Error* (191–196).
21. *Mind in Life*, 12.
22. Ibid., 11.

23. Bruce McConachie. *Engaging Audiences: A Cognitive Approach to Spectating in the Theatre* (New York: Palgrave Macmillan, 2008), 56.
24. See Brian Parkinson, Agneta H. Fischer, and Antony S. R. Manstead. *Emotion in Social Relations: Cultural, Group, and Interpersonal Processes* (New York and Hove: Psychology Press, 2005).
25. *Mind in Life*, 402.

3 The Actor's Tools

1. For an overview of the two models, see Dale Purves, et al. *Principles of Cognitive Neuroscience* (Sunderland: Sinauer Associates, Inc., 2008), 406–408.
2. Peter Rapp. "Structure and Organization of Memory in the Brain (and Other Stuff)." Presentation at the Humanities Institute at Stony Brook, Stony Brook University, video recording, December 12, 2007.
3. Esther Thelen and Linda B. Smith. *A Dynamic Systems Approach to the Development of Cognition and Action* (Cambridge, Mass., and London, UK: The MIT Press, 1996), 170.
4. Alan Baddeley. "The Magical Number Seven: Still Magic After All These Years." *Psychological Review*. Vol. 101, No. 2 (April 1994): 356; Nelson Cowan. "The Magical Number 4 in Short-Term Memory: A Reconsideration of Mental Storage Capacity." *Behavioral and Brain Sciences*. 24 (2000), 88.
5. "The Magical Number Seven," 355.
6. George A. Miller. "The Magical Number Seven, Plus or Minus Two: Some Limits on Our Capacity for Processing Information." *Psychological Review*. Vol. 101, No. 2 (1994), 350.
7. Gerald M. Edelman, *Bright Air, Brilliant Fire: On the Matter of the Mind* (New York: BasicBooks, 1992), 85-90.
8. "The Magical Number 4," 92.
9. Herbert Blau. *The Eye of Prey: Subversions of the Postmodern* (Bloomington, Ind.: Indiana University Press, 1987), 164.
10. Shaun Gallagher., *How the Body Shapes the Mind* (Oxford: Oxford University Press, 2005), 17-25, 30-39.
11. See Judith Butler., *Bodies that Matter: On the Discursive Limits of Sex* (London and New York: Routledge, 1993).
12. *How the Body Shapes the Mind*, 26.
13. Ibid., 24.
14. Ibid., 26.
15. Ibid., 118.
16. Defining categories is a necessary step in understanding phenomena, but it does a disservice to the complex, interactive nature of the system. Alain Berthoz uses a slightly different strategy in exploring the dynamic nature of movement. Proprioception and perception

are combined under the more global concept of kinesthesia—a source of environmental information that joins forces with memory and allows for a simulation of anticipated outcomes; see *The Brain's Sense of Movement*. trans. Giselle Weiss (Cambridge, Mass. and London, UK: Harvard University Press, 2000), 3. The projection of future events arises from the combination of past experiences (long-term memories) with current perceptual data in working memory, allowing for an appraisal and modification of movements in the immediate circumstances. His example is of a skier coming down a slope. She is aware of what is happening (snow conditions, changes in the topography, sense of balance, etc.); at the same time, she has a sense of the next stages in navigating the hill. Fresh perceptual information requires adjustments in the immediate activity of skiing and perhaps a reassessment of the overall trajectory. The movement of the skier occurs within the parameters of these boundary conditions. The more skillful she is, the more accurate and swift will be the adjustments for a successful downhill run. The actor in performance also needs to feel sufficiently comfortable with the score, so that it can be retrieved and performed easily and so that she can respond to the inevitable variations that arise over the course of the theatre event.

17. Jerome A. Feldman. *From Molecule to Metaphor: A Neural Theory of Language* (Cambridge, Mass.: The MIT Press, 2008), 96.
18. Ibid., 194.
19. Ibid., 200.
20. Ibid., 204.
21. See Antonin Artaud. "Correspondence with Jacques Riviere." *Artaud Anthology*. Ed. Jack Hirschman. Trans. Bernard Frechtman. (San Francisco: City Lights Books, 1965); and for a discussion of the letters: John Lutterbie. *Hearing Voices: Modern Drama and the Problem of Subjectivity* (Ann Arbor: University of Michigan Press, 1997), 33–37.
22. Dylan Thomas. *Selected Poems, 1934–1952*, Revised edition (New York: New Directions, 2003), 122.
23. *From Molecule to Metaphor*, 323.
24. Gilles Fauconnier and Mark Turner. *The Way We Think: Conceptual Blending and the Mind's Hidden Complexities* (New York: Basic Books, 2002), 17.
25. Roland Barthes. *Image, Music, Text* (New York: Hill and Wang, 1977), 188.
26. David McNeill. *Gesture and Thought* (Chicago and London: University of Chicago Press, 2005), 93.
27. Ibid., 56.
28. Ibid., 212.
29. Ibid., 19.
30. Ibid., 4.

31. Ibid., 107.
32. Ibid., 18.
33. Ibid., 107.
34. Ibid., 107.
35. Ibid., 125.
36. Ibid., 124.
37. Ibid., 18.
38. *A Dynamics Systems Approach*, 180.

4 Technique

1. See Hubert L. Dreyfus and Stuart E. Dreyfus. *Mind Over Machine: The Power of Human Intuition and Expertise in the Era of the Computer* (New York: Free Press, 1986).
2. Robert P. Crease and John Lutterbie. "Technique." *Staging Philosophy: Intersections of Theater, Performance, and Philosophy.* Ed. David Krasner and David Z. Saltz (Ann Arbor: The University of Michigan Press, 2006), 166.
3. Ibid., 166.
4. The basal ganglia includes the striatum (caudate nucleus and putamen), thalamus, globus pallidus, and substantia nigra.
5. Eric R. Kandel, James H. Schwartz, and Thomas M. Jessell. *Principles of Neural Science*. Third edition (New York, Amsterdam, London, and Tokyo: Elsevier Science Publishing Co., Inc., 1991), 652.
6. Elias Khoury. *Gate of the Sun*. Trans. Humphrey Davies (New York: Picador, 2006), 160.
7. Herbert Blau. *The Eye of Prey: Subversions of the Postmodern* (Bloomington, Ind: Indiana University Press, 1987), 164.
8. Shaun Gallagher. *How the Body Shapes the Mind* (Oxford: Oxford University Press, 2005), 24.
9. Ibid., 43.
10. Ibid., 44.
11. Ibid., 24, fn.
12. Ibid., 37.
13. Ibid., 37.
14. Maxine Sheets-Johnstone. "Kinetic Tactile-Kinesthetic Bodies: Ontogenetical Foundations of Apprenticeship Learning." *Human Studies*. Vol. 23, No. 4 (Netherlands: Kluwer Academic Publishers, 2000), 345.
15. Gallagher, 36.
16. "Kinetic Tactile-Kinesthetic Bodies," 343.
17. Maxine Sheets-Johnstone. *The Primacy of Movement* (Amsterdam and Philapdelphia: John Benjamins Publishing Company, 1999), 270.
18. "Technique," 165.
19. Antonio Damasio. *Descartes' Error: Emotion, Reason, and the Human Brain* (New York: Avon Books, Inc, 1994), 159.

20. "Kinetic Tactile-Kinesthetic Bodies," 358.
21. Alan Baddeley. *Human Memory: Theory and Practice*. Revised edition (Hove and New York: Psychology Press, 1997), 369.
22. Marcel Mauss. *Sociology and Psychology: Essays*. Trans. Ben Brewster (London, Boston, and Henley: Routledge and Kegan Paul, 1979), 97.
23. Marcel Mauss. *Techniques, Technology and Civilisation*. Ed. Nathan Schlanger (New York and London: Durkheim Press/Berghahn Books, 2006), 80.
24. *Sociology and Psychology,* 101–102.
25. Ibid., 120.
26. Eugenio Barba. *The Paper Canoe: A Guide to Theatre Anthropology*. Trans. Richard Fowler (London and New York: Routledge, 1995), 15–16.
27. Kristen Linklater. *Freeing the Natural Voice* (New York: Drama Book Publishers, 1976), 7.
28. Arthur Lessac. *The Use and Training of the Human Voice: A Practical Approach to Speech and Voice Dynamic*. Second edition (New York: DBS Publications, Inc., 1967). xii.
29. Ibid., xii.
30. *Freeing the Natural Voice*, 3.
31. *Training of the Human Voice,* xi, 18, 22.
32. Ibid., 17.
33. Ibid., 18.
34. Ibid., 18–20.
35. Ibid., 20–21, 131–35.
36. Ibid., 91, 95.
37. Ibid., 18 fig. 1.
38. Ibid., 22.
39. Ibid., 20.
40. *Training of the Human Voice,* xvii; *Freeing the Natural Voice,* 3.
41. Ibid., 2.
42. Ibid., 11.
43. Ibid., 5, 11.
44. *Training of the Human Voice,* 117.
45. Ibid., 5.
46. Ibid., 9.
47. Ibid., 4.
48. Ibid., 77, 80, 109, 140.
49. Anna Kisselgoff. "After 12 Years in Exile, Twyla Tharp Shifts Gears Again." *New York Times* (July 6, 2000), 5.
50. These observations are based on the video "Baryshnikov by Tharp." Dance in America. Public Broadcasting System (1984).
51. E. T. Gendlin. "Crossing and Dipping: Some Terms for Approaching the Interface between Natural Understanding and Logical Formulation." *Minds and Machines*. Vol. 5, No. 4 (1995): 547–560. Also available from Web: The Focusing Group http://www.focusing.org/Gendlin.html. October 1, 2001

52. "Crossing and Dipping,"
53. *Human Memory,* 369.
54. Gui Xue, Dara G. Ghahremani, and Russell A. Poldrack. "Neural Substrates for Reversing Stimulus-Outcome and Stimulus-Response Associations." *The Journal of Neuroscience.* Vol. 28, No. 44 (October 29, 2008), 11196–11204; and Dara G. Ghahremani, John Monterosso, J. David Jentsch, Robert M. Bilder, and Russell A. Poldrack. "Neural Components Underlying Behavioral Flexibility in Human Reversal Learning." *Cerebral Cortex.* Vol. 20, No. 8 (2010), 1843–1852.
55. Two performances of "Push Comes to Shove" were available on You Tube at the time of writing. The earlier version is available at http://www.youtube.com/watch?v=5mUd3lk2iJI&feature=related, and the later at http://video.google.com/videoplay?docid=-212565168490747815&q=baryshnikov+push&ei=wphbSIKtNJPs-gHbnsyTDw.
56. Peter R. Rapp. Presentation at the Science and Art Seminar, Humanities Institute at Stony Brook University. Videotape. December 12, 2007.
57. Margarita Espada. Interview with John Lutterbie. Stony Brook University. Tape recording, November 11, 2001.

5 Improvisation

1. Tim Etchells. *Certain Fragments: Contemporary Performance and Forced Entertainment* (London and New York: Routledge, 2002), 53.
2. Gilles Deleuze and Félix Guattari. *A Thousand Plateaus: Capitalism and Schizophrenia.* Trans. Brian Massumi (Minneapolis: University of Minnesota Press, 1987), 9.
3. See Marcel Mauss. "Techniques of the Body." *Techniques, Technology and Civilization.* Ed. Nathan Schlanger (New York and Oxford: Durkheim Press/Bergbahn Books, 2006).
4. See Louis Althusser. *Lenin and Philosophy and Other Essays.* Trans. Ben Brewster (New York and London: Monthly Review Press, 1971).
5. Gilles Deleuze and Félix Guattari. *A Thousand Plateaus: Capitalism and Schizophrenia.* Trans. Brian Massumi (Minneapolis: University of Minnesota Press, 1987), 303.
6. See Augusto Boal. *The Rainbow of Desire: The Boal Method of Theatre and Therapy.* Trans. Adrian Jackson (London and New York: Routledge, 1995), 40–46.
7. Miranda Tufnell and Chris Crickmay., *A Widening Field: Journeys in Body and Imagination* (Hampshire: Dance Books, 2004), 53.
8. Deborah Mayo. Interview with John Lutterbie. Stony Brook University. Tape recording, December 5, 2001.

9. Margarita Espada. Interview with John Lutterbie. Stony Brook University. Tape recording. February 4, 2002.
10. Deborah Mayo. Interview with John Lutterbie. Stony Brook University. Tape recording. July 3, 2003.
11. Margarita Espada. Interview with John Lutterbie. Stony Brook University. Tape recording. February 4, 2002.
12. See Maxine Sheets-Johnstone. "Thinking in Movement." *The Primacy of Movement* (Amsterdam and Philadelphia: John Benjamins Publishing Company, 1999), 483–517.
13. Susan Sontag, ed., *Antonin Artaud: Selected Writings*, Trans. Helen Weaver. (Berkeley and Los Angeles: University of California Press, 1976), 571.
14. Eugenio Barba. *The Paper Canoe: A Guide to Theatre Anthropology*. Trans. Richard Fowler. (London and New York: Routledge, 1995), 15–16.
15. Deborah Mayo. Interview with John Lutterbie. Stony Brook University. Tape recording. November 7, 2001.
16. I am deeply indebted to Amy Cook for clarifying so beautifully the complexity of the conceptual blends in these seemingly simple examples.
17. Amy Cook. *Shakespearean Neuroplay: Reinvigorating the Study of Dramatic Texts and Performance through Cognitive Neuroscience* (New York: Palgrave Macmillan, 2010), 11.
18. Amy Cook. "Interplay: The Method and Potential of a Cognitive Scientific Approach to Theatre." *Theatre Journal*. Vol. 59, No. 4 (2007), 579–594.
19. Seana Coulson and Todd Oakley. "Blending Basics." *Cognitive Linguistics*. Vol. 11, Nos. 3–4 (2000), 187.
20. *Shakespearean Neuroplay*, 11.
21. *Certain Fragments*, 49.
22. Tim Etchells. *Forced Entertainment: On Making Performance*. http://www.youtube.com/watch?v=m2fRfN5U7GA. December 31, 2010.

6 The Actor's Score

1. See John Tytell. *The Living Theatre: Art, Exile, and Outrage* (New York: Grove Press, 1997), 225–278.
2. See Chrisann Verges and Mark Obenhaus. *Einstein on the Beach: The Changing Image of Opera*. Videotape, 1984.
3. Thomas Richards. *At Work with Grotowski on Physical Actions* (New York and London, UK: Routledge, 1995), 122.
4. For the linguistic definition of performative utterances, see J. L. Austin., *Philosophical Papers*. third edition (Oxford: Oxford University Press, 1990), 233–52.
5. Some will argue that this definition is based on traditional text-based performances. I am ambivalent about how to respond to this critique. There are, of course, incredible performances that do not

make use of an existing text or which depend on emotional connections to remembered pasts. Moreover, there are performances, such as those of *The Living Theatre*, that actively resist the development of a score, focusing specifically on responding to what is occurring onstage without regard for previous performances or the rehearsal process. I am more interested in presenting the most complex and sophisticated definition possible, in order to adequately argue for the significance of cognitive science in understanding the work of the actor. My approach, therefore, is additive rather than subtractive. To validate the approach used to talk about acting, I am more interested in showing that dynamic systems theory and phenomenology are up to the task of dealing with the most complex set of circumstances. In saying this, I am in no way suggesting that because a certain score is more complex it is in any way better or more aesthetically pleasing than a less layered score.

6. William Shakespeare. *The Complete Works.* Ed. Alfred Harbage (Baltimore: Penguin Books, 1969), 951.
7. David McNeill. *Gesture and Thought* (Chicago and London: University of Chicago Press, 2005), 107.
8. Tori Haring-Smith. "Dramaturging Non-Realism: Creating a New Vocabulary." *Theatre Topics.* Vol. 13, No. 1 (2003), 46.
9. See David L. Saltz. "How to Do Things on Stage." *Journal of Aesthetics and Art Criticism.* Vol. 49, No. 1 (1991), 31–45.
10. "Dramaturging Non Realism," 52.
11. Saviana Stanescu and Daniel Gerould. eds. *roMANIA after 2000: Five New Romanian Plays* (New York: Martin E. Segal Theatre Center Publications, 2007), 244–245, emphasis added.
12. Heiner Müller. *Hamletmachine and Other Texts for the Stage.* Trans. Carl Weber (New York: Performing Arts Journal Publications, 1984), 56–57.
13. Hans-Thies Lehmann. *Postdramatic Theatre.* Trans. Karen Jürs Munby (London, UK and New York: Routledge, 2006), 27.
14. Ibid., 21.
15. *Einstein on the Beach: The Changing Face of Opera.*
16. Ibid.
17. Tim Etchells, *Forced Entertainment, "On Making Performance"* (http://www.youtube.com/watch?v=m2fRfN5U7GA). December 31, 2010.
18. See Claudia Castellucci, Romeo Catellucci, Ghiara Guidi, Joe Kelleher, and Nicholas Ridout. *The Theatre of Socìetas Raffaello Sanzio* (London, UK and New York: Routledge, 2007).
19. Andrew Quick. *The Wooster Group Work Book* (London, UK and New York: Routledge, 2007), 216.
20. *The Theatre of Socìetas Raffaello Sanzio*, 1.

21. Nelson Cowan. "The Magical Number 4 in Short-Term Memory: A Reconsideration of Mental Storage Capacity." *Behavioral and Brain Sciences*. 24 (2000), 92.
22. See Hans Robert Jauss., *An Aesthetics of Reception* (Minneapolis: University of Minnesota Press, 1982).
23. "The Magical Number 4," 89.
24. Ibid., 93.
25. Howard B. Richman, James J. Staszewski, and Herbert A. Simon. "Simulation of Expert Memory Using EPAM IV." *Psychological Review*. Vol. 102, No. 2 (1995), 306.
26. Ibid., 315.
27. There is no certainty about how this process works. Cowan speculates, "The recall process could proceed in phases, each of which may involve the subject scanning the memory representation, transferring several items to the capacity-limited store, recalling those items, and then returning to the representation for another limited-capacity 'handful' of items." ("The Magical Number 4," 106).
28. Eugenio Barba. *The Paper Canoe: A Guide to Theatre Anthropology*. Trans. Richard Fowler (London and New York: Routledge, 1995), 55, 57.
29. "The Magical Number 4," 92.
30. Dara G. Ghahremani, John Monterosso, J. David Jentsch, Robert M. Bilder, and Russell A. Poldrack. "Neural Components Underlying Behavioral Flexibility in Human Reversal Learning." *Cerebral Cortex*. Vol. 20, No. 8 (2010): (November 13, 2009), 1848.
31. Ibid., 8.
32. Glenn R. Wylie, John J. Foxe, and Tracy L. Taylor. "Forgetting as an Active Process: An fMRI Investigation of Item-Method-Directed Forgetting." *Cerebral Cortex*. Vol. 18, No.3 (March, 2008), 678.
33. Ibid., 678.

7 In Performance

1. David McNeill., *Gesture and Thought* (Chicago and London, UK: University of Chicago Press, 2005), 100.
2. Antonin Artaud., *The Theatre and Its Double*. Trans. Mary Caroline Richards (New York: Grove Press, Inc., 1958), 52.
3. Hollis Huston. *The Actor's Instrument: Body, Theory, Stage* (Ann Arbor: The University of Michigan Press, 1992), 89.
4. Esther Thelan and Linda B. Smith., *A Dynamic Systems Approach to the Development of Cognition and Action* (Cambridge, Mass. and London, UK: The MIT Press, 1996), 216.
5. Maurice Merleau-Ponty. *The Visible and the Invisible*. Trans. Alphonso Lingis (Evanston: Northwestern University Press, 1968), 144.

6. Eugenio Barba. *The Paper Canoe: A Guide to Theatre Anthropology*. Trans. Richard Fowler (London, UK and New York: Routledge, 1995), 176 fn, 30.
7. Janne Risum. "The Impulse and the Image: The Theatre Laboratory Tradition and Oden Teatret." *Odin Teatret 2000*. Ed. John Andreasen and Annelis Kuhlmann (Åarhus: Aarhus University Press, 2000), 49.
8. Chrisann Verges and Mark Obenhaus. *Einstein on the Beach: The Changing Image of Opera*. Videotape. 1984.
9. John Moran. *Book of the Dead (2nd Avenue)*. New York Public Library for the Performing Arts. Videotaped in Martinson Hall, Public Theatre, by Theatre on Film and Tape Archive at the New York Public Library for the Performing Arts. December 14, 2000. The Joseph Papp Public Theater/New York Shakespeare Festival, George C. Wolfe, producer.
10. Gilles Deleuze and Félix Guattari. *A Thousand Plateaus: Capitalism and Schizophrenia*. Trans. Brian Massumi (Minneapolis: University of Minnesota Press, 1987), 19.
11. Jean Decety. "To What Extent Is the Experience of Empathy Mediated by Shared Neural Circuits?" *Emotion Review* Vol. 2, No. 1 (2010), 1.
12. Ibid., 3.

Bibliography

Althusser, Louis. *Lenin and Philosophy and Other Essays*. Trans. Ben Brewster. New York and London: Monthly Review Press, 1971.
Artaud, Antonin. "Antonin Artaud." *Ubuweb: Sound*. http://www.ubu.com/sound/artaud.html. March 13, 2011.
———. *Artaud Anthology*. Ed. Jack Hirschman. Trans. Bernard Frechtman. San Francisco: City Lights Books, 1965.
———. *The Theatre and Its Double*. Trans. Mary Caroline Richards. New York: Grove Press, Inc., 1958.
Austin, J. L. *Philosophical Papers*. Third edition. Oxford: Oxford University Press, 1990.
Baars, Bernard J. *In the Theater of Consciousness: The Workspace of the Mind*. Oxford: Oxford University Press, 1997.
Baddeley, Alan. *Human Memory: Theory and Practice*. Revised edition. Hove and New York: Psychology Press, 1997.
———. "The Magical Number Seven: Still Magic After All These Years." *Psychological Review*. Vol. 101, No. 2 (April 1994): 353–356.
Barba, Eugenio. *The Paper Canoe: A Guide to Theatre Anthropology*. Trans. Richard Fowler. London and New York: Routledge, 1995.
Barthes, Roland. *Image, Music, Text*. New York: Hill and Wang, 1977.
Berthoz, Alain. *The Brain's Sense of Movement*. Trans. Giselle Weiss. Cambridge, Mass. and London: Harvard University Press, 2000.
Blau, Herbert. *The Audience*. Baltimore, Md. and London: The Johns Hopkins University Press, 1990.
———. *The Eye of Prey: Subversions of the Postmodern*. Bloomington, Ind.: Indiana University Press, 1987.
Boal, Augusto. *The Rainbow of Desire: The Boal Method of Theatre and Therapy*. Trans. Adrian Jackson. London and New York: Routledge, 1995.
Braun, Edward, ed. and trans. *Meyerhold on Theatre*. New York: Hill and Wang, 1969.
Brecht, Bertolt. *Brecht on Theatre*. Trans. John Willett. New York: Hill and Wang, 1964.
Butler, Judith. *Bodies that Matter: On the Discursive Limits of Sex*. London and New York: Routledge, 1993.

Castellucci, Claudia, Romeo Catellucci, Ghiara Guidi, Joe Kelleher, and Nicholas Ridout. *The Theatre of Societas Raffaello Sanzio*. London and New York: Routledge, 2007.

Chekhov, Michael. *To the Actor*. New York, Evanston, and London: Harper and Row, 1953.

———. *On the Technique of Acting*. New York: Harper Collins, 1991.

Cook, Amy. "Interplay: The Method and Potential of a Cognitive Scientific Approach to Theatre." *Theatre Journal*. Vol. 59, No. 4 (2007): 579–594.

———. *Shakespearean Neuroplay: Reinvigorating the Study of Dramatic Texts and Performance through Cognitive Neuroscience*. New York: Palgrave Macmillan, 2010.

Coulson, Seana and Todd Oakley. "Blending Basics." *Cognitive Linguistics*. Vol. 11, Nos. 3–4 (2000): 175–196.

Cowan, Nelson. "The Magical Number 4 in Short-Term Memory: A Reconsideration of Mental Storage Capacity." *Behavioral and Brain Sciences*. 24 (2000): 87–185.

Crease, Robert P. and John Lutterbie. "Technique." *Staging Philosophy: Intersections of Theater, Performance, and Philosophy*. Ed. David Krasner and David Z. Saltz. Ann Arbor: The University of Michigan Press, 2006.

Damasio, Antonio R. *Descartes' Error: Emotion, Reason, and the Human Brain*. New York: Avon Books, Inc., 1994.

———. *The Feeling of What Happens: Body and Emotion in the Making of Consciousness*. New York, San Diego, and London: Harcourt Brace & Company, 1999.

Decety, Jean. "To What Extent Is the Experience of Empathy Mediated by Shared Neural Circuits?" *Emotion Review* Vol. 2, No. 1 (2010): 1–4.

Deleuze, Gilles and Félix Guattari. *A Thousand Plateaus: Capitalism and Schizophrenia*. Trans. Brian Massumi. Minneapolis: University of Minnesota Press, 1987.

Dreyfus, Hubert L. and Stuart E. Dreyfus. *Mind Over Machine: The Power of Human Intuition and Expertise in the Era of the Computer*. New York: Free Press, 1986.

Espada, Margarita. Interview with John Lutterbie. Stony Brook University. Tape recording. February 4, 2002.

———. Interview with John Lutterbie. Stony Brook University. Tape recording. November 11, 2001.

Etchells, Tim. *Certain Fragments: Contemporary Performance and Forced Entertainment*. London and New York: Routledge, 2002.

———. *Forced Entertainment: On Making Performance*. http://www.youtube.com/watch?v=m2fRfN5U7GA. December 31, 2010.

Fauconnier, Gilles and Mark Turner. *The Way We Think: Conceptual Blending and the Mind's Hidden Complexities*. New York: Basic Books, 2002.

Feldman, Jerome A. *From Molecule to Metaphor: A Neural Theory of Language*. Cambridge, Mass.: The MIT Press, 2008.

Gallagher, Shaun. *How the Body Shapes the Mind.* Oxford: Oxford University Press, 2005.

Gendlin, Eugene T. "Crossing and Dipping: Some Terms for Approaching the Interface between Natural Understanding and Logical Formulation." *Minds and Machines.* Vol. 5, No. 4 (1995): 547–560.

Ghahremani, Dara G., John Monterosso, J. David Jentsch, Robert M. Bilder, and Russell A. Poldrack. "Neural Components Underlying Behavioral Flexibility in Human Reversal Learning." *Cerebral Cortex.* Vol. 20, No. 8 (2010): 1843–1852.

Grotowski, Jerzy. *Toward a Poor Theatre.* Ed. Eugenio Barba. New York: Simon and Schuster, 1968.

Hagen, Uta. *A Challenge for the Actor.* New York: Scribner, 1991.

Haring-Smith, Tori. "Dramaturging Non-Realism: Creating a New Vocabulary." *Theatre Topics.* Vol. 13, No. 1 (2003): 45–54.

Hethmon, Robert H. ed. *Strasberg at The Actors Studio.* New York: Theatre Communications Group, Inc., 1995.

Huston, Hollis. *The Actor's Instrument: Body, Theory, Stage.* Ann Arbor: The University of Michigan Press, 1992.

Jauss, Hans Robert. *An Aesthetics of Reception.* Minneapolis: University of Minnesota Press, 1982.

Jefferies, Stuart. "Inside the Mind of an Actor (Literally)." *The Guardian.* http://www.guardian.co.uk/science/2009/nov/24/fiona-shaw-neuroscience. November 24, 2009.

Johnson, Mark. *The Body in the Mind.* Chicago and London: The University of Chicago Press, 1987.

Kandel, Eric R., James H. Schwartz, and Thomas M. Jessell. *Principles of Neural Science.* Third edition. New York, Amsterdam, London, and Tokyo: Elsevier Science Publishing Co., Inc., 1991.

Karneva, Oksana ed. *Konstantin Stanislavsky: Selected Works.* Moscow: Raduga Publishers, 1984.

Khoury, Elias. *Gate of the Sun.* Trans. Humphrey Davies. New York: Picador, 2006.

Kisselgoff, Anna. "After 12 Years in Exile, Twyla Tharp Shifts Gears Again." *New York Times.* July 6, 2000, E-1, 5.

Lakoff, George and Mark Johnson. *Philosophy in the Flesh: The Embodied Mind and Its Challenge to Western Philosophy.* New York: Basic Books, 1999.

———. *Metaphors We Live By.* Chicago and London: The University of Chicago Press, 1980.

Lecoq, Jacques. *Theatre of Movement and Gesture.* Ed. David Bradby. London and New York: Routledge, 2006.

———, Jean-Gabriel Carasso, and Jean-Claude Lallias. *The Moving Body: Teaching Creative Theatre.* Trans. David Bradby. London and New York: Routledge, 2001.

Lehmann, Hans-Thies. *Postdramatic Theatre.* Trans. Karen Jürs-Munby. London and New York: Routledge, 2006.

Lessac, Arthur. *The Use and Training of the Human Voice: A Practical Approach to Speech and Voice Dynamics*. Second edition. New York: DBS Publications, Inc., 1967.

Lewis, Marc D. "Bridging Emotion Theory and Neurobiology through Dynamic Systems Modeling." *Behavioral and Brain Sciences*. 28 (2005): 169–245.

Linklater, Kristen. *Freeing the Natural Voice*. New York: Drama Book Publishers, 1976

Lotar, Eli. "Abattoir." *Documents*. 6 (1929): 328.

Lutterbie, John. "Gestus and Acting Style in *The Good Person of Szechwan*: A Case Study." *Gestus: A Quarterly Journal of Brechtian Studies*. Vol. 1, No. 3–4 (1985–86): 77–91.

———. *Hearing Voices: Modern Drama and the Problem of Subjectivity*. Ann Arbor: University of Michigan Press, 1997.

Mayo, Deborah. Interview with John Lutterbie Stony Brook University. Tape recording. December 5, 2001.

———. Interview with John Lutterbie. Stony Brook University. Tape recording. July 3, 2003.

———. Interview with John Lutterbie. Stony Brook University. Tape recording. November 7, 2001.

Mauss, Marcel. *Sociology and Psychology: Essays*. Trans. Ben Brewster. London, Boston, and Henley: Routledge and Kegan Paul, 1979.

———. *Techniques, Technology and Civilization*. Ed. Nathan Schlanger. New York and Oxford: Durkheim Press/Bergbahn Books, 2006.

McConachie, Bruce. *Engaging Audiences: A Cognitive Approach to Spectating in the Theatre*. New York: Palgrave Macmillan, 2008.

McNeill, David. *Gesture and Thought*. Chicago and London: University of Chicago Press, 2005.

Meisner, Sanford and Dennis Longwell. *Sanford Meisner on Acting*. New York: Random House, 1987.

Merleau-Ponty, Maurice. *The Visible and the Invisible*. Evanston: Northwestern University Press, 1968.

Miller, George A. "The Magical Number Seven, Plus or Minus Two: Some Limits on Our Capacity for Processing Information." *Psychological Review*. Vol. 101, No. 2 (1956): 343–355.

Moran, John. *Book of the Dead (2nd Avenue)*. New York Public Library for the Performing Arts. Videotaped in Martinson Hall, Public Theatre, by Theatre on Film and Tape Archive at the New York Public Library for the Performing Arts. December 14, 2000. The Joseph Papp Public Theater/New York Shakespeare Festival, George C. Wolfe, producer.

Müller, Heiner. *Hamletmachine and Other Texts for the Stage*. Trans. Carl Weber. New York: Performing Arts Journal Publications, 1984.

Noice, Helga and Tony Noice. "Two Approaches to Learning a Theatrical Script." *Memory*. Vol. 4, No. 1 (1996): 1–17.

———. "Long Term Retention of Theatrical Roles." *Memory*. Vol. 7, No. 3 (1997): 357–382.

Parkinson, Brian, Agneta H. Fischer, and Antony S. R. Manstead. *Emotion in Social Relations: Cultural, Group, and Interpersonal Processes.* New York and Hove: Psychology Press, 2005.

Purves, Dale, Elizabeth M. Brannon, Roberto Cabeza, Scott A. Huettel, Kevin S. LaBar, Michael L. Platt, and Marty G. Woldorff.. *Principles of Cognitive Neuroscience.* Sunderland: Sinauer Associates, Inc., 2008.

Quick, Andrew. *The Wooster Group Work Book.* London and New York: Routledge, 2007.

Ramachandran, V. S. and Sandra Blakeslee. *Phantoms in the Brain: Probing the Mysteries of the Human Mind.* New York: Harper Perennial, 1999.

Rapp, Peter R. "Structure and Organization of Memory in the Brain (and other stuff)." Presentation at the Humanities Institute at Stony Brook, Stony Brook University. Videotape. December 12, 2007.

Richards, Thomas. *At Work with Grotowski on Physical Actions.* London and New York: Routledge, 1995.

Richman, Howard B., James J. Staszewski, and Herbert A. Simon. "Simulation of Expert Memory Using EPAM IV." *Psychological Review.* Vol. 102, No. 2 (1995): 305-330.

Risum, Janne. "The Impulse and the Image: The Theatre Laboratory Tradition and Oden Teatret." *Odin Teatret 2000.* Ed. John Andreasen and Annelis Kuhlmann. Åarhus: Aarhus University Press, 2000.

Rizzolatti, Giacomo, Leonardo Fogassi, and Vittorio Gallese. "Mirrors in the Mind." *Scientific American.* Vol. 295, No. 5 (November 2006): 54-61.

Saltz, David. "How to Do Things on Stage." *Journal of Aesthetics and Art Criticism.* Vol. 49, No. 1 (1991): 31-45.

Sheets-Johnstone, Maxine. "Kinetic Tactile-Kinesthetic Bodies: Ontogenetical Foundations of Apprenticeship Learning." *Human Studies.* Vol. 23, No. 4 (2000): 343-370.

———. *The Primacy of Movement.* Amsterdam and Philadelphia: John Benjamins Publishing Company, 1999.

Sontag, Susan ed. *Antonin Artaud: Selected Writings.* Trans. Helen Weaver. Berkeley and Los Angeles: University of California Press, 1976.

Stanescu, Saviana and Daniel Gerould, eds. *roMANIA after 2000: Five New Romanian Plays.* New York: Martin E. Segal Theatre Center Publications, 2007.

Stanislavski, Konstantin. *An Actor's Work on a Role.* Trans. Jean Bendetti. London and New York: Routledge, 2010.

Su,Tsu-Chung. "The Occidental Theatre and Its Other: The Use and Abuse of the Oriental Theatre in Antonin Artaud." *NTU Studies in Language and Literature.* Vol.1, No. 22 (December 2009): 1-30.

Thelen, Esther and Linda B. Smith. *A Dynamic Systems Approach to the Development of Cognition and Action.* Cambridge, Mass. and London: The MIT Press, 1996.

Thomas, Dylan. *Selected Poems, 1934-1952.* Revised edition. New York: New Directions, 2003.

Thompson, Evan. *Mind in Life: Biology, Phenomenology, and the Sciences of Mind*. Cambridge, Mass. and London, England: Harvard University Press, 2007.

Tufnell, Miranda and Chris Crickmay. *A Widening Field: Journeys in Body and Imagination*. Hampshire: Dance Books, 2004.

Tytell, John. *The Living Theatre: Art, Exile, and Outrage*. New York: Grove Press, 1997; 225–278.

Verges, Chrisann, director, and Mark Obenhaus, producer, *Einstein on the Beach: The Changing Image of Opera*. Videotape, OCLC No. 182958578. 1984.

Wylie, Glenn R., John J. Foxe, and Tracy L. Taylor. "Forgetting as an Active Process: An fMRI Investigation of Item-Method-Directed Forgetting." *Cerebral Cortex*. Vol. 18, No. 3 (March 2008): 670–682.

Xue, Gui, Dara G. Ghahremani, and Russell A. Poldrack, "Neural Substrates for Reversing Stimulus-Outcome and Stimulus-Response Associations." *The Journal of Neuroscience*. Vol. 28, No. 44 (October 29, 2008): 11196–11204.

Index

Abdoh, Reza, 11, 223
Act Up, 11
acting
  becoming the character, 71, 170, 186
  Brecht, not becoming the character, 44–49
  Chekhov, 59–60
  Grotowski, 53–54
  Hagen, 64–67
  Meisner, 67–69
  Meyerhold, 36–39
  Stanislavski, 30–36
  Strasberg, 62–64
  creating a role, 31–34, 40, 45, 148
  inside out, 10, 23, 28, 61, 73, 153
  outside in, 11, 28, 59, 61, 73, 152–153
  pre-acting, 39
  relationships, 29, 39, 174, 198–200, 202, 217, 219, 221
  warm-up, 212–213
action
  arc of action, 184, 206
  consonant action, 150–151; *see also* Lessac
  physical actions, 29, 32–35, 39–41, 53–55, 58–61, 72, 148, 152, 182, 202, 203, 224, 236 n. 70, 245 n. 3
  structural action, 150–151; *see also* Lessac
  tonal action, 150–51; *see also* Lessac

actor
  self-presentation, 37, 147
Actors Studio, The, 61, 237 n. 109
Adams, Paul, 7, 16
Adler, Stella, 11, 234
aesthetics
  aesthetic practice, 144
affect, 223–224
affective
  affective states, 35, 101
AI (Artificial Intelligence), 23
Albee, Edward, 27
Althusser, Louis, 164, 244 n. 3
amateurs, 26
analysis, 22, 34–35, 40, 60, 70, 98, 117–118, 148–149, 153, 187, 194, 197
Anderson, Ray, 8
animate, 22, 65–67, 141–142, 169, 223
Anti-Oedipal, 164
appraisal, 89, 92–97, 101–102, 241
arboreal, 165
  see also Deleuze; Guattari
art, 7, 10, 12, 14–15, 22–23, 29–30, 35–36, 51, 53–54, 61–64, 102–103, 131–133, 159, 192
Artaud, Antonin, 10, 11, 21, 42, 47–52, 55, 59, 120, 138, 176, 211, 236 n. 56–69, 241 n. 21, 245 n. 12, 247 n. 2
  alchemy, 47, 52
  Balinese dancers, 49

Artaud, Antonin—*Continued*
  body without organs, 24, 48–50
  double, the, 47–50
  theatre of cruelty, 47, 50–51
"as if," 67–70
associations
  chain of associations, 178
atrophy, 107, 135, 144, 153, 158, 209
attention
  center of attention, 178, 228
  circle of attention, 110, 170–172, 205–206, 209, 215, 219, 229
  divided attention, 56
attitudes, 80, 113–114, 178, 186, 200
attractor states, 13, 176
audience, 2, 14–15, 26
  vigilant observer, 37

Baars, Bernard J.
  In the Theater of Consciousness, 79–80
Baddeley, Alan, 106, 111, 145, 240 n. 4, 243 n. 21
  see also working memory
balance, 40, 56–57, 64, 153
ballet, 114, 132, 154–155, 158, 230
Barba, Eugenio, 2, 10, 11, 147, 163, 170, 204, 220, 231, 243 n. 26, 245 n. 13
  Daily body techniques, 147, 170
  extra-daily energy, 147, 159, 214, 227
  Extra-daily techniques, 147, 170
  Sats, 204
Barthes, Roland, 38, 122, 241
  the grain of the voice, 38, 122
Baryshnikov, Mikhail, 154, 193, 230
Bausch, Pina, 192
beat, 170, 183–184, 187–200, 203–207, 210, 213, 218–219, 224
Beckett, Samuel, 7, 10, 11, 27, 187, 204
  Happy Days, 187

behavior
  emerging pattern, 91–92, 111, 126, 128, 172, 206, 209
  pattern of behavior, 91, 94, 128, 186, 196–197
Behn, Aphra, 27
being in the moment, 4, 5, 167–168, 214
Bensussa, Simone, 27
Berry, Cecily, 10
bicycle, 134–135, 138, 140, 221, 239
biology, 7
biomechanics, 11, 36, 39–41, 45
  see also Meyerhold
Blakeslee, Sandra, 9, 234
Blanchett, Cate, 230
Blau, Herbert, 6, 15, 137, 212, 240 n. 9, 242 n. 7
  The Audience, 212
  Eye of Prey, 137
blending, *see* Fauconnier
blocking, 183–184, 186, 196, 200, 203, 204, 213, 215
Blue Man Group, 11, 27
Boal, Augusto, 2, 11, 26, 163, 167, 213, 244 n. 5
  cop in the head, 167
  invisible theatre, 26, 213
body
  actor's instrument, 22, 62, 73, 138, 152, 247
  body memories, *see* Chekhov, Michael
  mind-full body, *see* Sheets-Johnstone
  neutral body, *see* Lecoq
  physical tension, 70, 152
body image, 113–117, 135, 138, 140–142, 144–148, 155, 157–158, 193
  see also Gallagher
body schema, 113–117, 135, 138–142, 144, 148, 157–158, 193
  see also Gallagher
body without organs, 24, 48, 169
  see also Artaud

Bogart, Ann, 11, 163
Bond, Edward, 27
Borges, Jorge Luis, 173
boundaries, 93–94, 113, 140, 166–167, 176–177
brain
   amygdale, 7, 82
   association cortex, 136
   basal ganglia, 136, 242 n. 4
   brainstem, 81, 116
   Broca's area, 124
   cerebellum, 81, 116, 136
   cingulate gyrus, 82
   frontal lobe, 124
   hardwiring, 79, 94
   hippocampus, 7, 82
   inferior frontal gyrus, 124
   inhibition, 110, 136, 158
   lateralization, 81
   limbic system, 81–82, 136
   prefrontal cortex, 82, 109
   premotor area, 136
   primary motor cortex, 136
   reptilian brain, 81
   soft wiring, 94
   somatosensory cortex, 136
   speech centers, 124–125
   supplementary motor area, 136
   thalamus, 82, 136, 242 n. 4
   see also neocortex
breath
   breathing, 50, 81
Brecht, Bertolt, 10, 11, 27, 42–47, 59, 61, 71, 94, 138, 152, 154, 203, 223, 231, 235 n. 46
   alienation, 42–46
   complex seeing, 44
   critical reflection, 43
   distancing effect, 44
   gestus, 45–46, 203
   quotation, 45–46
   Verfremdungseffekt, 43–45, 72, 154
Brenner, Patricia, 12
Breton, André, 47
   Nadia, 47
   Surrealism, 47

Bricoleur, 156
Brook, Peter, 10
Büchner, Georg, 11, 27
Builders Association, 11, 192
Buñuel, Luis, 47
   Le Chien Andalou (The Andalusian Dog), 47
Butoh, 163

Castellucci, Claudia, 195, 246 n. 18
categories, 22, 24, 26–27, 81, 96, 105, 108, 128, 132, 145, 169, 240
change, 94–95, 141, 221
character, 4, 11, 30–39, 41, 44–46, 52, 57–68, 71–72, 170–171, 173, 183–187
Chekhov, Anton, 27, 185
   Cherry Orchard, The, 184
   Three Sisters, The, 216
Chekhov, Michael, 10, 11, 50, 51, 59, 112, 201, 203, 231, 237
   psychological gesture, 51, 59–60, 201, 203–204
   will power, 59
   will-impulses, 59
choreography, 133, 154–155, 157–158, 193
chunking, 108–109, 198–209, 215–216, 218–219, 224–225
Churchill, Caryl, 27
Cieslak, Ryszard, 53, 163
Cirque du Soleil, 11, 27
Clarke, Martha, 192
cognition, 80, 83–84, 92, 96–97
   mental construction, 125
cognitive science, 5, 7, 23, 73, 246
cognitive studies, 8, 13, 15, 16, 78
collaboration, 185
comedy, 162, 166, 173, 215
communication, 21, 31, 37, 39, 41, 48–49, 52, 69, 72–73, 98, 103, 106, 116–118, 120–122
complexity, 84–85
   DST, 118–120

concentration, *see* attention
concepts
   cognitive sciences, 78–79, 84
conceptual blending
   blended space, 174
   compression, 174
   elaboration, 175
   input space, 174
   mental space, 123, 174, 175
   projections, 174
   running the blend, 174–175
consciousness
   divided consciousness, 62, 64
   subconscious, 38, 63
   unconscious, 12, 38, 47–48, 51–52, 62–64, 72, 73, 80, 97–98, 100, 105, 107, 146–147
consolidation, 82, 98, 109, 202, 206, 229
content, 5, 35
   Artaud, 48–49
   Brecht, 46
   memory and emotional content, 67, 136, 151
   Meyerhold and formalism, 36, 38–39
context, 90–92
   gesture and utterance, 121–122
   importance of context in improvisation, 172–173, 187
   technique and memory, 145–146
   see also world-making
convention(s), 48
   Hagen's realism, 65
   nonrealism, 186–187
costumes, 184, 189, 200, 221, 223
Cowan, Nelson, 106, 184, 240, 246 n. 21
   see also working memory
craft
   Stanislavski on craft, 29–32
   Strasberg, craft as imitation, 62
Crease, Robert, 16, 242 n. 2

creativity
   creative impulse, 22, 58, 59, 66, 88, 166, 176
   creative process, 5, 23, 27, 32, 79, 88, 162, 169, 176, 178
   creative states, 170
Crickmay, Chris, 163, 167, 244 n. 6
critical reflection, *see* Brecht
crossroads, 11
cues, 14, 110, 140, 152, 153, 188, 197, 200, 203, 208–209
   see also score, acting score; trigger
cultural norms, 118
curtain call, 228

Dah Theatre, 181
Dali, Salvador, 47
Damasio, Antonio, 6, 9, 16, 22, 72, 78, 239
   Descartes' Error, 22, 78, 239
   Feeling of What Happens, The, 6, 16–17
Dance Theatre, 192
De Chirico, Georgio, 47
de la Barca, Calderón, 2, 27, 53
   The Constant Prince, 53
Decety, Jean, 226–227, 239 n. 3
decision-making, 78, 81, 82, 96, 110
Deleuze, Gilles, 163–165, 167, 176, 225, 244 n. 4, 248 n. 10
Dennehy, Brian, 230
Descartes, Rene, 79, 82, 118
   mind body split, 48
Desire
   Desiring, 225
devising, 89, 112, 167, 177, 182, 185
dialectic, 43–44, 46, 125–127, 185, 211
   synthesis, 43, 46, 125
Diderot, Denis, 148
director, 25, 206, 220–221
   role of director in Grotowski, 52
disability, 114
   disabled performers, 27

disequilibrium, 25, 57, 84, 92–93, 96, 97, 99
dramaturg, 89, 105, 190, 210
Dreyfus, Hubert, 12, 233, 242, 250
Dreyfus, Stuart, 12, 233, 242, 250
Dynamic Systems Theory, 5, 7, 9, 25, 77, 79, 81–85, 91, 96, 98, 101–104, 112, 120, 197–198, 231
  attractor states, 13, 176
  attractors, 13–14, 93–94, 98–99, 104, 107, 110–111, 117–118, 120, 124, 128, 147, 170–171, 197, 206–209, 218–219, 225, 229
  best fit, 121–123
  boundary conditions, 13–14, 91, 93–95, 97–102, 104, 107, 111, 118, 120, 122–125, 128, 135, 144, 147, 156–157, 170
  circular causality, 90, 94–95, 97–99, 114
  control parameters, 135
  emergent patterns, 93, 128
  limit conditions, 94
  metastability, 91
  perturbationn, 13, 25, 90–95, 98, 100, 102, 105, 107, 112, 115, 117, 120, 123, 126–127, 197, 201, 210, 229, 231
  phase synchrony, 95, 98–99
  phase transition, 93–94, 97–99, 124, 206, 209
  phase-locking, 95
  primitives, 91

Edelman, Gerald, 110, 240
  reentrance, 110
Ekert, Rinde, 11
embodiment, 23, 35, 113
  see also body image; body schema
emergent, 93, 97, 128
  emergent structure, 174
Emotion
  emotional centers, 34, 148
emotional depth, 68; see also Meisner
emotional identification, 10, 29–32, 101
emotional intensity, 31, 38, 41, 60–61, 86, 186, 197–198
emotional recall, 24, 29, 32, 35, 52, 61, 66–67, 72, 190, 201
empathy, 42–46, 78, 101–102, 226–227
encoding, 201–202, 206
  recoding, 108–109, 201–202, 206
energy
  energetic relaxation, see Lessac
  extra-daily energy, see Barba
  psychological energy, 45, 65
  relaxed energy, see Lessac
  vectors of energy, 225
engagement(s), 3, 38, 41, 44, 100, 102, 112–113, 119, 142
  improvisation, 166, 168–169, 178
environment
  environmental constraints, 94, 126
  external environment, 104, 166, 209, 218–220
  internal environment, 113, 117
equilibrium, 57, 84, 92
Escher, M. C.
  Drawing Hands, 225
Espada, Margarita, 2, 5, 16, 163, 168, 169, 193, 195, 233 n. 3–7, 244 n. 8, n. 57, 245 n. 10
Etchells, Tim, 116, 244 n. 1, 245 n. 21
evaluation, 5, 96, 152, 156, 166, 168, 171
everyday
  everyday life, 37, 41–42, 47–48, 51, 55–57, 65, 80, 112, 116, 133, 137, 147
  techniques, 133, 137, 139, 145, 164, 193

evolution, 79, 81, 101, 112, 116, 143
  evolution of personae, 195
  evolution of score, 182, 184
excitation, 40, 84, 92, 95, 136, 156
executive
  executive control, 14, 104,
    109–112, 128, 214, 229
exercises, 2, 40, 52, 151–153, 163,
    214, 235
expectations, 22, 44, 73, 75, 104,
    111, 121, 133, 135, 169,
    198–199, 212–213, 226
experience
  autobiographical, 60, 80,
    105, 142
expertise, 12–13, 107, 155, 158, 230
experts, 132, 176–177
expression
  body as vehicle of, 32–33, 62–63
  Gallagher, 115–117
  Grotowski, 52–53
  Lessac, 151–152
  Meyerhold, economical
    expression, 36, 40
expressionism
  Brecht's turn away from, 42
  Robert Wislon's
    neoexpressionism, 223
exteroceptive, 139

facilitation, 110, 144
falsifiability, 9
Fauconnier, Gilles, 122, 241
feelings
  inner feelings, 62
Feldman, Jerome A., 118–120,
    241 n. 24
  neural theory of language,
    118–119, 241 n. 17
flesh, 6, 23–25, 47, 100, 135,
    140, 229
  Maurice Merleau-Ponty, 25,
    140, 220
flow, 88, 90, 92, 175–176, 178,
    194, 210, 215
fMRI, 22, 157, 247 n. 32

Fo, Dario, 10
focus
  dual focus, 216
Forced Entertainment, 11, 27, 163,
    185, 192–193, 196, 244 n. 1,
    245 n. 21, 246 n. 17
  Bloody Mess, 185
Foreman, Richard, 11, 27, 192, 195
forgetting, 109, 184
  intentional, 109, 184, 198,
    207–208
form, 10, 11, 26, 27, 36–37, 42,
    45, 55, 64–65, 99, 103, 117,
    118, 122, 124, 126, 133,
    137, 155, 162, 185, 187,
    191–192, 194, 196, 199, 223
  opposition between form and
    content in supremacist
    work, 36
  see also formalism
formalism, 64–65
Fornes, Marie Irene, 10
Forsythe, William, 27
Fosse, Bob, 133
frames
  frame of reference, 166
Freud, Sigmund, 59
  repression, 48
  unconscious, 47, 48

Gallagher, Shaun, 113–115,
    139–142
  How the Body Shapes the Mind,
    113, 240 n. 10
Garrick, David, 148
gender, 114, 187
Gendlin, Eugene, 98, 154–155,
    243 n. 51
  carry forward, 98, 155
  crossing, 154–155
gestalt, 95, 97–98, 101–102, 119,
    135, 143, 239 n. 15
  see also Brecht
gesture
  gestus, 45–46, 203, 236; *see also*
    Brecht

growth point, 125
iconic, 124–125
psychological gesture, 51, 59–60, 201, 203–204
psychological predicate, 126
stop order, 125–126
unpacking, 125–127, 203
Gibson, William, 23
given circumstances, 32–36, 68–71
Gladwell, Malcolm, 97
Blink: The Power of Thinking Without Thinking, 97
Glass, Phillip, 184
Goat Island, 192
Government Inspector, The, 29
Grapes of Wrath, The, 6, 124, 181, 183
Granpa Joad, 6, 124, 183
Grotowski, Jerzy, 10, 11, 47, 50–55, 57, 59, 71, 137, 152, 163, 176, 183, 203, 211, 236 n. 70, 237 n. 72
art as vehicle, 51, 53–54
carnal prayer, 51, 54–55
Constant Prince, The, 53, 163, 181–182; *see also* de la Barca
paratheatre, 51
theatre of presentation, 51–52, 54
theatre of sources, 26, 51
via negative, 51–52, 55, 72, 117, 137
Guattari, Félix, 163–167, 176, 225, 244 n. 4, 248 n. 10

habit
habit of mind, 164–165
habit strength, 185
habitual patterns, 28, 91, 137, 150
secondary impulses, 152
habitus, 145–146
Hagen, Uta, 11, 64–67, 131, 138, 251
formalism, 64–65, 84
outer technique, 64
particularization, 67
selected behavior, 65
transference, 65
see also naturalism
Hamlet, 8, 21, 121, 126
Ophelia, 184
Haring-Smith, Tori, 185, 187, 246
harmony
harmonic patterns, 97
Hart, F. Elizabeth, 7, 15
Hegel, Georg, 43
dialectic, 43
Heidegger, 143
hermeneutic cycle, 143
Hoffman, Philip Seymour, 230
homunculus, 6, 110
human spirit, 30, 32, 34–35, 37, 41, 42, 47, 55, 58, 64, 223

Ibsen, Henrik, 27, 185, 186
Rosmersholm, 186
identity, 12, 94, 132, 147–148, 167
ideology, 164
illusion
Brecht, 44–45
Grotowski, 54
Plato, allegory of the cave, 30
image mapping, 214–215
imagination, 15, 28, 37, 56, 66–67, 70, 73, 102, 153, 163, 178, 182
imitation
Brecht, two types of acting, 43
realism as imitation in Hagen, 65
Sheets-Johnstone, human development, 142–146
Strasberg, imitation as craft, 61–62
technique, 135
improvisation
improvisational techniques, 178; *see also* technique
improvise, 32, 167, 172, 178
impulses
inner impulses, 51
inhibition, 110, 136, 158
inspiration, 30, 55, 66, 149, 193
instinct, 52, 71

instrument, 22, 40, 118, 133, 138
  Hagen, 66
  Lessac, voice as instrument, 150
  Linklater, 152–153
  Strasberg, 62–63
intellect, 5–6, 31–35, 40, 48–49, 61, 152–153
intensities, 101, 170, 218
intention, 13, 39–40, 203
interior monologue, 209
interiority, 38
International Phonetic Alphabet (IPA), 151
interpretation, 98–99, 120–121
intersubjectivity, 100, 102, 140
intuition, 82, 127, 221, 233
Ionesco, Eugene, 10, 11, 223
  Bald Soprano, The, 223
Irwin, Bill, 11, 223
  Regard of Flight, The, 223

Jarry, Alfred, 11, 230
Jennerod, Marc, 100
Jennerod, Pierre Jacob, 100, 101
Jesurun, John, 11
Jeter, Derek, 115
journey
  flight, 164–167, 170, 172, 176
  path, 111, 119, 126, 136
  river, 68–69
  stream, 44, 68, 71, 200
Jung, Carl, 59
  anima and animus, 59
  archetype, 59
  shadow, 59

Kandel, Eric, 136, 242, 251
Kane, Sarah, 11, 184, 204, 223
  4.48 Psychosis, 184, 223
Kantor, Tadeuz, 11
Kelso, J. A. Scott, 77, 83, 91, 93, 239
Kennedy, Adrienne, 10, 11
knowledge, 78, 80, 91, 134–135, 143, 164
KRAKEN, 11
Kroetz, Franz Xaver, 204

landscape, 100, 214
  emotional landscape, 100
  physical landscape, 100, 214
language, 14, 24, 25, 41, 48, 49, 74, 82, 83, 90, 91, 101, 102, 106, 117–123, 185, 187, 231
  language and gesture, 124–127
LeCoq, Jacques, 3, 4, 10, 11, 26, 50–51, 55–58, 137, 152, 231, 237
  counter-mask, 58
  countermovement, 57
  mimages, 57
  mimodynamic process, 57
  neutral creative state, 51
  neutral mask, 3, 55–56, 58, 69, 137
  universal poetic sense, 55, 57–58
LeDoux, Joseph, 9
  The Synaptic Self, 9
Lehmann, Hans-Thies, 11, 27, 192, 234 n. 7
Leonard, Robert Sean, 230
Lessac, Arthur, 149–153, 243 n. 28
  consonant action, 150–151
  energetic relaxation, 150
  inverted megaphone, 151
  relaxed energy, 150
  structural action, 150–151
  tonal action, 150–151
  Use and Training of the Human Voice, The, 149
Leung, Hoi-Chung, 8, 16
Lewis, Marc, 83, 85, 92, 96, 239 n. 5
lighting, 216–218
linear systems, 84, 99
lines of flight, 164–166, 167, 170, 172, 176
linguistics, 8–9, 13, 118, 124
Linklater, Kristen, 10, 149, 152–153
  blocks, 152
  Freeing the Natural Voice, 152
  touch of sound, 153
lip-synch, 224

living human spirit, 32, 34–35, 41–42, 47, 51, 55, 58, 223
Living Theatre, The, 10, 47, 181, 196, 215
  Paradise Now, 215
logic, 98, 169–170, 186–187, 218
looping, 205
Lotar, Eli, 47, 236
  Abattoir, 47

Mabou Mines, 192
MacNeill, David, 123
Maeterlinck, Maurice, 27, 36, 38
  Blue Bird, 32
Magritte, René, 47
Mangano, Nick, 6, 16
mapping, 82, 111, 116, 120, 122–123, 214–215
Marceau, Marcel, 14
mask
  counter-mask, 58; *see also* Lecoq
  gas mask, 161, 170, 173
  inner mask, 38, 41
  neutral mask, 3, 55–56, 58, 69, 137; *see also* Lecoq
Matrix, The, 121, 225
Mauss, Marcel, 138, 145–146, 164, 243, 244, 252
Mayo, Deborah, 1–5, 10, 16, 163, 168–169, 172, 222, 233, 244
McConachie, Bruce, 7, 15, 16, 100, 240 n. 23
  Engaging Audiences, 100
Mee, Charles, 195
  Bobrauschenbergamerica, 195
Meisner, Sanford, 11, 67–71, 112
  canoe, 68
  emotional depth, 68
  emotional dialogue, 69–70
  inner character, 71
  inner life, 70
  particularization, 68–71
  preparation, 68–71, 213
  Sanford Meisner on Acting, 68

memory
  autobiographical memory, 80
  chunks, 108–109, 198, 200, 206–207, 209, 218, 224–225
  consolidation, 82, 98, 202, 206, 229
  declarative memory, 80
  echoic memory, 106
  episodic memory, 105–106, 108
  explicit memory, 105, 107, 201
  forgetting, 109
  implicit memory, 8, 107–108, 135, 139, 156–157
  kinesthetic memory, 150
  long-term memory, 82, 98, 105–107, 109, 157, 196, 198, 207
  perceptual memory, 25, 198
  peripheral memories, 198
  retrieval, 83–84, 109, 157, 197–198, 202–203
  semantic memory, 108
  spatial memory, 82
  visual memory, 63–64, 66–67
  working memory, 106, 108–109, 121, 218–219
Mendes, Sam, 184
Merleau-Ponty, Maurice, 25, 140, 220, 234 n. 5
metaphor
  affection is warmth, 119
  canoe, *see* Meisner
  causes are forces, 119
  change is motion, 119
  Container (containment, containing), 5, 24, 32–33, 38, 62
  embodied schemas, 122
  metaphorical associations, 29
  mind as theatre, 80
  mixed metaphors, 122–123, 175
  schemas, 119–122
  source-path-goal schema, 119
  states are locations, 119
metaphysics, 57
Method, The, 10, 61–62, 67, 94

methodology (methodologies), 11, 26, 28, 65, 68, 103, 131, 148, 149, 150, 153, 192, 193, 195, 203, 230
Meyerhold, Vsevelod, 10, 11, 29, 32, 39–42, 45, 59, 235 n. 40
   actor-tribune, 41
   affective centers, 40
   mystical vibrations, 39
   N=A1 + A2, 39
   plasticity, 37, 58, 178
   pre-acting, 39
   Russian Constructivism, 36
   stylized theatre, 36
   Symbolist Theatre, 36
   vigilant observer, 37
   see also biomechanics
Miller, Arthur, 27, 95, 185
   After the Fall, 187
   The Crucible, 95
   Death of a Salesman, 187
Milosevic, Dijana, 181
mime, 10–11, 195, 213
mind
   mind-body split, 22–24, 79, 84, 118; *see also* Descartes
mirror neurons, 78
   mirror neuron function, 227
   Mirror Neuron System (MNS), 227
Mitchell, Katie, 11, 88–89
   Waves, 85–90
Mnouchkine, Ariane, 10, 11, 27, 163
   Les Éphémères, 163
molar, 165
molecular, 165
Molière (Jean-Baptiste Poquelin), 11, 27, 185
Molina, Alfred, 230
Monk, Meredith, 192
Monsieur Hulot, 57
Moran, John, 224, 248
   Book of the Dead (2nd Avenue), 224
Moscow Art Theatre, 37, 61
motor control, 81, 136

movement
   countermovement, *see* Lecoq
   expressive, 115
   instrumental, 115–117
   locomotive, 115
   reflex, 115–117
Müller, Heiner, 11, 27, 189–191, 246
   Hamletmachine, 189–191, 246

narrative, 84–85
National Theatre, 84–85, 88
naturalism, 37, 65
nature
   second nature, 13, 109, 115, 133–135, 141, 145
neocortex
   associational cortex, 82
   auditory cortex, 82
   motor cortex, 82
   prefrontal cortex, 82
   visual cortex, 82
neuro-muscular system, 137
neurons
   neural assemblies, 93, 95, 99, 102
   neural networks, 78, 83, 95–96, 106–110, 117, 137, 143, 147, 156, 158, 202–203, 206
   neural pathways, 176
neuropsychology, 9, 79
neuroscience, 5, 9, 16, 22, 25, 76, 77, 79
neutral, 3–5, 51, 55–58, 69, 137, 168
Newson, Lloyd, 113
Nichols, Peter, 211
   A Day in the Life of Joe Egg, 211
Noh, 138, 213
   Hashigakari, 214
Noice, Helga, 22, 234
Noice, Tom, 22, 234
non-linear systems, 83–84
non-realism, 11, 184, 186–189, 195, 234
non-text based performance, 181
novelty, 209

objective, 4, 40–41, 50–52, 170–171, 176, 200–201
Odin Theatre, 26
Oedipus, 164
Olga's House of Shame, 195
O'Neil, Eugene
   Long Day's Journey into Night, 215
Open Theatre, 2, 10

paradigm, 15, 27, 77–78, 81, 83, 191–192
parallel processing, 78, 83, 121
parameters, 68, 135, 148–149, 159, 162–163, 167, 170–171, 186, 191
Parkinson, Brian, 101, 240, 253
passion(s), 31, 34, 45, 122
passive, 4, 25
patterns, 25, 27–28, 30, 82–85
   patterns of behavior, 12, 14, 84, 110, 112, 126, 128, 147, 172, 197, 209, 213, 218, 220, 222
Peirce, Charles Sanders, 49
perception (perceives)
   oral perception, 25
   perceptual data, 197–198, 200, 220, 225, 241
   tactile perception, 25, 162, 171
   visual perception, 100, 139, 143
   see also Merleau-Ponty
performance, 7
   actor's score, 14, 191–192
   Artaud, 49–51
   Brecht, 42–44
   DST, 112–116
   Grotowski, 51–53
   Meisner, 68–69
   Meyerhold, 38–41
   Stanislavski, 29–35
   Strasberg, 62–64
   super objective, 170
   technique, 132–133
phenomenology, 7, 9, 16, 83
philosophy, 13, 30, 83, 113, 163, 165, 234

physical actions, 33–35, 39, 41, 53–55, 60–61, 124, 148, 152, 182, 224, 236
physicalization, 37, 183, 196
Ping Chong, 11
Pinker, Steven, 9
Pinter, Harold, 117, 204
   No Man's Land, 117
Pirandello, Luigi, 10, 11, 27
Plato
   allegory of the cave, 30
   The Republic, 30
play analysis, 117
playwright, 36, 38–39, 64–65, 149, 187
plot, 186
politics, 11, 41–42, 46, 164–165, 187
Pollock, Jackson, 8
postdramatic, 11, 14, 26–28, 184, 191–194, 234, 246, 251
poststructuralist theory, 9, 163
prime, 203–209, 218
Prince, Harold, 196
Principle of Falsifiability, 9
process
   creative process, 5, 23, 27, 32, 79, 88, 162, 169, 176, 178, 196, 211, 222
   dynamic process, 30, 120, 173
proprioception (proprioceptive), 25, 72, 91, 100, 106, 113–119, 128, 140, 143, 150, 198, 210, 229
props, 184, 189, 200, 212–213
psychological realism, 10
psychology, 22, 186, 243

race, 187
Rajaram, Suparna, 8, 16
Ramachandran, V. S., 9, 234
Rame, Franca, 10
Rapp, Peter R., 158, 240, 244
rational, 5, 40, 43, 152–153
realism
   dialogic structure, 185
   multi-dimensional characters, 185

reason
  abstract reason, 110
reception theory
  horizon of expectations, 198
reciprocal, 24, 26, 33
  reciprocity, 223
Red, 230
Redgrave, Vanessa, 215, 230
Redmayne, Eddie, 230
Rehearsal(s)
  rehearsal process, 3–4, 68–69, 88–90, 98–99, 219, 230
  technical rehearsals, 217
relaxation, 62, 150–153, 214
remembering, 106–108, 145, 184, 197, 196–197, 208
repetition, 2, 13, 51, 61, 89–91, 132, 135
  habitus, 146
  human development, 142–144
  score, 182–183, 187, 193, 196–197, 200, 208–209, 222, 224
rhizome, 165
rhythm, 39, 54
  actor's score, 200–201, 205, 207, 221; *see also* chunking
  Beckett, 187–188
  Lessac, 151; *see also* Lessac, tonal action
Richardson, Sir Ralph, 1, 117
Richman, Howard B., 202, 247, 253
risk, 34, 65, 97–98, 176–177
  see also Deleuze; Guattari; lines of flight
Rivère, Jacques, 49
role
  becoming the role Strasberg, 62–64
  creating the role, 31–34, 40, 45, 148; *see also* acting
Rosenthal, Rachel, 11
Rostand, Edmond, 185
Ruhl, Sarah
  Eurydice, 223
Rush, Geoffrey, 10

Saussure, Ferdinand de, 49
Schiller, Friedrich, 27
science
  cognitive science, 5, 23, 73, 246 n. 5
  intersections between sciences and the humanities, 7–9
  neurobiology, 8, 239 n. 5
  see also Principle of Falsifiability
score, 181–220
  acting score, 82, 91–92, 98–100, 104, 111–112, 224–226, 230, 241 n. 16
  creating a score, 14, 52–55, 60, 64, 71, 80, 84, 116, 163, 181–191, 197–198, 210, 212
  rehearsal score, 199–201, 213
  skill sets, 138, 148, 156
script, 5, 52, 185, 234 n. 2
second nature, 13, 115, 133–135
  habitus, 145
self
  autobiographical self, 142–143
  free the self, 34
  self-organization, 85, 92, 239 n. 1
senses
  hearing, 25
  olfactory, 39, 93–94
  taste, 25, 106
  touch, 25, 106
    body schema, 139
    Linklater, 153
  vision, 25, 56–57, 100–101, 106
sequence of actions, 46, 62, 111–112
  as actor's score, 181, 218
  chunking, 197–200, 225
  DST Theory, 197
  dynamic body, 156
sexuality, 114, 187
Shakespeare, William, 11, 27, 132, 174, 185, 246 n. 6
  Hamlet, 8, 121
  Hamletmachine, 189–191, 226
Shaw, George Bernard, 67
Shaw Fiona, 22, 234 n. 3

Sheets-Johnstone, Maxine, 24, 138, 141–144, 169, 234 n. 4, 242 n. 14
   apprenticeship to the body, 144–145
   I cans, 115, 134, 142, 144, 146–147
   imitation, 142–146
   joint attention, 142–143
   turn taking, 142–143
Shepard, Sam, 10, 27
signs
   Artaud, 48–49
   Grotowski, 52
   Lecoq's theory of neutrality, 55
Simon, Herbert A., 202
skill, 12
   as technique, 132–133
Snow, C. P., 7
Societas Sanzio Raffaello, 11
   Tragedia Endogonidia, 193, 195
society
   Althusser, ideology, 164
   Atraud, repression, 47–48
   body image, 114, 146–148; *see also* gender; race
   Brecht, critique of capitalism, 42–43
   Deleuze and Guattari, 164–165
   emotional restraint, 69
   Marcel Mauss, 145–146
space
   liminal space, 54, 214
   mental space, 123; compression, 174–175
   neural space, 202
   physical as constraint in improvisation, 178
   space of performance, 212, 214, 216
   spatial relationship, 32, 120, 214, 225
   stage space, 225
spectator, *see* audience
speech
   Hagen, vocal mechanism, 66
   Lessac's three energies, 149–151, 243 n. 28
   relationship with gesture, 14, 116, 122–126
   see also Lessac; Linklater; voice, vocal production
Spirit X, 195
Split Britches, 27
sports
   baseball, 13–14, 141
   bicycling, 134–135, 138, 140, 221
   football, 43
   tennis, 12–13
stage manager, 213, 229
Stanescu, Savania
   Waxing West, 187, 246 n. 11
Stanislavski, Constantine, 10, 24, 28–39, 113, 137, 152, 223, 226, 235 n. 15
   Actor Prepares, The, 61
   actor's creative state, 31–33
   An Actor's Work on a Role, 29, 32, 235 n. 15
   emotional identification, 10, 29–32
   emotional recall, 24, 29, 32, 35, 66–67, 72, 201
   influence on Artaud and Brecht, 42–45, 47, 49, 50
   Chekhov, 59–60, 61
   Grotowski, 50–53
   Lecoq, 58
   Lee Strasberg, 61, 64
   Sanford Meisner, 67
   Vsevolod Meyerhold, 37
   inner creative state, 31–35
   Moscow Art Theatre, 37, 61
   "On Various Trends in Theatrical Art," 29
   presenting a role, 29
Staszewski, James J., 247 n. 25
Stein, Gertrude, 11
   Doctor Faustus: Lights the Lights, 195
Stelarc, 23

Strasberg, Lee
  emotional recall, 61, 66–67
  inner technique, 61–66
  Method, 10, 61–62, 67, 94
  see also subtext
Strindberg, August, 27
Style, 10–11
  Brecht, 42–43
  Chekhov, 59
  dancing, 154–155
  Hagen, 64
  technique, 131–132
subtext, 50, 64, 194
super objective, 170–171
Surrealism, 47
Swamp Gravy, 11
synapse, 7, 77, 98, 109, 158
  ion gates, 7
  synaptic cleft, 98, 101
  synaptic connections, 98–99, 106–107, 109, 144, 157–158, 206–209
system
  actor's score, 209–210, 212
  Artaud, 48–49
  body/mind as interdependent system, 22–24
  cast, 220–221
  curtain call, 228
  dynamic system, 13–14, 25, 88–91, 99–100, 103, 107, 118, 128, 172, 176
  Lecoq, 56–57
  linear and non-linear systems, 84, 99
  Stanislavski, 29, 35–36
  see also brain, limbic system; Dynamic Systems Theory

talent, 21, 28, 128, 199
Tasic, Sanja Krsmanovic, 181
Taylor, Frederick, 40
Teatret Gruppe, 38, 192
technique
  analytical, 60, 83, 89, 148–150, 194

body, 145, 244 n. 2
daily body techniques, 147, 170; *see also* Barba
extra-daily techniques, 147, 159, 170; *see also* Barba
improvisational techniques, 176
inner technique, 61–62, 64–66; *see also* Strasberg
outer technique, 64
physical technique, 149, 208
riding a bicycle, 135, 138, 140
technology
  imaging, 78, 124
  technologies of theatre, 184, 195, 210
template, 14, 111–112, 128, 135, 159, 176, 202, 215, 221, 226, 229
text(s)
  communication of the text, 39–41
  embodying the text, 35–36
  text-based theatres, 11, 14
Tharp, Twyla
  modern dance, 154–155, 157–158, 193, 230, 243 n. 49, n. 50
Theatre Complicite, 11
Theatre of Sources, 26, 51
  Grotowski, 26, 51
theatricality, 41, 65, 89, 188
theory
  theory of mind, 7, 9, 21–25, 34, 43
Thompson, Evan, 83, 97, 100, 102, 138
  Mind in Life, 7, 239 n. 7
through-line, 79, 182–184, 187, 195
  emotional, 53, 61, 71–72, 123, 170
Toole, David
  The Cost of Living, 113
  DV8, 113
top-down, 97
training
  voice training, 66, 118, 151–153
  see also biomechanics; Lessac; Linklater

trajectory, 33, 87, 164, 199–200, 206, 210, 216, 218
transcendence, 22, 23
  Grotowski, 51
transformation
  Grotowski, 51
    actor's score, 183
  improvisation, 175
  postdramatic theatre, 192
  recoding, 202
  Stanislavski, 35–36
  The Waves, 88–89
trigger, 67, 84, 90–93, 98–99, 112, 120, 201, 203–209, 222–223, 225
  Marc Lewis, 92
  "tagged," 156
truth-value, 74, 78
Tufnell, Miranda, 163, 167, 244 n. 6
Turner, Mark, 122, 241 n. 24

Unclean, The, 195
unconscious
  cognitive unconscious, 97–98
unfolding, 204–207, 209–210, 212–213, 216, 218–225, 227, 228
universal poetic sense, 55, 57–58, 202
  see also Lecoq
universals, 12

values, 24, 46, 73, 113–114, 147–148, 156, 164–165
Viewpoints, 192
  see also Bogart
vision
  visual perceptions, 100, 139, 143
  visual representations, 100–101

voice
  intonation, 198, 200
  phrasing, 123, 200
  rhythm, 188, 200, 205, 207–208, 215, 221
  tempo, 89, 188, 214
  vocal production, 118, 132, 149–150, 153, 156

Waltz, Sasha, 192
Wasserstein, Wendy, 27, 185
Waterman, Ian, 139, 140
Wellman, Mac, 27
Wesker, Arnold, 27
Whose Line Is It Anyway, 162
Wilde, Oscar, 11, 185
  Importance of Being Earnest, The, 223
Williams, Tennessee, 27, 95, 185
  Camino Real, 187
  The Glass Menagerie, 187
  Streetcar Named Desire, 27, 28, 95, 230
Wilson, Robert, 14, 27, 184, 192, 196, 223
  Einstein on the Beach, 27, 181, 185, 193, 207, 215, 223–224, 230, 245 n. 2, 246 n. 15, 248 n. 8
  Quartett, 27, 28
Wood, John, 115
Woolf, Virginia
  The Waves, 85–86, 88–90
Wooster Group, 11, 27, 192, 193, 246 n. 18
  House/Lights, 195
working memory, 106–109, 121, 198, 215, 218–219, 240–241 n. 16
world-making, 214–215